HANRATTY

THE A6 MURDER AND ITS AFTERMATH

Leonard Miller

Zoilus Press

A Zoilus Press paperback
First published in Great Britain by Zoilus Press in 2022

A CIP catalogue record for this book is available from the British Library.

ISBN 9781838489854

Cover design by The Ever-Shifting Subject

Typeset by Electrograd

ZOILUS PRESS
York, England

Contents

I have interviewed several journalists connected with the case, all of whom surprised me by insisting on Hanratty's guilt.

Paul Foot (1971)

It's impossible to think about this story without feeling that there is a mystery here with a hidden explanation. But the mystery is that there is no explanation and that, as unlikely as it may seem, that's how it happened.

Emmanuel Carrère, *The Adversary* (2000)

Introduction

The A6 murder was one of the most notorious and mysterious crimes of postwar England. As dusk fell on a warm August evening in 1961, Michael Gregsten, a 36-year-old married man, and his lover, 22-year-old Valerie Storie, were together in a small Morris Minor car parked off-road in a field in Buckinghamshire. It was a quiet rural location, popular as a place for courting couples to go in a car. They had been there a while and it was growing dark. The time was probably around 9.30pm-9.45pm. Unexpectedly, a smartly dressed young man appeared right beside the car. He rapped on the window. When Gregsten wound down the window the man pointed a handgun at him – later determined to be a .38 revolver. He was standing so close to the car window that they could not see his face. The man climbed into the back of the car and forced Gregsten to drive further into the field. There he engaged in a rambling monologue. After perhaps two hours had elapsed he ordered Gregsten to start the engine and drive off. The trio then went on a strange and apparently haphazard journey through the night, which ended when the gunman ordered Gregsten to pull over into a lonely lay-by on the A6 at a place called, with macabre irony, Deadman's Hill, in Bedfordshire. There, probably at around 2am (but possibly later), he shot the driver dead. Afterwards he raped the driver's young female companion. The rapist then talked to his victim in a conversation which lasted some twenty minutes. Then he told her to drag Michael Gregsten's body out of the car. She couldn't manage it unaided, so the killer helped her. The body was dumped on the ground. The killer asked to be shown how the gears worked on the car. Valerie Storie showed him. She urged him to make his getaway and leave her. The killer seemed about to do so when he suddenly fired several times. Hit, she collapsed on to the ground.

The killer fired more shots. When he was satisfied she was dead he drove off. The car was found later that same day, abandoned near an underground station in outer London.

This horrific yet mysterious sequence of events had major news potential. It fitted the news values and the news medium of its time. In the words of crime reporter Duncan Campbell, writing in 2009:

> The supremacy of crime in popular newspaper coverage in the 1950s and 1960s was reflected in the amount of space devoted to court cases, once a staple of the now fast-declining local newspaper. For the nationals, a murder trial, preferably with some sort of sexual frisson to it, could be guaranteed thousands of words of copy filed by teams of court reporters. "If it bleeds, it leads," became the motto of a thousand newsrooms.

Valerie Storie did not die, despite being repeatedly shot, although she was paralysed and never walked again. The police were initially baffled as to the identity of the gunman. The crime seemed motiveless and the long car journey to Deadman's Hill without any logic to it. After three weeks of feverish newspaper speculation about what kind of person the killer was, an initial suspect was identified. He was a drifter called Peter Alphon, who had been reported to the police for behaving strangely in the days after the crime. When two cartridge cases ejected from the killer's gun were discovered in a room at the Hotel Vienna in Maida Vale it transpired that Alphon had stayed there the night after the murder. This seemed damning circumstantial evidence, even though Alphon had not stayed in the room where the cartridge cases were found. However, none of the three witnesses who claimed to have seen the killer at the wheel of the Morris Minor identified Alphon as the man. Valerie Storie also failed to pick him out in an identity parade and Alphon was released. Attention then turned to the guest who had stayed in the relevant room the night before the abduction in the field. He had signed in as "Jim Ryan" and given a false address. This man turned out to be a 24-year-old career criminal named James Hanratty. His previous offences included housebreaking and vehicle theft. None had involved violence or sex.

Miss Storie was in no doubt that he was the man who had raped her. Two other witnesses picked out Hanratty from an identification parade as the man they had seen driving the stolen Morris Minor, very badly, shortly before it was dumped on a quiet residential street. Hanratty was duly charged with murder. After what was at that time the longest trial in British criminal history the prisoner was convicted and executed by hanging at Bedford Prison on 4 April 1962. Hanratty was among the last handful of prisoners to suffer the death penalty before it was abolished in the United Kingdom in 1965.

Hanratty died protesting his innocence – a claim strongly supported by his family, who insisted that he was incapable of such a horrific crime. Although at this time there was a substantial body of opinion that the death penalty was a barbaric form of punishment in a supposedly civilised society, and although there was a grassroots radical campaign against hanging in the form of the National Committee for the Abolition of Capital Punishment, Hanratty's execution did not provoke protests or large-scale public unease. It "passed uneventfully; there were no scenes outside the prison". The case "raised little public feeling". It was not controversial in the way that, say, the hanging of Derek Bentley in 1953 had been, or Ruth Ellis, in 1955.

I am old enough to remember the A6 murder case. I still have a vivid childhood memory of the report of the jury's verdict in the newspaper which my parents had delivered every week – *The Sunday Express*. I was too young to understand what it was all about but I recall the photograph of Hanratty's face staring out from the newspaper. I am not sure why I remember it so vividly. I imagine my father must have talked about the case. He had been a career soldier when war broke out and his years in the army and his wartime experiences would have left him with little sympathy for a criminal like James Hanratty. He was a man of strong and conservative views and he would have had no objections to Hanratty's execution. On the contrary, he would have welcomed it.

I forgot about the case until years later I bought a paperback about the case, by Paul Foot. At that time in my life I was not particularly interested in non-fiction crime books – or for that matter crime fiction – but I had previously gone along to hear Foot speak when he visited the university where I was a student. I remember the lecture theatre where he spoke was packed out, with every seat taken and people standing in the aisles and at the back. Paul Foot was a radical – a revolutionary socialist and a prominent journalist with something of a public profile. He was an electrifying speaker – passionate, amusing, showering his audience with facts and statistics. I cannot now remember what his precise topic was but it touched on the state of the nation. There was corruption and injustice and exploitation! At question time there were objections to his analysis from some in the audience but Foot dealt with them charmingly, wittily, convincingly. I came away with warm feelings towards the speaker, although with no inclination to join the fringe Trotskyist organisation of which he was a leading figure and for which he was keen to recruit new members.

When I came across a paperback he had written about the A6 case I bought it and read it. It was racy, compelling and, I thought, utterly persuasive. The book left me in no doubt at all that a terrible miscarriage of justice had occurred. The state had executed the wrong man, and had been covering up its mistake ever since. Another paperback by Foot appeared, about the violent, mysterious death of a young English nurse, Helen Smith, in Saudi Arabia and I bought that too. This book was also highly readable and convincing, although in the end the truth surrounding this troubling death never seemed to emerge and this particular tragedy faded from public view.

The A6 case remains lodged in public consciousness largely because of the effectiveness of the campaign which was mounted on James Hanratty's behalf. Paul Foot was perhaps its most effective advocate. The campaign received high-profile sympathetic coverage across the media spectrum – all the way from the popular satirical magazine *Private Eye* to BBC television and *The Sunday Times*. Many MPs were persuaded by the case made for Hanratty's innocence and this in turn obliged successive governments and the legal establishment reluctantly to engage with the claim that a massive miscarriage of justice had occurred. The campaign coincided with growing unease about some spectacular miscarriages of justice which occurred against the background of "the Troubles" in Northern Ireland. It seemed entirely plausible that Hanratty's conviction had simply been the prelude to many others which were unsustainable. In his 1991 anthology *Truth to Tell*, Ludovic Kennedy asserted that "Because truth was suppressed" James Hanratty was among those hanged "for murders committed by others". Hanratty's conviction was a gross miscarriage of justice, comparable to others including "the cases of the Guildford Four, the Maguire Seven and the Birmingham Six".

In returning to the A6 murder case I have various motives. Firstly, my 2001 book *Shadows of Deadman's Hill*, which asserted that Hanratty was guilty and that the arguments of the campaigners were devoid of substance, was only ever available as a hardback, in a small print-run. It is long out of print and is today a very rare book – perhaps the rarest of all the books on the case. At the time of writing a single copy is available for sale on the Amazon UK website for £365.99 (plus postage). This new book, *Hanratty's Guilt*, incorporates much of its text, although I have at times taken the opportunity to polish the style, correct typos, cut some sentences and paragraphs, and expand certain sections. It also contains some new material about the case, including information about what James Hanratty was probably doing in a cornfield in Buckinghamshire on the night he abducted Michael

Gregsten and Valerie Storie. The most influential books on the case, by Paul Foot and Bob Woffinden, although out of print, remain in circulation and are easily obtained in cheap second-hand editions, therefore I would like my critique of them to be equally available. My book was the first (and indeed the last) to subject the accounts and arguments of the campaigners to detailed critical scrutiny.

Secondly, the years have rolled by, allowing a new perspective on this case. All the central figures are now dead. Some new information has come to light, although there is nothing which significantly alters an already existing under-standing of the strange saga which began on the night of 22 August 1961. However, in re-engaging with this subject I have taken the opportunity to offer some updated reflections on the case and also to comment on two new books about it which have appeared in recent years. It is also the case that the myth of James Hanratty's innocence lingers on and appears in unexpected places. Ronan McGreevy's recent well-received book on the 1922 assassination of Sir Henry Wilson in passing mentions Hanratty as "dubiously executed for murder", including his case alongside those of Timothy Evans and Derek Bentley.

After *Shadows of Deadman's Hill* was published I received many communications from a variety of individuals. Most were simply from people who agreed with me and who said how pleased they were to see the campaigners' case demolished in such a forensic fashion. One such letter of congratulation came from a relatively high-profile figure who decades earlier had become involved in the case. Another was from someone who had known one of the witnesses. Two were of special interest in that they contained fresh information about the case, shedding light on two of its darkest and most intriguing corners. Thus, although much in this book will be familiar to true A6 obsessives, even they, I hope, will find something new in it.

1   Complicity

To write a thriller, you begin with improbability.

John Braine (1974)

In his famous essay "Decline of the English Murder" George Orwell analysed what he claimed was a common complaint of readers of Sunday newspapers that "you never seem to get a good murder nowadays". The perfect murder, he suggested, was committed by a respectable professional man – perhaps a dentist or a solicitor – enmeshed in an adulterous passion. In order to conceal and perpetuate his furtive love affair the murderer only committed the crime "after long and terrible wrestles with his conscience". The murder would be carried out with meticulous planning and the victim would be poisoned. The killer would only be found out because of "some tiny unforeseeable detail". What was agreeable about this kind of crime was that it possessed "dramatic and even tragic qualities which make it memorable and excite pity for both victim and murderer".

Orwell, whose essay was written in 1946, compared this type of crime with the then notorious "Cleft Chin Murder", committed during wartime. A 22-year-old US Army deserter and his 18-year-old English girlfriend went on a short rampage of theft and assault which climaxed with the shooting dead of a London taxi driver. It was, Orwell wrote, "a pitiful and sordid case" and a "meaningless story". He concluded "it is difficult to believe that this case will be so long remembered as the old domestic poisoning dramas, product of a stable society where the all-prevailing hypocrisy did at least ensure that crimes as serious as murder should have strong emotions behind them". The Cleft Chin Murder, he wrote on another occasion, was "uninteresting".

Orwell was only half-right. The Cleft Chin Murder was

11

not forgotten – it partly inspired a novel by Arthur La Bern, as well as two movies, *Good-Time Girl* (1948) and *Chicago Joe and the Showgirl* (1990) but neither the crime nor its incarnation in popular culture ever really gripped the public imagination in the way that other crimes and criminals have done. The couple involved in the Cleft Chin Murder were no Bonnie and Clyde.

Orwell's argument is that for a crime to be interesting it has to involve "strong emotions" and complexity. To him that meant that middle-class crime was usually more compelling than working-class crime. There was a sophistication and emotional depth present in carefully plotted middle-class murder which was lacking in the casual, spur-of-the-moment opportunistic violence of working-class killers.

One crucial aspect missing from Orwell's analysis is that for a crime to be compelling it helps if it contains ambiguity and mystery. Here, class and social status are of no consequence. Unsolved crimes are, arguably, far more intriguing than solved ones. The identity of Jack the Ripper continues to torment and obsess some people, even though it is surely obvious that he will never convincingly be identified. The same applies to the so-called "Jack the Stripper" serial killings of London prostitutes between 1959 and 1965. Those crimes inspired a number of books, including David Seabrook's powerful, idiosyncratic and wildly speculative *Jack of Jumps* and Robin Jarossi's quieter, more persuasive *The hunt for the 60s' Ripper*, which plausibly suggests that the murderer was a Metropolitan Police officer. Those killings also inspired a novel by Arthur La Bern, subsequently adapted by Alfred Hitchcock for his film, *Frenzy*. Meanwhile the murder of television celebrity Jill Dando remains unsolved, with no obvious motive. The disappearance of Madeleine McCann continues to provoke feverish speculation and purported scoops but at the time of writing no one has faced any charges.

Although exceptionally rare, an author writing about unsolved crime can actually be instrumental in the capture of the perpetrator. The outstanding example is that of Michelle

McNamara, author of *I'll Be Gone in the Dark*. Her all-consuming obsession with an unsolved and largely forgotten series of rapes and murders in California in the 1970s and 1980s inspired fresh interest in the case which led, after her death, to the identification of the elusive killer through his DNA. Her book's discussion of geographical profiling seems pertinent to the A6 case in relation to Hanratty's appearance at Dorney Reach, his choice of the highway to Bedford, and his dumping of the car in Ilford. *I'll Be Gone in the Dark* is an electrifying read and, unusually, it asks questions of those who choose to write about crime. As Jeremy Lybarger put it:

> In one of the book's many sharp insights, she likens herself and all amateur detectives to the killers they seek. Both perpetrator and sleuth share an uncommon and singular compulsion. One seeks to destroy, while the other seeks to create, however haphazardly, some kind of explanation.

Although the A6 murder was far from being unsolved it is precisely its enduring mysteries and ambiguities which have helped transform it into a minor classic of English "true crime". By Orwell's criteria it was "a pitiful and sordid case", albeit one with many unusual and special characteristics. But it was its very meaningless and lack of motive and purpose which made it so mysterious and intriguing. There were also some striking coincidences which seemed to strengthen the notion that just below the surface lay an alternative explanation of the crime.

The A6 murder case would probably have faded from sight had it not been for five individuals who each wrote books about it over the period 1963-1997: Louis Blom-Cooper, Jean Justice, Lord Russell of Liverpool, Paul Foot and Bob Woffinden. There were sometimes substantial differences in their approach to the subject but collectively they were agreed that justice had not been served by Hanratty's conviction and that the crime was a mysterious one, with a crucial secret dimension omitted from the trial. Four of these five books asserted that James Hanratty was a wholly innocent man and that a major miscarriage of justice had occurred.

The campaign to clear Hanratty spanned four decades, enjoying considerable success in PR terms, momentarily enlisting a prominent celebrity in the form of John Lennon and repeatedly getting widespread media coverage. It inspired sympathetic TV documentaries and provoked three Home Office inquiries into the case between 1967 and 1996. The campaign climaxed with the efforts of Bob Woffinden, a former rock music journalist who had reinvented himself as a campaigner on behalf of people he believed had been wrongly accused and convicted. Woffinden produced a powerfully emotional and manipulative TV documentary *Hanratty – The Mystery of Deadman's Hill*, first broadcast on Channel 4 in 1992 and shown again in 1994 and 1995. He followed it up with a book – *Hanratty: The Final Verdict*, published by a major publishing house in 1997. Both the documentary and the book insisted on James Hanratty's unambiguous, absolute innocence. To Woffinden "the final verdict" was beyond all doubt: *not guilty*.

Hanratty campaigners enthusiastically welcomed the new and developing science of DNA analysis. It brought a new, hitherto unimaginable scientific dimension to the understanding of crime scene material. Testing of semen stains from the crime, found on Valerie Storie's knickers would, the campaigners believed, provide the final exoneration of a much-traduced individual. Hanratty's mother Mary and his brother Michael both willingly supplied DNA samples, happy to assist in exonerating their infamous family member. But initial tests in 1995 failed to produce conclusive results. However, the analysis was slowly becoming more sophisticated, so there was still hope for a future definitive outcome. In 1997 the handkerchief used to wrap the murder weapon was discovered in police storage, which gave fresh hope for an unambiguous DNA analysis.

Meanwhile the Hanratty campaign presented the Home Office with fresh evidence which it was believed exonerated the dead man. A new police inquiry was initiated. Its conclusions were later leaked to the press. *The Independent* (27 January 1997) reported:

WRONGLY HANGED: HANRATTY IS FOUND INNOCENT

James Hanratty, hanged for one of the most notorious crimes this century, is about to be cleared 35 years after his execution for the A6 murder.

... Home Office officials are understood to have concluded that Hanratty was innocent. This follows an unpublished police enquiry which concluded last year that he was the victim of a miscarriage of justice and that the murder was probably part of a wider conspiracy.

The Home Office forwarded the papers in the case to the newly established Criminal Cases Review Commission. This body agreed that the conviction appeared to be unsound. In March 1999 the Commission referred the case to the Court of Appeal on the grounds of police conduct, lack of disclosure and flawed identification evidence.

Three months later new DNA tests were carried out. To the astonishment and dismay of the campaigners the analysis indicated that there was very strong evidence of a family match between the DNA supplied by Mary and Michael Hanratty and the DNA on the knickers and handkerchief. This indicated that James Hanratty had all along been the murderer and rapist. But to be absolutely certain of this conclusion it was necessary to use his own DNA – something which required the exhumation of his body. Suddenly the Hanratty family lost their enthusiasm for DNA testing and opposed this move, but were over-ruled by the

Lord Chief Justice, who said it was desirable in the interests of justice.

The Court of Appeal was still considering the case when, on 25 October 2001, my book *Shadows of Deadman's Hill: A New Analysis of the A6 Murder* was published. It presented a detailed critique of the earlier books on the case and set out to rip apart the idea that a miscarriage of justice had occurred. It asserted that even if the Court of Appeal ruled that the conviction was unsafe, on the basis of non-disclosure of evidence to the defence and other flawed procedures, this should not detract from the reality that James Hanratty was undoubtedly guilty of the crime for which he had been executed.

In fact (a little to my surprise, as not everything the campaigners had argued was wrong), some seven months later the Court of Appeal ruled that there was "overwhelming proof of the safety of the conviction" of James Hanratty and it was "beyond doubt" that he was the murderer of Michael Gregsten. Hanratty's own DNA had been found on Valerie Storie's knickers, along with the DNA of another male, assumed to be Michael Gregsten. That was damning evidence, reinforced by the discovery that the handkerchief used to wrap the murder gun contained only one individual's DNA – James Hanratty's. To anyone with an open mind it supplied the final, unambiguous proof of his guilt.

Faced with this stunning setback the campaigners argued that the crime scene samples must have been contaminated. It was a theory which the Court of Appeal had considered and rejected. Everything which campaigners like Paul Foot and Bob Woffinden had argued for now lay in shreds. *The Guardian* described the long-running campaign to absolve James Hanratty of the crime as having been "comprehensively dismissed" (11 May 2002). An editorial in *The Sunday Times* proclaimed *Case closed*. The newspaper acidly noted that some campaigners had "comprehensively blighted" the lives of two women centrally involved in the case. (12 May 2002) Valerie Storie had had to endure decades of opinionated men telling her that she was wrong about her identification of her rapist. The murdered man's widow, Janet Gregsten, had also had to suffer innuendo from some campaigners, who hinted that she was personally involved in the crime and bore a heavy responsibility for what had happened. *The Sunday Times* asked, somewhat rhetorically, if these campaigners (all men) would now have the good grace to offer an apology to the women they had defamed. Needless to say, no such apology was forthcoming.

Michael Hanratty, the dead man's brother, appealed to the House of Lords against the Court of Appeal's ruling. In July 2002 three law lords refused him leave to take his fight any further. In their view the DNA evidence alone was conclusive. This ruling more or less marked the end of this long-running saga. The case is closed, at least from the perspective of law.

But though the case is closed, the story is far from over. Surprisingly, even after the Court of Appeal's decision, a major national newspaper showed a reluctance to accept its conclusions. When Paul Foot's death was reported by *The Guardian* a little over two years after the Court of Appeal's verdict, it reported that "The list of books he wrote includes ... exposés of miscarriages of justice, including ... the execution for murder of James Hanratty" (19 July 2004). But there was no miscarriage of justice and it was perverse of the *Guardian* to suggest that in this instance Foot was anything other than deluded. *The Guardian* was not alone in stubbornly insisting on Hanratty's innocence, long after the DNA evidence had simply confirmed the overwhelming evidence of his guilt. In 2017, in his book on the campaigner Ludovic Kennedy, Richard Ingrams mentioned "the A6 murder, for which James Hanratty was wrongly executed in 1962".

Since the turn of the century and the Court of Appeal's dismissal of the case for Hanratty's innocence, the internet has given the A6 murder a new lease of life. Today there are substantial quantities of online commentary on the case. Some of it is interesting, much of it is not. There is a shrinking minority of people who continue loudly to insist that James Hanratty was innocent. Unfortunately social media is often not the place to encounter civility, reason or accuracy – merely very strong and sometimes very angry opinions. The internet affords every individual a platform and there is no shortage of material about the A6 case to be found online. Some of it is wildly inaccurate. To take a random example, you find assertions like this: "Alphon was the son of a highly ranking Scotland Yard detective. Was Scotland Yard trying to protect its own?" In fact, although Felix Alphon worked for the Metropolitan Police he was an office worker – a minor bureaucrat. He was not involved in any way with detective work. The notion that when his son Peter fell under suspicion as the A6 murderer senior police officers intervened to protect the suspect because his father was one of their own is a conspiracy theory which can be safely discarded as complete nonsense.

Carelessness and inaccuracy are not restricted to material found on the internet. *The Encyclopedia of Forensic Science* (2004) by Brian Lane includes a short, error-riddled section on the A6 murder. It puts Alphon in the same room as Hanratty at the Hotel Vienna "on the previous night"; it repeats the myth that Valerie Storie changed her description of her attacker's eyes; it claims Hanratty was only arrested when Storie picked him out at an identity parade; it describes "enormous doubt" based on Alphon's confessions and the Rhyl alibi (which was "almost certainly the truth") as having been expressed after the jury's verdict but *before* the hanging was carried out. This nonsense all too plainly originates in a sloppy, garbled reading of Paul Foot's *Who Killed Hanratty?*, which perhaps makes it unsurprising that the highly contentious conclusion is reached that "As of this writing, (September 2003), conclusive proof has yet to be offered by either side."

The A6 murder slowly accreted more and more commentary about its various aspects. There was the initially slow police investigation, which would later come in for wide-ranging criticism. There was the trial, which some felt failed to explain the crime and ignored aspects which might have been central to understanding it (such as the "friendship" of Michael Gregsten and Valerie Storie). Finally, there was the fact that the man first arrested for the crime, then released, subsequently proclaimed his own guilt after the execution of the second suspect in the case. These aspects helped inspire a sequence of books which re-examined the case, asserted that the legal system had failed the accused man, James Hanratty, and argued that a major miscarriage of justice had occurred.

It was also a case in which the class aspect of English society appeared in a heightened form. The convicted man, from a working-class family who lived on a council estate, was a semi-literate cockney. He became a career criminal devoid of education or social skills. He was a drifter, unattached, moving around mysteriously. The victims were middle-class: articulate, educated, law-abiding, in stable employment. Michael Gregsten was an accomplished pianist. The only transgression which existed in this relatively tranquil existence involved adultery – upsetting for one member of a romantic triangle, but not remotely criminal.

The brutal A6 case involved a clash of worlds, as the gunman erupted without warning into the tranquil setting of a couple sitting in a parked car. A working-class career criminal crashed into a quiet middle-class existence. But those who were first drawn to the case and became convinced that a miscarriage of justice had occurred tended to come from the upper class. One was the son of a diplomat; his wealth spared him the distraction of salaried employment. Another was a successful barrister. A third was the son of Sir Hugh Foot, the last Governor of Cyprus and Jamaica, and the nephew of Michael Foot, who was at one time leader of the Labour Party.

2 The Trial and Execution of James Hanratty

> Think of the connotations of "murder", that awful word: the loss of emotional control, the hate, the spite, the selfishness, the broken glass, the blood, the cry in the throat, the trembling blindness that results in the irrevocable act, the helpless blow. Murder is the most limited of gestures.
>
> John Hawkes, *Travesty* (1976)

In the early evening of Saturday 17 February 1962, after more than six hours of deliberation, the jury in the trial of James Hanratty for the murder of Michael Gregsten filed back into the courtroom of the Shire Hall, Bedford. The atmosphere was tense and expectant. A verdict was awaited and the prisoner had been brought up from the cells to take his place in the dock.

Having lasted for twenty-one days, it was the longest murder trial in British criminal history, and also one of the most sensational. Crowds waited in the street outside. Crime reporters were ready to rush out and telephone the news in time to make the headlines in the next day's Sunday papers. Would Hanratty be found guilty or not guilty?

This electrifying moment ended unexpectedly in anticlimax. There was no verdict. To everyone's surprise, after such an interminable wait, the jury had failed to arrive at a decision. They had simply returned in order to obtain advice from the judge, Mr Justice Gorman. The Foreman handed him a note, which read: "May we have a further statement from you regarding the definition of reasonable doubt? Must we be certain and sure of the prisoner's guilt to return a verdict?"

After such a long period of discussion this seemed to indicate that the jury was unable to agree and that at least some of its members felt indecisive about the evidence and were unsure about Hanratty's guilt. The jury's uncertainty seemed to be reflected in the advice which was sought from the judge. The jury requested that Mr Justice Gorman comment on the defence counsel's summing up with regard to circumstantial evidence from a different case and its bearing on two key aspects of the evidence presented in the trial. The first concerned identification of the accused by three witnesses; the second involved the two cartridge cases from the murder weapon found at the Hotel Vienna in the room where the defendant had stayed. "Would he also comment on the point made that where there is circumstantial evidence which admits of more than one theory, then the theory in favour of the defence must invariably be adopted?"

The jury could not make up its mind and was looking for some firm direction. What did the judge think of the mass of contradictory evidence which had been placed before the court? What is "reasonable doubt"? Of what value is circumstantial evidence? The judge duly supplied the jury with an explanation. Circumstantial evidence is evidence of circumstances, all of which point inevitably to one conclusion – the guilt of the accused. It might be regarded as akin to a series of roads, with each road leading to the same destination.

An hour and a half later the jury emerged from the jury room, and the court once more filled up. But this was another anticlimax. The jury had only emerged to request that tea be sent into them. Deliberations continued for another two hours and twenty minutes before a verdict was finally reached.

The jury's earlier indecisiveness and evident internal disagreement was understandable. In Britain in 1962 a guilty verdict on a charge of murder involving firearms and theft automatically resulted in a death sentence. It was an awesome responsibility to bring in a guilty verdict if there was any doubt at all about James Hanratty being the gunman who had shot Michael Gregsten.

The defendant himself had indignantly denied throughout that he was the murderer. What troubled some observers of the prosecution case was that no very persuasive explanation had been put forward as to why a petty criminal like Hanratty, with a record of burglary and car theft, should have suddenly turned into a murderer and rapist.

The trial had opened four weeks earlier, on Monday 22 January. There had been around one hundred witnesses or witness statements to be heard and nearly one-hundred-and-fifty exhibits. The transcript of the trial was equal in length to nine novels. The jury had been deluged with information, yet the case had loose ends, ambiguities, uncertainties and conflicting witness evidence. Serving on a jury, especially in a lengthy case, can be exhausting, stressful and require intense concentration. Although jurors can take notes it is easy enough to become overwhelmed by the mass of evidence presented to a court.

One juror had earlier asked if they could have a transcript to consult during their deliberations. This had been refused. No appropriate text which excluded legal submissions heard when the jury was not present was available, nor could one be quickly prepared. Besides, if jurors cannot make up their mind after listening to all the evidence put before them, and judging for themselves the veracity of witnesses and the defendant and the persuasiveness of the case for the prosecution and that for the defence, it is unlikely that pouring over thousands of pages of typescript would have provided any help. This, after all, was one of the difficulties of the A6 case: information overload combined with a number of perplexing voids, strange coincidences and an absence of crystal-clear motive.

"Members of the jury, at a little after half-past six, on the morning of Wednesday 23 August of last year, there found at Deadman's Hill, on a concrete extension of the A6 road, in this county, the dead body of Michael Gregsten. Near to him, and most gravely injured, was Miss Valerie Storie." This was how the trial judge began his summing-up, in which he endeavoured to focus the minds of the jury members on all the evidence heard during the trial. It took him three days to take them back through all the evidence.

Some facts were not disputed (although the only source for this narrative of events was Valerie Storie). Late in the evening of Tuesday 22 August 1961 Michael Gregsten, a married man of 36, and Valerie Storie, a single woman of 22, were sitting together in the front seats of a Morris Minor car which had been driven a few yards off the road and parked in a cornfield between the village of Dorney and the nearby hamlet of Dorney Reach, bordering the River Thames in Buckinghamshire. The couple both worked at the Road Research Laboratory near Slough and had been having an affair for some three or four years. However, the jury were simply informed that they were good friends who had parked in the field to discuss a works motor rally. This concealment of the couple's true relationship subsequently fed the suspicions of those writers and campaigners who would later come to believe that the crime was not a random one but was directly connected to Gregsten and Storie's affair.

They had been sitting in the car for around half an hour when out of the darkness came a sudden tap on the window. When Gregsten wound down the window he found himself faced by a man who was holding a gun. The man was standing so close to the car that Gregsten could not see his face.

"This is a hold-up," the man said. "I am a desperate man." He demanded that Gregsten hand over the ignition key and then climbed into the back of the Morris. He pointed the gun at Gregsten and told the couple to stare ahead and not turn round. It later emerged that the gunman's face was partly masked by a handkerchief worn cowboy-style beneath his eyes.

After a short conversation he returned the key to Gregsten and ordered him to drive further into the field. He then demanded their cash and their watches. Storie managed to keep back seven one-pound notes, stuffing them down her bra.

After more rambling conversation the gunman decided they should go for some food. He gave instructions about which route to take. Gregsten drove to the nearby A4, where they turned right. As they travelled down the high street in Slough, Valerie Storie noted that the clock on the Post Office showed that it was 11.45pm.

Near London Airport they stopped to get two gallons of petrol at a garage, then continued towards London. Turning left through Hayes they crossed what was then the A4010 and continued along Western Avenue. Somewhere in Harrow they stopped and Gregsten bought a packet of cigarettes from a machine. At last they left London and travelled on via Watford and the A5 to St Albans.

As he directed them, the gunman talked about himself. "He said he had been in institutions since he was eight. He'd been to a remand home, he'd been to Borstal." Gregsten made surreptitious attempts to attract the attention of other drivers by flashing the reversing light and the headlights. This worked with one driver, who was behind them. When the car overtook the occupants pointed at the back of the Morris. But it was night and they had evidently failed to notice the masked figure in the back seat of the Morris, or the gun he was holding.

At St Albans, Gregsten, still obeying the gunman's instructions, headed due north along the A6. After they had passed through Luton the gunman announced that he was tired and needed "a kip". Twice they pulled off the road but neither spot was deemed sufficiently safe from scrutiny.

A mile beyond the village of Clophill the gunman ordered Gregsten to turn off into a lay-by which ran parallel to the A road, separated from it by a low grassy embankment. At the end of the lay-by the car was turned round, facing back in the direction from which they had come.

The gunman explained that he would need to tie them both up before he went to sleep. Storie's wrists were clumsily bound with Gregsten's tie and a piece of rope from the car boot.

Looking for something else suitable with which to tie up Gregsten, the gunman ordered him to pass over a duffel bag which was lying on the car floor at Storie's feet. As Gregsten turned to pass over the bag the gunman opened fire, shooting him in the side of the head at point blank range. Gregsten slumped over the steering wheel, blood gushing from his wounds.

"You shot him, you bastard!" Storie shrieked. "Why did you do that?"

"He frightened me. He moved too quick," the gunman replied.

Storie insisted that a doctor was needed, urgently. The gunman told her to shut up. "Be quiet will you. I am finking." For some fifteen or twenty minutes they argued about Gregsten's condition before the gunman decided he must be dead. The gunman removed a pair of pyjama trousers from the duffel bag and put it over his victim's face. He then ordered Storie to kiss him, or be shot. He removed the handkerchief from across the lower part of his face. It was at this moment, as she faced him, that the headlights of a passing vehicle briefly washed over the gunman's face.

Having kissed her, the man ordered her to get into the back of the car with him, otherwise he would shoot her. He forced her to remove her knickers and loosen her bra and then raped her.

Afterwards, for perhaps another twenty minutes, they continued talking and arguing. Storie pointed out it would soon be daybreak and told the man to take the car and go. The man seemed to agree, and together they dragged Gregsten's blood-drenched corpse from the driver's seat and laid it on the edge of the concrete strip where the car was parked. The gunman then asked her to start the car for him and show him how the gears worked. It stalled. She got the car going again, then went back to the body of her lover. The gunman followed her. "I think I had better knock you on the head or something," he remarked, "or else you will go for help."

Storie promised not to and produced a one-pound note, telling him he could have it if he left quickly. The gunman seemed surprised that she was still in possession of money. He took the banknote and walked away. Then, without warning, he turned and shot her. She collapsed and lay still. The gunman fired more shots. In all, he shot her five times. Remarkably, she was still alive. Storie was aware of the gunman approaching. He stood over her. She lay absolutely still, pretending to be dead. Finally the man prodded her, then, evidently convinced she was not alive, walked away. He got into the car, put the headlights on, and drove away to the south.

Valerie Storie was discovered, crying out for help, some three and a half hours after the killer and rapist had fled. She had survived her brutal attack, although tragically one bullet hit her spine. At the age of just twenty-two she was permanently paralysed from the waist down. She used a wheelchair for the rest of her life. Although wounded, she was able to give police a full account of the bizarre sequence of events which had taken place. One immediate difficulty for the police was the apparent lack of motive. If the intention was murder and rape, why force the victims to travel almost to Bedford when they were just as vulnerable in the field where their ordeal had begun? The unidentified assailant was, it was assumed, some kind of crazy psychopath – or as one of the papers later colourfully put it, a "moon maniac".

At first the criminal investigation moved swiftly. The stolen Morris car was discovered at 6.30pm the same day, 23 August, parked on Avondale Crescent in Ilford, Essex, very close to Redbridge Station on the London Underground's Central Line. Three witnesses later reported seeing a grey Morris Minor being driven very badly, at speed, near this location early that morning. They had each caught a glimpse of the driver. The very next day, 24 August, a bus cleaner for London Transport found a gun and ammunition hidden under the upstairs back seat of a 36A double-decker bus. This was quickly identified as the murder weapon.

The officer in charge of the case was Detective Superintendent Basil Acott, usually known as Bob Acott. Although a Scotland Yard officer D.S. Acott initially based his investigation in Bedford, the nearest town to the crime scene. But after the initial discovery of the stolen car and the murder weapon, the trail went cold. A pair of identikit pictures were released, one based on Valerie Storie's impression of her attacker, the other on the face of the man seen driving a Morris Minor badly close to the place where the car used in the crime had been later abandoned. A number of suspects were questioned but all had alibis or were able to persuade the police that the crime had nothing whatever to do with them.

After almost three weeks, and despite massive publicity about the case, the police were nowhere near to catching the killer. Forensic examination of the Morris Minor had yielded little of value. The killer had carefully and successfully wiped away all traces of his fingerprints (which perhaps hardly existed at all, since the man had worn gloves throughout, except when assaulting Valerie Storie). He had avoided leaving behind any clothing fibres or hairs. Modern forensic investigation would probably have found traces of some kind but the science was in its infancy in 1961, added to which the standard police treatment of a crime scene was, by current standards, often slapdash and amateurish. The most tangible evidence of the identity of the attacker was his semen, but in 1961 DNA testing did not exist.

It began to look as if the gunman would not be identified and this shocking, high-profile crime would go unsolved. Then, unexpectedly, on 11 September, there was a sensational new development which was to bring two men under suspicion. Two empty cartridge cases from the murder weapon were found in a basement room at the Hotel Vienna in Maida Vale. This was fortuitous for the police, as by this time the trail had gone cold and they were getting nowhere in identifying a suspect.

When the investigation team examined their files they discovered that a man who had already been questioned in connection with the A6 murder had actually stayed at the hotel on the night, although not in the room where the cartridge cases were found. This man, Peter Louis Alphon (1930-2009), was alleged by a hotel employee called Jack Glickberg (whose real name was actually William Nudds) to have had access to the basement and to have seemed agitated and dishevelled when seen in his hotel room at about mid-day on Wednesday 23 August. Alphon was a drifter who had no regular employment and he resembled one of the identikit images of the killer. He had originally been questioned because of his odd behaviour at a different hotel in the days after the crime. The police were now convinced that they had their man and put out a public alert for him. Alphon promptly surrendered himself. When he was put on an identification parade Valerie Storie picked another man. The case against him dissolved and Nudds later withdrew his incriminating statement. The credibility of Valerie Storie's eyewitness testimony was also thrown into question.

After the debacle of their over-hasty identification of Alphon as the prime suspect, the police now focused their attention on the guests who had actually stayed in the room where the cartridge cases were found. It turned out to have been a little-used basement room. Only one guest had briefly had access to it in the period between the murder and the discovery of the cartridge cases. Since he was Vigan Rapur, an Indian from Delhi, he could be safely excluded from suspicion; the killer was unquestionably a young white man. That left one other person to be considered – the man who had slept there the night before the abduction. The name in the hotel register was "J. Ryan" of 72 Wood Lane, Kingsbury. When Detective Superintendent Acott went there the man who had occupied this address for twenty-five years said no one of that name had ever lived there. However, he had recently received a letter addressed to Ryan, which he passed over. The envelope came from Ireland and contained documentation from a car rental business in Dublin relating to a car which "Ryan" had hired.

The police (for reasons which remain a little opaque and which will be discussed later) were swiftly able to connect "Ryan" with a petty criminal called James Francis Hanratty, aged 24, whose family home was not far from 72 Wood Lane, Kingsbury. Hanratty's first conviction dated back to 1954, when he was 17. The following year he was convicted of housebreaking and theft and sentenced to two years in prison. Five months after his release he was convicted of stealing a car and sentenced to six months. Shortly after his release he was convicted of two more cases of car theft and sentenced to three years Corrective Detention (or "C.T."). This was highly significant as the gunman had told Valerie Storie that not only had he done "C.T." but that he had "done the lot". This meant nothing to Storie, who was unaware that "done the lot" was prison slang for serving the whole of a sentence with no remission. Detective Superintendent Acott discovered that there were only five men in Britain who had recently served an entire sentence of corrective training without remission. One of them was James Hanratty.

When he heard that the police wanted to question him in connection with the A6 murder, Hanratty went on the run. He telephoned Acott and told him that he was innocent and had spent the night of the murder with three men in Liverpool. He refused to give Acott the names of these men because they had told him they didn't want to get involved, and one of them was wanted on a warrant for non-payment of a fine. He was also not prepared to give himself up because by this time he had learned the police were after him for housebreaking and because of his criminal record he knew that this time he would get a five-year sentence.

Hanratty was captured on 11 October, in Blackpool. Two days later he was put on an identification parade before three witnesses believed to have seen the Morris Minor with the killer driving it. Two identified Hanratty as the driver. The next day thirteen men were put on an identification parade before Valerie Storie. She picked out Hanratty and at 6.15pm the same day he was charged with the murder of Michael Gregsten.

Between 22 November and 5 December 1961 the prosecution outlined its case before magistrates at Ampthill, Bedfordshire. They decided there was a case to answer at a higher court. On 14 January 1962 to the charge of the murder of Michael Gregsten was added the attempted murder and rape of Valerie Storie. On the opening day of the trial, 22 January 1962, these two additional charges were dropped.

There was no obvious forensic evidence to tie Hanratty to the crime. The prosecution rested its case on evidence of identification, on circumstantial evidence, and on the evidence of Roy Langdale, a fellow prisoner at Brixton Prison, who claimed that Hanratty had directly admitted to him that he was guilty of the crime. Valerie Storie was unshakeable in her certainty that Hanratty was the gunman whom she had momentarily seen without his mask in the headlights of a passing vehicle. John Skillett was equally sure that Hanratty was the man he had seen driving the Morris Minor shortly before it was dumped in Ilford. James Trower was certain that it was Hanratty he had seen at the wheel of the Morris being driven into Avondale Crescent shortly after 7am on 23 August.

There was also a mass of circumstantial evidence to connect Hanratty to the crime, not least the discovery of two cartridge cases from the murder weapon in the hotel room Hanratty had stayed in the night before the crime. The accused also admitted talking to a criminal associate about getting hold of a gun (although he claimed he had not been serious). There was also the prisoner's admission that he had indeed told a friend that under the upstairs back seat of a London double-decker bus was a good place to hide stuff you wanted to get rid of. Since that was precisely where the murder weapon and a stock of bullets were discovered, this fact seemed damning. Hanratty could not produce the suit jacket he had been wearing at the time of the murder, which, if he was the killer, might well have been stained with the victim's blood. He claimed he had torn it and thrown it away in a park.

Hanratty originally claimed to have been in Liverpool at the time of the murder, with criminal associates he did not want to name. During the course of the trial he admitted his alibi was bogus and instead claimed he had spent the nights of 22 and 23 August at a boarding house in Rhyl, a Welsh seaside resort some fifty miles from Liverpool by road. But though a landlady, Grace Jones, was found who agreed that the accused might have stayed at her guesthouse on the nights in question, none of the other guests had seen him there. Hanratty claimed to have visited a sweetshop in Liverpool on the day of the abduction but though a shop assistant was found who matched his account she insisted this could only have occurred on the day before, when he was apparently in London. Finally, there was the testimony of Roy Langdale, who alleged that Hanratty had confessed his guilt.

Hanratty's defence team argued that the identification evidence was unreliable. The first person to speak to Valerie Storie after her ordeal was teenager John Kerr. As she lay wounded in the lay-by he claimed that she had described her attacker as having "light, fairish hair". He said he had written down the key information she had given him and later handed this first witness account to a uniformed police officer. It was never subsequently found. At the first identification parade Valerie Storie had mistakenly picked a man with light, fairish hair. But Hanratty's hair was dyed black at the time of the murder. The defence suggested that her first description of her attacker was a much better match for Peter Alphon, the man first arrested on suspicion of the crime. It was also argued that Alphon had access to the basement room where the incriminating cartridge cases were found.

In short, the defence argued, the eye-witness testimony and the circumstantial evidence failed to stack up against James Hanratty. As for his supposed confession to a fellow prisoner, that was a cock and bull story fabricated by the "wretch" Roy Langdale, whose evidence was contradictory. Detective Superintendent Acott was guilty of "inaccuracies and omissions" in his account of interviews with Hanratty after his arrest and was bluntly accused of not having told the truth. The defence hinted that Hanratty had perhaps been framed. After all, if he was really the killer, why leave cartridge cases in his hotel room *before* the murder? And wasn't it the case that whoever put the gun and ammunition under the bus seat was not hiding them but actually *wanted* them to be found?

There was no objective, scientific evidence to link Hanratty to either the murder weapon or the car. Moreover his behaviour throughout the period of the murder and afterwards had been quite unsuspicious. Hanratty was a truthful witness and incidents which he had described and which at first appeared to be invention later turned out to be true. Besides, Mrs Jones believed that Hanratty had stayed at her guesthouse on the night of the murder and the following night. His alibi enjoyed third-party support. His counsel, Michael Sherrard, implored the jury to bring in a verdict of not guilty.

Graham Swanwick QC then reiterated the prosecution case against Hanratty, and the judge provided a lengthy summing-up, lasting from Thursday afternoon to early on Saturday 17 February. Some observers felt that the judge was more sympathetic to the defence case than that of the prosecution and that his summing-up invited the jury to acquit the accused. At 11.22am the jury was sent out to consider its verdict. When it returned after six hours to seek clarification and advice, this was felt to favour the defence. To spectators in the courtroom, even those convinced of Hanratty's guilt, it seemed that he would be found not guilty. If the jury was unable to agree on a verdict after six hours then plainly it was divided, with at least one member unconvinced by the prosecution case. In 1962 majority verdicts were not permissible in British courts. A jury's verdict had to be unanimous. If even one juror stuck to the view that James Hanratty was innocent he could not be convicted and the case would require a re-trial.

The judge responded to the foreman's note by explaining that the phrase "no reasonable doubt as to his guilt" was unsatisfactory because the expression "reasonable doubt" gives rise to a variety of definitions. He directed that before convicting Hanratty of the charge of murder the jurors must be *sure* of his guilt. He added, "If you have a reasonable doubt, then you are not sure. You understand that, do you not?"

As for circumstantial evidence. It needed to be "quite good evidence" but it must point "inevitably" to only one conclusion: the guilt of the accused. Two cartridge cases from the murder weapon were found in the hotel room occupied by Hanratty on the night before the murder, but the judge pointed out that others had access to this room prior to their discovery. "You must not jump to the conclusion that the mere finding of those cartridge cases there denotes that they were left there by the prisoner unless you are quite sure that all the roads lead to that one place."

Having listened to this advice, the jurors filed out again and returned upstairs to the plush red-carpeted Grand Jury Room on the first floor of the Shire Hall, overlooking the River Ouse. After further deliberation the jury returned to the packed courtroom. Once again, the atmosphere was electric. Once again, the expectation of a verdict was dashed: the jury had simply returned to request some refreshment. The judge was clearly not pleased but the request was granted and the jurors once more returned to continue their discussion. Finally, at 9.10pm, they returned with their verdict. Among those present there was the feeling that the length of the jury's deliberations – almost ten hours – suggested serious concern about the evidence and the likelihood that Hanratty would be acquitted.

The foreman of the jury stood up and was asked if they had reached a verdict. They had. "Guilty, my lord."

James Hanratty was asked if he had anything to say. After stumbling over his words he said that he was innocent and would appeal. The judge, the black cap by now placed over his wig, pronounced the only sentence allowed under English law at that time: death by hanging.

The only hope for the defendant now was that the verdict would be overturned by the Court of Appeal or that the Home Secretary would grant a reprieve.

None of the jurors in the trial of James Hanratty ever spoke of what happened during those long hours of discussion. In the absence of any account we can only speculate about what shaped their verdict. Perhaps it is not surprising that the jury found him guilty. After all, three witnesses, including the surviving victim, had picked Hanratty out in identification parades, insisting that he was the man in the car. He did not deny that he had talked to a criminal associate about getting hold of a gun, or that he had stayed in the hotel room where the cartridge cases had been found, or that he had shown a friend how the upstairs back seat of a double-decker bus was a good place to hide things. Finally, Hanratty had claimed to have been in Liverpool at the time of the crime and then, during the course of the trial, confessed that this was a lie. He now said he had been in Rhyl, at a bed and breakfast establishment which he was unable to identify. But though one such place resembled his very general description, none of the other guests had seen him during the two days he claimed to have stayed there.

Every criminal trial is a tale of conflicting narratives which boil down to two opposing versions of what happened. It is for the jury to decide which version is most plausible. In the end jury members judge a case on their own life experiences. Who is lying? Who is telling the truth? Does the circumstantial evidence amount to a pattern which indicates guilt, or is it random or coincidental and unconnected to the crime? What rings true and what doesn't?

It is also difficult to say what will impress a particular individual. Did any member of the jury really believe the evidence of Roy Langdale, the petty criminal who claimed that Hanratty had confessed to him in the exercise yard of Brixton Prison? Langdale's evidence seemed all too obviously an attempt to curry favour with the authorities by supplying some helpful "evidence" in return for which he would receive lenient treatment for his crimes – as indeed happened. Writing after the trial, and equipped with the knowledge that Langdale had subsequently been described as "normally ... very helpful to the police" in order to mitigate his sentence, Louis Blom-Cooper believed that Langdale was probably a police informer "planted next to Hanratty to glean what evidence he could from the man they accused of the A6 killing". He questioned whether the jury would have accepted Langdale's evidence at all had they known this. Nevertheless Blom-Cooper concluded, perhaps surprisingly, that "The confession made by Hanratty to Langdale was ... almost certainly true". However, he based this belief on the evidence of a prison warder who had overheard Langdale and who believed that he had obtained information which had not been reported in the newspapers and which could only have been known to the murderer. This assumption later proved to be open to debate.

At his trial Hanratty denied he had ever talked to Langdale about the A6 case. He insisted that Langdale's evidence was "all false, every word of it". But, astonishingly, one of those who believed that Hanratty *had* talked to Langdale about the case was Jean Justice, the man who pioneered the campaign to clear Hanratty's name. Justice excused Hanratty's conversation on the grounds that "the fact he revealed particular details about the A6 murder to a stool-pigeon meant no more than that he was repeating what he had gathered from newspaper reports concerning the murder". If even Jean Justice disregarded Hanratty's denial of ever having spoken to Langdale about the case, why should not members of the jury?

And what of the Rhyl alibi, now a central plank of the campaign to clear Hanratty's name? At the time Jean Justice didn't seem to believe it either. In his first book on the case he recalled "Superintendent Acott's satisfied grin when Hanratty tried out his unconvincing Rhyl alibi". That, remarkably, was Justice's only reference to Hanratty's claim that he was nowhere near the crime scene.

Lord Russell of Liverpool speculated that the jury had "lingering doubts" about Hanratty's guilt.

> It is difficult to escape the conclusion that had the murder of Gregsten been committed a few hundred miles further north and Hanratty had been tried under Scottish law, which provides for a verdict of "not-proven", he would still have been alive today, even though under a cloud of suspicion.

He presumably based this notion on the length of time the jury had taken to reach a decision. On the other hand, they had a massive amount of evidence to sift through and decide on. Besides, the jury faced an uncomfortable choice. If they acquitted James Hanratty they would, in effect, be asserting that Valerie Storie was quite wrong in her insistence that the man in the dock was the person who shot Michael Gregsten and then raped her. They would also be indicating that the two other witnesses, who swore that they recognised Hanratty as the man at the wheel of the Morris Minor, were equally wrong. And they would be saying that all the other circumstantial evidence – even the discovery of the cartridge cases in the room Hanratty had stayed in at the Hotel Vienna – was sheer coincidence and nothing at all to do with him.

A verdict of not guilty would have meant that the crime remained unsolved, with no identifiable suspect, and no one punished for one of the most high profile and shocking cases of the decade.

In such circumstances perhaps it is not surprising that even the one or more doubters among the jury – if there were any – were finally swayed by the arguments of the others, so that in the end all eleven unanimously agreed that Hanratty was guilty as charged.

Hanratty's only grounds for a successful appeal against his conviction were technical ones: that the legal process of the trial had been tarnished in some way. This was what his barrister, Michael Sherrard, duly argued. On 13 March 1962 he put it to the three Appeal Court judges that the jury's verdict was perverse and was not supported by the evidence in the case. Furthermore, he asserted, Mr Justice Gorman's summing-up was defective and some of the material placed before the jury had been inadmissible.

The Court of Appeal brusquely dismissed every one of these arguments. The trial judge's summing up was "not only fair, but favourable" to the defendant (as some observers felt at the time, not least Louis Blom-Cooper). Indeed, Hanratty had been lucky to have Mr Justice Gorman as the judge, as he was noticeably solicitous to the defendant's interests. The prisoner was fortunate narrowly to have avoided appearing before Mr Justice Melford Stevenson, a notoriously harsh and bigoted judge, who was fond of making inflammatory and highly prejudicial remarks. The appeal judges further stated that the identification evidence against Hanratty was conclusive and it was not unreasonable for the jury to be influenced by it. Finally, they asserted that even if the material which Sherrard regarded as inadmissible had been discounted, "the case against Hanratty is not a jot weaker". Indeed, in its view so strong was the case against Hanratty that the Appeal Court judges chose not to hear any submissions from Graham Swanwick QC in rebuttal of Sherrard's seven and a half hours of legal argument.

Following the rejection of the appeal, the Home Office stated that the execution of James Hanratty would take place at Bedford Prison on 4 April 1962. His only chance now lay in a reprieve. His defence lawyer Michael Sherrard duly visited the Home Office, armed with new information not mentioned at the trial. This showed that there were other witnesses in Rhyl who remembered seeing Hanratty there on 22 and 23 August 1961. However, on 2 April the Home Office released a statement that the Home Secretary, R. A. Butler, "has most carefully considered all the circumstances of this case, but regrets that he has failed to discover any sufficient grounds to justify him in advising Her

Majesty to interfere with the due course of law".

"Who killed Hanratty?" Paul Foot was later to ask. It was a rhetorical question. The answer, he suggested, was the Establishment (police, judiciary, the Home Office, politicians) and, implicitly, the conspirators who, he believed, had arranged for Michael Gregsten to be intimidated into ending his adulterous relationship with Valerie Storie. But the literal answer to Foot's question was the hangman, Harry B. Allen, aided by an assistant.

The cold, brutal, dehumanized ritual of state hanging had evolved over centuries. Once public, by the twentieth century it was hidden from view behind prison walls. The hangman and his assistant arrived the day before the execution and often stayed overnight in the prison. The prisoner would be taken to another part of the prison, so as not to hear the crash of the trapdoors being tried out. The rope was tested with a sandbag, which was left overnight to stretch the rope. A mathematical formula based on the prisoner's weight and height was used to calculate the drop.

In the morning the condemned man was led from his cell into the execution chamber and hanged before he hardly knew what was happening. Once the prisoner was inside the execution chamber the process was often accomplished in less than ten seconds. Albert Pierrepoint, the best known of all public hangmen, enjoyed puzzling prison warders and new assistants by lighting a cigar just before going off to carry out an execution. After taking a few puffs he would put the cigar down, go off and hang someone, and return to his cigar, which would invariably be still alight. He would then take a few ostentatious puffs before the eyes of startled and very impressed prison warders and his assistant. This performance was intended to emphasize his speed and professionalism.

Those in attendance at the execution would usually include the prison governor, the Under Sheriff and the chaplain. The prisoner, his hands bound behind him, was asked to stand on chalk marks, one foot on each trapdoor, while the hangman placed a linen hood over the prisoner's head. The hood was partly to calm the prisoner while the final adjustments were made, and partly to spare onlookers the sight of the dead man or woman's horribly contorted face after death.

The hangman stepped off the trap, pulled down a lever, and the trapdoors opened, crashing loudly against the brick walls below. The prisoner plummeted down into the pit beneath and met an instant death from dislocation or fracture, usually between the second and third cervical vertebrae.

Public opinion slowly shifted against hanging in the post-war years. This was due in part to a growing campaign against state executions on the part of intellectuals, writers and political activists. One of the most eloquent essays ever written against capital punishment is George Orwell's "A Hanging". It describes the execution of an unnamed prisoner, for an unidentified crime, in colonial Burma in the 1920s, where the author famously served as a police officer. One of the best things Orwell ever wrote, this brilliantly vivid and atmospheric essay portrays an execution as a grotesque and macabre episode, involving a moment of black comedy with a stray dog. Its defining moment is when the prisoner on his way to the gallows steps aside to avoid a pool of water on the path.

> It is curious, but till that moment I had never realized what it means to destroy a healthy, conscious man. When I saw the prisoner step aside to avoid the puddle, I saw the mystery, the unspeakable wrongness, of cutting a life short when it is in full tide. This man was not dying, he was alive just as we were alive. All the organs of his body were working – bowels digesting food, skin renewing itself, nails growing, tissues forming – all toiling away in solemn foolery. His nails would still be growing when he stood on the drop, when he was falling through the air with a tenth of a second to live. His eyes saw the yellow gravel and the grey walls, and his brain still remembered, foresaw, reasoned – reasoned even about

puddles. He and we were a party of men walking together, seeing, hearing, feeling, understanding the same world; and in two minutes, with a sudden snap, one of us would be gone – one mind less, one world less.

The prisoner is anonymous and his crime is unmentioned but Orwell humanizes him and makes him an object of compassion and sympathy.

This essay had little or no impact when it was first published in a small literary magazine in 1931, when Eric A. Blair was an unknown writer who had yet to publish his first book or to adopt the pen-name "George Orwell". But it was republished in 1946 (after the publication of *Animal Farm*) and again, posthumously, in 1950, 1956 and in Orwell's *Collected Essays* in 1961. Orwell's friend Arthur Koestler was a leading campaigner against capital punishment, and in that same year – the year of the A6 murder – he co-authored the polemic *Hanged By The Neck*, which the publishers twinned with another, Leslie Hale's *Hanged In Error*. Both polemics were published as distinctive scarlet-jacketed Penguin Specials – a popular, widely distributed series of paperback originals specalising in contemporary social issues.

The central arguments had now been comprehensively articulated: hanging was uncivilised, it did not deter people from killing, and it was a punishment which could not be reconsidered at a later date if a miscarriage of justice had occurred. The execution of James Hanratty, however, did not provoke the scenes of public unrest which accompanied some other hangings of the era. A small early morning crowd gathered outside Bedford Prison prior to the conventional execution time of 8am but it seems most were there out of morbid curiosity rather than to protest. There was no trouble, as there had been a few years earlier when Ruth Ellis was hanged at Holloway Prison and police had to force back a crowd of angry protesters. The only explicit dissent came from four students with placards, who stood in silent dignified protest beside the prison entrance. They were not there to protest that James Hanratty was innocent of the crime for which he had been convicted but to assert that the death penalty was barbaric and wrong.

The sentence was duly carried out. The crowd dispersed. The A6 murder case seemed to be over.

> In this case now I have got three friends: that is my
> counsel and my family. The rest of the world are [sic]
> against me. The papers have seen to that.
>
> James Hanratty at his trial

If there was one thing that the hanging of James Hanratty did not bring it was closure.

In the year following Hanratty's execution. *The A6 Murder* by Louis Blom-Cooper (1926-2018), a lawyer, appeared as a Penguin Special. Blom-Cooper had attended the trial, presumably in his capacity as the legal correspondent of *The Guardian* and *The Observer* newspapers. He claimed that "Most lawyers were of the opinion that on the evidence, as adduced before the eleven-man jury, Hanratty should not have been convicted". He shared this view, although this was not because he thought James Hanratty was innocent of the crime.

On the contrary, he believed that Hanratty was the murderer, and he regarded his Rhyl alibi as "palpably false". He felt that if some of the evidence which had been ruled inadmissible had been put before the jury – statements by the Brixton Prison officer who had overheard Roy Langdale describing Hanratty's confession, and statements supplied by Hanratty's associate Louise Anderson – then "the gap in the Crown's case might have been filled sufficiently to merit a conviction on the evidence". However, speaking as a lawyer, he felt that "on the evidence before the court and, with the heavy onus of proof on the Crown borne in mind, it is doubtful whether he should have been convicted." He described the trial judge as appearing "deeply affected" after pronouncing the death sentence, adding "one almost suspects that he disagreed with the verdict".

Blom-Cooper was troubled by what he perceived as baffling aspects of the crime. The final chapter of *The A6 Murder* was entitled "The Lingering Doubts". How did an urban criminal like Hanratty "come to be wandering pointlessly in Buckinghamshire"? and "what was the explanation of the long nightmare drive"? What were Michael Gregsten and Valerie Storie really up to in that cornfield? The trial had explored none of these aspects of the case. Blom-Cooper hinted that Hanratty's arrival in the field might not have been a purely random event but could have involved what he darkly and cryptically called "perverted design". Later, he elaborated on what he meant. He theorised that perhaps someone wanted to scare Michael Gregsten into ending his relationship with Valerie Storie. Hanratty was a hired gun, sent on a mission by someone else. No harm had probably been intended but matters had spiralled out of control.

Blom-Cooper conceded that such a theory might seem "fantastic" but asked "should we not explore it?" However, he left that project to others. His only further contribution to this conspiracy theory was to draw attention to the strange suicide of Hanratty's criminal associate, Charles France. It had been suggested, Blom-Cooper remarked (without saying who had suggested it, or where, or when) that France was the middle-man who had arranged for Hanratty "to be hired to go out and scare the couple in the cornfield". This was "wildly fantastic" (but if so, why bother mentioning it?). Or perhaps, more plausibly, France had supplied Hanratty with the gun. But perhaps not. In which case, "If France did not supply the gun, he may nevertheless have told Hanratty where he could get hold of one."

The A6 Murder is a somewhat idiosyncratic book. It was subtitled *Regina v. James Hanratty, The Semblance of Truth* (alluding to a quotation from Shakespeare's *Cymbeline* on the theme of misleading circumstantial evidence, which prefaces Blom-Cooper's final chapter). As an account of Hanratty's trial it is a patchy and superficial one. Blom-Cooper's book had a wider agenda: a plea for reform of the English judicial system, which, he argued, excluded material in criminal trials which might shed light on the background and motive of an offender's action.

Much of the A6 case is treated as a peg on which to hang a variety of suggestions for the reform of criminal investigation and judicial process. Blom-Cooper lent his support to the campaign for abolition of the death penalty, arguing that Hanratty might have been rehabilitated and "behavioural scientists" could have then persuaded him to explain what his crime had really been about. There were other matters arising from this case which vexed him, such as the lay-out of English courts. Blom-Cooper felt the dock should be abolished since it carried a "distinct aura of guilt" and defendants should be allowed to sit alongside their counsel, American-style.

Some of Blom-Cooper's interests now seem distinctly weird. At one point he considers "the question of victim-precipitation – that is, to what extent the victim contributes to his own death". He claimed that research had shown that a woman who screams on encountering a burglar in her home is more likely to be assaulted than one who calmly tells the burglar to leave. This led him to the solemn observation that "if old women in this predicament can learn that their lives may be saved by the exercise of considerable presence of mind in not shouting for help or screaming, then murders may be prevented".

What seems to have bothered Blom-Cooper more than anything is that he couldn't *understand* the crime. It was "inexplicable". As he put it, alluding to what he believed was the probable involvement of Hanratty's criminal associate Charles France, if "the real story" was known then the fight against crime might be improved. But the real story behind France, Hanratty and the murder weapon remained as elusive as Hanratty's appearance in the cornfield. Blom-Cooper articulated his doubts and indicated that Hanratty might not have been alone in his criminal enterprise but said no more. Of course if Hanratty *had* been hired to scare Michael Gregsten in order to persuade him to end his affair with Valerie Storie, this invited the obvious question: which person or persons had done the hiring? Blom-Cooper did not ask this question, let alone attempt to answer it.

The problematic evidence and the fundamental mystery of the crime indicated to Blom-Cooper inadequacies in the legal process which required reform. Others drew a completely different conclusion – namely that James Hanratty was entirely innocent of the crime. Hanratty's parents firmly believed that murder and rape were completely alien to their son's character and history as a petty criminal. His convictions were for burglary and car theft – not violence, still less sexual violence. Spectators at the trial had mixed feelings. The barrister Jeremy Fox at first "thought him not all a savoury character, and assumed that he must have committed the murder". Every crime correspondent for the national newspapers believed Hanratty was guilty as charged. The jury, of course, unanimously found him guilty. But others were impressed by Hanratty's apparently open, honest disposition. His barrister Michael Sherrard believed Hanratty would make a good impression in the witness box and would show that he was not the psychopathic monster who had apparently carried out the crime. Under questioning by the prosecution Hanratty stoutly maintained his innocence and poured scorn on the suggestion that he was a robber who had gone out to steal:

> It is quite obvious if I did that I would not be looking for a car in a cornfield, as you put it to the court. I will be looking for some cash, a bank, a shop, something to that effect. I would not be looking for a car in a cornfield for some cash for a stick-up.

It appeared a convincing argument. At another moment, when Graham Swanwick went through Hanratty's criminal record with him, he retorted:

Sir, I must put this point quite clear. I ain't a man the court approved of as of good character, but I am not a murderer. This is a murder trial, not a housebreaking trial.

Hanratty also ridiculed the notion that he was a rapist, acting from pent-up lust:

If I wanted a woman I could have gone in the West End and had a woman for a fortnight. If I wanted a woman I could get one for a fortnight … The man who committed this is a maniac and a savage … I am not a man the court can approve of, but I am not a maniac of any kind.

Among those watching and listening was Dr David Lewes, an Australian consultant at Bedford General Hospital. He was very impressed by Hanratty's defence and after the verdict vociferously asserted the condemned man's innocence of the crime.

There was one other man who had attended the trial and who had likewise become convinced of Hanratty's innocence. This was Jean Justice (1930-1990), an affluent 31-year-old dilettante who some years earlier had dropped out of a law course at Oxford. Justice's efforts to clear Hanratty of the crime were to end in failure but in the long run they were astonishingly successful in terms of influencing more high-profile figures and, through them, wider public opinion. His impact on later campaigners was immeasurable. There are lengthy and admiring descriptions of his pioneering attempts to clear Hanratty of the crime in Paul Foot's *Who Killed Hanratty?*, which reached an audience no other book on the case has matched, before or since, and Bob Woffinden's *Hanratty: The Final Verdict*. In the years and decades that followed the political and legal establishment might resist calls for the quashing of Hanratty's conviction, but in the popular mind, thanks to those early efforts of Jean Justice, there seemed little doubt that James Hanratty's name belonged in what by the 1990s had become a lengthening roll-call of miscarriages of British justice.

Jean Justice was all too clearly searching for some kind of meaning in his life, something to focus on and make sense of what had otherwise been a privileged and self-indulgent lifestyle. He had dabbled very successfully in property dealing; he painted; he aspired to write music. He was also a flamboyant homosexual and a heavy drinker, brash and extrovert, known as "Boomy" to his friends. In 1957 he began to live with a gay barrister named Jeremy Fox. This was an era when gay men endured widespread institutional prejudice. They were often harassed and entrapped by homophobic police officers and were prosecuted in the courts. Whereas Jean Justice flaunted his sexuality, Jeremy Fox preferred reticence and discretion.

Justice, evidently at heart a frustrated barrister (and born with a surname that must have seemed highly charged with his own private destiny), was drawn to high-profile court cases. In 1961 he had briefly managed to smuggle himself into the Portland spy trial at the Old Bailey, which concerned five people accused of passing Royal Navy secrets to the Soviet Union. He was found to have used a wig and gown borrowed from his lover, Jeremy Fox. Later that year, when the committal proceedings of the A6 murder case opened at Ampthill, Justice instructed his chauffeur to drive him to Bedfordshire and observed proceedings from the public gallery. He was troubled by the apparent absence of motive for the crime and quickly decided that the case didn't add up. His suspicion that something was amiss was underlined by the announcement that the notes jotted down by teenager John Kerr could not be found. Kerr said he had handed them to a senior officer, but his identity remained elusive. As Kerr was the first person to hear Valerie Storie's description of her attacker, this was arguably vital evidence – especially when the suspicion grew that her description of the gunman later changed, with inconsistencies that amounted to blatant contradictions. If Storie was an unreliable eye-witness then this completely undermined her subsequent confident identification of the accused man.

After Hanratty was committed for trial in the New Year, Justice set out to find more about the case. He visited Hanratty's old Soho haunt, the Rehearsal Club. He met and talked to Hanratty's parents. In February 1962, with the trial in full flow, Justice tried to track down the first suspect, Peter Alphon. He finally made contact on 11 February and the two men went for a drink. On 17 February the jury brought in their verdict of guilty.

Five days later Justice went to visit Peter Alphon at the Regent Palace Hotel, where he was staying uner the pseudonym "Peter McDougal". Alphon dramatically handed Justice a drawing. It was

> an extraordinary surrealist affair of criss-crossing horizontal and vertical lines, tiny squares and oblongs, meandering squiggles and curious splodges. I looked at it long and earnestly, but at first could make nothing of it. Then, something prompted me to hold the paper flat just below eye-level and peer along it. Its message became immediately, terrifyingly apparent.
>
> The longer lines, fore-shortened, formed letters and the letters spelled out words. One way I could clearly distinguish "PETER McDOUGALL". The other way I could see "MURDERER" and beneath it the tell-tale place-name "BEDFORD".

To Justice this was nothing less than a confession – dramatic evidence that Peter Alphon was, as the police had first suspected, the A6 murderer.

Shortly before the day of Hanratty's execution Justice, Fox and Alphon went to the Old Station Inn, Taplow, where Michael Gregsten and Valerie Storie had been for a drink before going on to the cornfield. Justice quietly quizzed the manageress,

Mary Lanz, who said that Alphon had visited the Inn on several occasions the previous summer. Later, travelling via Dorney Reach, Alphon shouted "Stop!" and Fox turned into a field by the side of the road. It was the cornfield from which Gregsten and Storie had been abducted. From that night on Justice became utterly convinced that Alphon was indeed, beyond all doubt, the A6 killer. Fox remained sceptical but later also came to believe it.

On May 15 Alphon at last gave Justice what he had long desired: a set of notes which hinted at what had happened and which amounted to a written confession. Alphon indicated that he had conspired with the Hotel Vienna employee William Nudds to frame Hanratty. In October 1962 Justice had his last face-to-face meeting with Alphon, but communication between the two continued by telephone. By this time Justice had interested others in his belief that Hanratty was innocent and that Alphon had been the real murderer all along. Fenner Brockway, the Labour MP for Slough, was sympathetic, as was a local journalist named Tony Mason. Martin Ennals, general secretary of the National Council for Civil Liberties, also became involved. Ironically this keen libertarian suggested that Justice secretly tape his telephone conversations with Alphon – advice which Justice accepted and proceeded to implement.

In the spring of 1963 Justice, Fox, and Tony Mason put together a file of material on Alphon and the A6 case which Fenner Brockway passed on to the Home Secretary. He also presented a petition signed by over a hundred Members of Parliament calling for an inquiry. A debate was held in the House of Commons on 2 August. The Home Secretary, Henry Brooke, rejected the call for an inquiry. He pointed out inconsistencies in Alphon's supposed "confession" which cast doubt on its probity and said it was "impossible" that he could have been the perpetrator of the crime. He also cuttingly pointed out that the two individuals at the heart of the campaign – Jean Justice and Peter Alphon – were "people of precarious mental balance". Moreover Justice was known to be a heavy drinker.

Following this rebuff Justice set about writing a book on the case. He was at work on it when, on 18 March 1964, there was a dramatic new development. In the course of one of their long telephone conversations Alphon named for the first time a man who, he alleged, had paid him to carry out the crime. His "mission", Alphon explained, was to terminate the relationship between Gregsten and Storie on behalf of this man. When Justice questioned the man about this accusation he replied that Alphon was a "lunatic". He said he had never met Peter Alphon.

Justice completed his book in 1964 and it was published three months later. *Murder vs. Murder: The British Legal System and the A6 Murder Case* is as much autobiography as it is criminological inquiry. Justice supplied a feverish, passionate account of his tortured relationship with Peter Alphon. The book describes Alphon's confessions of involvement in the crime and reveals salacious details allegedly suppressed by Valerie Storie. *Murder vs. Murder* had two central arguments. One was that Peter Alphon was the A6 killer and rapist. The second was that the evidence for James Hanratty's innocence was "overwhelming" and that he had unquestionably been framed. The book was hostile to Valerie Storie, accusing her of letting her evidence be affected by "a slow and insidious process of police conditioning". But Justice was more cautious when it came to the new information he had been given.

Louis Blom-Cooper never identified where he had come across the "wildly fantastic" theory that the gunman had been hired to frighten Gregsten and Storie. This formed a key part of Peter Alphon's supposed "confession" to the murder, which Justice publicised. But in *Murder vs. Murder* Justice made no mention of the individual who Alphon had lately claimed commissioned the crime. Instead Justice's conspiracy theory involved Peter Alphon knowing both James Hanratty and his criminal associate Charles France. He said "a reliable witness" (whom he did not name) had told him of once seeing Hanratty and Alphon together. The cartridge cases found in the room at the Hotel Vienna which Hanratty had stayed in on the night before the crime were "deliberately planted" there by Alphon.

Murder vs. Murder: The British Legal System and the A6 Murder Case reads like the story of an intense gay love affair which has turned sour. It is also laced with paranoia. Justice claimed that the man leading the investigation, Superintendent Acott, was "told by superior authorities that Alphon was not to be touched". In fact Alphon was dropped as a suspect as the result of the identification parade when Valerie Storie failed to identify him as her attacker. In any case, Alphon was middle-class and well-spoken, whereas the gunman had been working-class, with a cockney accent (Justice got round that difficulty by claiming that Alphon was a clever mimic, who had deliberately impersonated a working-class man while carrying out his crime.) Justice also believed that "Whitehall" was out to get him for exposing the truth.

Murder vs. Murder was published in Paris by Olympia Press, a notorious press run by Maurice Girodias. Three-quarters of the books on his list were "pornographic trash". Girodias delighted in publishing books which no one else wanted to touch, the more offensive the better. When no one wanted *Lolita* he was happy to publish it – especially since he believed that Nabokov was a paedophile and that his book would encourage "a change in social attitudes toward the kind of love described in *Lolita*, provided of course that it has this authenticity, this burning and irrepressible ardour". Justice's own racy, largely autobiographical book was not short of burning passion. The intensity of his relationship with Peter Alphon seems to have unbalanced both men, with Alphon feeding Justice ostensible titbits of juicy detail to maintain the other man's interest in him.

One of the mysteries of the A6 murder case is what the gunman's motive was in getting into the car in the cornfield and doing nothing but talk to Gregsten and Storie for almost two hours. After listening to Peter Alphon's confessions, Jean Justice believed he had the answer. There had been more than just talk.

What happened during that period was so nauseating that I can understand why Miss Storie has so far said nothing of the matter ... Although I have never spoken to Valerie Storie, I have been told precisely what took place in the Morris Minor in the cornfield. If Valerie will admit that I am right when I state that she and Gregsten were forced to have sexual intercourse together, then she will also realise that only one person could have given me the information.

The murderer.

This salacious detail, which was nothing more than Alphon's own private sexual fantasy, makes it rather apt that Justice's book was published by a notorious pornographer. Justice did not know that Valerie Storie had been entirely frank with the police about her relationship with Michael Gregsten. She freely admitted that she and her lover sometimes went to the cornfield to have sex and had done so just two evenings earlier, on Sunday 20 August. But on the evening of the abduction they had gone there simply to talk. Had the gunman forced them to copulate while he watched, Valerie would certainly have told the police so. But she did not, because that never happened. She was a very strong woman, with a robust personality, and she was unshamed by her involvement in an adulterous triangle. Reticence was not her style. She told the police everything.

It is possible, of course, that Valerie Storie was completely unaware of Justice's coarse challenge at the time, since the book was published abroad. Its publication in Paris by a disreputable fringe publisher helped to ensure that its appearance passed without notice in Britain. Few, outside a handful of people with specialised knowledge of the A6 trial, probably even knew that this book existed. *Murder vs. Murder*, one suspects, sold very few copies and, unlike *Lolita*, it was not reprinted by Girodias. In time, however, Justice and his book would become hugely influential over two campaigners who would pick up where he left off. Apart from its central thesis that Hanratty was the innocent victim of a conspiracy and that Peter Alphon was the real killer, *Murder vs. Murder* helped perpetuate basic errors about the case. As part of his argument that Valerie Storie was an unreliable witness, Justice reproduced this courtroom exchange between the defence lawyer, Michael Sherrard, and Storie, relating to the ID parade at which she picked out Hanratty:

> SHERRARD. On that occasion, I am right in saying, am I not, that you made no identification for as long as twenty minutes?
> STORIE. I don't think it was that long.
> SHERRARD. In fact, you made no identification for twenty minutes?
> STORIE. I didn't specify the man I recognised until that time was up.

This was classic defence lawyer strategy. When Storie said "I don't think it was that long" she was entirely right. She had initially been wheeled up and down the line (later confiding that she had recognised Hanratty immediately). She was then wheeled up and down a second time. She requested that each man say the words "Be quiet will you, I'm thinking." She was wheeled along the line again, with each man speaking in turn. She requested a repeat performance. When this was all over Storie was asked if she recognised any of the men as the attacker. She identified Hanratty.

This somewhat attenuated ID parade had taken eleven minutes – not twenty. Valerie Storie had recognised Hanratty's face immediately and the sound of his voice merely confirmed her certainty that he was the gunman and rapist. But for decades afterwards the Hanratty campaigners falsely suggested that the ID parade had taken twice as long as it actually had done, and that after twenty minutes an uncertain, dithering Valerie Storie had made a wild guess based on the colour of Hanratty's hair.

Of rather more consequence than *Murder vs. Murder*, in the short term, was the publication the following year of the second book-length analysis of the A6 murder to be published in Britain. It came just two years after Blom-Cooper's Penguin Special paperback.

Deadman's Hill: Was Hanratty Guilty? (1965) was written by Lord Russell of Liverpool, otherwise known as Edward Frederick Langley Russell, 2nd Baron Russell of Liverpool (1895-1981). He was a qualified and experienced legal professional, as well as the author of non-fiction bestsellers about Nazi and Japanese war crimes. *Deadman's Hill* was a very well written book which provided the first substantial account of the case. Lord Russell had not attended the A6 murder trial but he benefited from being the first author defending Hanratty to have access to a full transcript of the trial, loaned to him by Hanratty's defence lawyer, Michael Sherrard. Hanratty's parents also let him see their son's prison letters and gave him permission to publish extracts. Dr David Lewes, the Bedford consultant who had attended the trial and proclaimed Hanratty's innocence, gave him a copy of his unpublished essay, "Reflections upon the Hanratty Trial".

Jean Justice's influence was evident in the book's central thesis that James Hanratty was a wholly innocent man. Indeed, in his Acknowledgements, Lord Russell expressed his thanks to "Mr Jean Justice for providing me with certain information". As far as Lord Russell was concerned it was "a case which bristled with red herrings" and in his opinion there was nothing to justify a conviction.

Lord Russell, though very much aware of Peter Alphon's confessions, did not describe them in his book. He did not argue that Peter Alphon was the real murderer, and indeed mentioned him only in passing. Lord Russell was not concerned with conspiracy theories, the notion that Hanratty was framed, or who the real murderer might have been. Instead he concentrated his fire solely on exonerating Hanratty.

The eye-witness evidence, he argued, was unpersuasive

and depended only on fleeting glimpses of the accused. The cornerstone of the case was Valerie Storie's identification of Hanratty, but women could be unreliable, as was illustrated by the notorious case of Adolph Beck, wrongly identified as a criminal by no less than fourteen women. In Russell's view "The identification of Hanratty by Miss Storie as the man who shot Gregsten dead was the cornerstone of the case" but "There is no class of evidence more liable to fall victim to the frailties of human judgement than that relating to identity."

As for the rest of the prosecution case. There was no evidence that Hanratty was in the cornfield in Buckinghamshire at 9.30pm, nor was there any credible motive for him to have been. Two empty cartridge cases from the murder weapon had been found in a hotel room occupied by Hanratty, who had used an alias, but it was "fantastic" to suggest that only James Hanratty could have been responsible. There was no evidence that Hanratty had ever owned a gun. Superintendent Acott had described Hanratty as "a typical gunman" but no evidence had ever been put forward to support this claim. Indeed, Lord Russell was convinced that "he was not the kind of young man who would ever want to do so". Moreover, Hanratty's behaviour in the six weeks following the crime was entirely inconsistent with guilt. There was not the slightest evidence he was a sex maniac.

Lord Russell ended his book with what were essentially two character references. In an Appendix he included two poignant letters from Hanratty to his parents and brother Michael, written shortly before his execution. These indicated that Hanratty came from a decent, caring family and continued to the very last moment to insist on his innocence and forecast that the truth "will one day be proved to the world".

Deadman's Hill, originally published in hardback by Secker and Warburg, was republished the following year as a paperback, by Icon Books of London and by Tallis Press of Oxford. It indicated a certain level of popular interest in the case, although after 1966 it was not republished, and it would soon be superseded by the biggest-selling and most influential A6 murder book of them all.

In the same year that Lord Russell's book first appeared hanging was abolished in the U.K., provisionally for five years, but in reality permanently. The families of hanged prisoners were given permission to have the bodies of their loved ones exhumed from unconsecrated pits in prison grounds and reburied in public cemeteries. On 22 February 1966 James Hanratty's remains were re-interred at Carpenders Park Lawn Cemetery in Watford.

During the summer of 1966 the A6 murder was in the news again when, during a debate in the House of Lords, Lord Russell publicly named Peter Alphon as a man who had confessed to the crime. Lord Stonham, Parliamentary Under Secretary at the Home Office, dismissed the possibility of Alphon being the murderer and questioned whether anything new was being said which was not considered by the trial jury.

There followed a flurry of publicity about Alphon's involvement and the possibility of Hanratty's innocence. In September 1966 Paul Foot published his first article on the A6 case in *Queen* magazine, naming Alphon as the real murderer. In November, BBC TV's prestigious current affairs programme *Panorama*, with five million viewers, questioned whether Hanratty was really guilty. Peter Alphon was interviewed but denied he was the murderer and said that his conversations with Jean Justice were merely scenarios for a book. Grace Jones, her previous hesitancy having evaporated, now asserted that Hanratty had definitely stayed at her boarding house. Newspaper-seller Charlie Jones miraculously remembered a man who one evening in August, probably a Tuesday, asked for "Terry" and the whereabouts of the fairground, who returned to ask him where he could find digs. Jones said he had directed him to Mrs Jones's establishment on Kinmel Street. Mrs Jones and Charlie Jones were paid ten guineas for their contributions. Quite why Hanratty would need to have asked for the whereabouts of the fairground in a tiny resort like Rhyl, when he had previously worked there (albeit briefly) was not explained. Valerie Storie appeared on the programme, insisting that she was certain of her identification of Hanratty as the gunman. But the thrust of the programme was to suggest that she was mistaken and there were serious questions to be asked about the safety of the conviction. It put Storie off giving any more interviews; she felt she had been tricked by the programme makers.

The momentum of a campaign to establish Hanratty's supposed innocence of the crime was gathering speed, assisted by sympathetic and influential media figures. As a consequence it was announced in January 1967 that Detective Superintendent Douglas Nimmo would be conducting an inquiry into Hanratty's Rhyl alibi. The following month Paul Foot reported in *Private Eye* that Lord Russell of Liverpool had attended Marylebone Magistrates Court and taken out a summons against Peter Alphon and his solicitor Sidney Eden, alleging breach of "recognisance" in relation to nuisance calls. According to Foot the police had declined to prosecute lest it "prejudice the investigation into the Rhyl alibi claimed by James Hanratty". Foot scented a cover-up. "Now what," he melodramatically asked, "could a routine prosecution in relation to the Post Office Act have to do with James Hanratty's alibi in Rhyl?"

Detective Superintendent Nimmo's report was completed in March. According to *The Daily Express* (23 March 1967), Nimmo found no evidence to substantiate Hanratty's alibi. In response the so-called "A6 Committee", which largely consisted of Hanratty's parents, his brother Michael, Jean Justice, Jeremy Fox and Paul Foot, went to Rhyl in search of new alibi witnesses. As a result of the Committee's claims to have found fresh evidence, Chief Superintendent Nimmo was sent back to investigate these new witnesses. He made what were described as "detailed and exhaustive investigations covering all possible lines of inquiry into the alibi" and concluded that he had found "no further evidence which, if put before the jury, might have influenced the verdict".

Paul Foot returned to the subject of the A6 murder in April. In *Private Eye*, under the punning headline *What's It All About, Alphon?*, he described a random encounter on a number 83 bus between James Hanratty senior and Peter Alphon on 14 April. It was not the first time their lives had randomly collided. Eighteen months earlier Alphon had been behind Hanratty's father in the queue at the White City greyhound racing stadium. On that occasion he remarked, "Mr Hanratty, every time I see you I feel the police are going to put their hand on my shoulder." Alphon had failed to appear in reply to Lord Russell's February summons and was therefore wanted by the police. Foot concluded (with hints of malpractice):

> Hanratty reported the matter to the police, who are "keeping a watch out". Scotland Yard, who have taken charge of the Marylebone summons have also been informed, yet have taken no action of any kind.

A fortnight later, on 12 May, Peter Alphon held a press conference in Paris and confessed to being the A6 killer. He also publicly named the man who, he alleged, had commissioned the crime. The British media withheld the name, aware that without evidence this was plainly a highly defamatory allegation. Alphon later reiterated his guilt on Independent Television's *Dateline* programme. Within a fortnight the Sunday newspaper *The People* reported that Peter Alphon had now retracted his confession. In November the Home Secretary, Roy Jenkins, brushed aside media calls for an inquiry, referring to Detective Superintendent Nimmo's unequivocal conclusion that the original verdict was safe.

The following year, 1968, was a relatively quiet one for the Hanratty campaigners. Jean Justice's second book on the case came out but not only was it once again published in France, this time it was written in French. *Le Crime de la Route A6* was basically a revised and expanded edition of *Murder vs. Murder* but was published by a different printing house. Although on this occasion it was put out by Robert Laffont – a far more reputable mainstream publishing house – the book probably had as little impact in Britain as in its original incarnation. It was a far more handsome production than the earlier Olympia Press text. It included photographic plates of key locations and individuals in the case, and a map showing the route taken from Dorney Reach via Harrow, Elstree, St Albans and Luton, all the way to Deadman's Hill. It also included several of Hanratty's letters written in the Bedford gaol prior to his execution.

Le Crime de la Route A6 was not a book ever likely either to be distributed in the U.K. or sold to a British publisher and translated into English because it was very vulnerable to an action for libel. For the first time the shadowy and somewhat abstract conspiracy theory which purported to explain the crime was unambiguously articulated:

> *Au cours d'une conference de presse donnée à Paris, à l'Hôtel du Louvre, le 12 mai 1967, Peter Alphon a ouvertement accuse un certain William Ewer de l'avoir engage pour metre un terme à la liaison de Michael Gresten et de Valérie Storie.*

> During a press conference at the Hôtel du Louvre in Paris on 12 May 1967, Peter Alphon openly accused one William Ewer of having hired him to put an end to the affair between Michael Gregsten and Valerie Storie.

Who was William Ewer? This individual, who had until now never been mentioned in connection with the A6 murder, was the brother-in-law of the murdered man, married to Janet Gregsten's sister. Who might have wanted to involve him in a scheme to break-up the affair? The answer was the murdered man's widow, Janet Gregsten.

Le Crime de la Route A6 included a suggestive photograph of a woman, the murdered man's widow, who had

59

barely featured in the A6 story. At the time both the trial and the accompanying newspaper coverage had maintained the fiction that Michael Gregsten and Valerie Storie were simply good friends. It was an illusion reinforced by Janet Gregsten's sympathetic visits to Valerie Storie in hospital. Few knew the tangled human story which lay behind the fact of married man Michael Gregsten sitting in a car with a much younger woman in a farmer's field at nightfall on a warm summer evening.

Janet Gregsten had been persuaded (presumably by a journalist) to pose in a chair in her living room, hands clasped, staring into space. In the background is the piano which her dead husband had once played. Janet looks young and attractive. She is smartly but casually dressed, with a pleated skirt extending well below the knees. On the carpeted floor beside her is a cup and what resembles a large ash tray or oval saucer filled with what looks like ash and cigarette ends. Nearby, artfully arranged so that it could be read by anyone looking at the photo, is the front page of a broadsheet newspaper with the headline HANRATTY TO DIE, beside a head and shoulders shot of the condemned man.

It is an image which invites decoding. Janet Gregsten's face is expressionless. She could be lost in grief, or traumatised and numb. But the positioning of the newspaper is disturbing. Although the framing of the image was surely nothing at all to do with Janet Gregsten it perhaps indicates a lack of emotion on her part that her husband's killer would soon be executed. It could be read as coldness, perhaps even as signifying satisfaction at his fate. In the context of Jean Justice's book this picture is surely included to suggest just that – or perhaps even complicity in a conspiracy.

Le Crime de la Route A6 seems to have made little impact in Britain and today it remains one of the most obscure titles on this subject. It is missing from the bibliography of the latest book on the A6 murder. Even though Bob Woffinden idolised Jean Justice and dedicated his own 1997 book on the case to him, he evidently never read it. He passes by its publication in a single sentence, erroneously stating that it was published "again by

Girodias". This indicates that he never saw a copy of the book, which is astonishing.

What made far more impact was the momentary involvement of a Beatle in the case. In 1969 John Lennon announced that he was joining the A6 Committee, and also financing a film about the case. This celebrity endorsement ensured the campaign remained in the headlines. Lennon and Yoko Ono were photographed meeting Hanratty's mother and father and beside them was a poster reading BRITAIN MURDERED HANRATTY.

Meanwhile Paul Foot kept plugging away at the case in the pages of *Private Eye*. It should be remembered that in its early years this fortnightly satirical magazine was a marginal and transgressive publication. W. H. Smith refused to stock it. I remember first buying it from a man who sold a variety of fringe underground publications, including *Oz* magazine, which were laid out for display on a city pavement, under a railway bridge. By 1969 the circulation of *Private Eye* had reached 48,624. That year Paul Foot published a piece entitled "A6 Murder: Breaking the Commons Law". He reported that members of the A6 Murder Committee had assembled outside the St Stephens entrance to the House of Commons, displaying three placards. No unauthorised demonstration is permitted within a mile of Parliament Square but when asked to move on the protestors refused. No action was taken against them. When the police were invited to arrest them, they declined. A senior officer told them, "That's what you want. If I arrested you, it would give you a political platform to express your views."

Foot once again scented a cover-up. He pointed out that one of the placards "made some very serious allegations against a senior police officer connected with the A6 murder enquiry". (He chose not to supply the name but it seems probable that the unidentified officer was Detective Superintendent Acott.) Foot was also indignant that Jean Justice's book *Murder vs. Murder* was also being sidelined. It had been identified on the placard as the source of allegations against the policeman. An MP, William Hamling, asked the Attorney General if he would take proceedings against the author and publisher "in view of the criminal libels therein on members of the Metropolitan Police". The response was that "in the Attorney-General's opinion he would not be justified in instituting such proceedings in this case".

Foot indignantly compared this to the case of Peter Forbes, who was sentenced to three years' imprisonment for criminal libel on the basis of a letter he had sent to the Prime Minister alleging harassment by a police officer. But this was very much Foot making a mountain out of a molehill. Apart from the fact that his book had been published outside the U.K., Jean Justice was hardly worth bothering with. His obscure and emotional book was seamed with paranoia. He portrayed Acott as the puppet of "superior authority" which had ordered him to leave Alphon alone and find someone else to charge with the A6 murder. Justice also accused Acott of manipulating Valerie Storie to ensure that she picked out Hanratty as her attacker. These allegations were ludicrous. Acott's supposedly seductive powers even extended to the courtroom: Justice denounced the officer's "histrionic performance" in the witness-box, which he grumbled "went down well with the jury".

Jean Justice, like his admirers, had little sense of irony. He reported that a senior officer at Scotland Yard had advised him to drop his obsession with the A6 case and Peter Alphon, otherwise "it will be the loony bin for you and no mistake". The policeman suggested that Justice take a holiday, which, Justice complained, implied that he "was the victim of a nervous breakdown". But that is exactly the impression given by *Murder vs Murder*. It's an impassioned and often hysterical narrative, rooted in Justice's obsessions, prejudices, gross errors of fact, and overall delusion that he alone had cracked the mystery of the A6 murder.

The following month Foot returned to the attack. He announced that Peter Alphon had written to the Home Secretary demanding a public inquiry into the A6 murder. If this was refused Alphon threatened to call a press conference on 22 October, in London, repeating the allegations he had made in Paris two years earlier. On that occasion, Foot informed *Private Eye* readers, "Alphon confessed to the murder and named the man who, he said, persuaded him to do it for money". Foot supplied a much abbreviated history of events which would have left anyone thinking something very fishy had gone on in the aftermath of the crime. He added that the officer in charge of the case, Detective Superintendent Acott, "resigned last month".

This was simply more attention-seeking bluster on Alphon's part. The Home Secretary, unsurprisingly, ignored him. There was no press conference. In any case, no newspaper would risk a libel action by naming someone as the brains behind the A6 murder – not without unambiguous evidence which would stand up in court. The lurid claims of an unstable publicity-seeker like Peter Alphon amounted to nothing. As a story it lacked legs.

The following year Hanratty's parents served a writ for negligence on R. A. Butler, who as Home Secretary had declined to grant a reprieve from execution for their son. Butler's decision had been determined by advice from civil servants; he could have over-ruled that advice, but only if there had been compelling political or legal reasons to do so. There had not been any. The writ was duly and predictably dismissed by the Court of Appeal.

Paul Foot's interest in the A6 murder had been gestating for five years. He now produced the most influential and popular of all the books ever written on this crime, first published in May 1971. In its various editions, including mass market paperbacks, it undoubtedly sold far more copies than any other book on the A6 murder. Even today, half a century later, second-hand copies can easily and cheaply be obtained. Foot's passionate belief in Hanratty's innocence cast (and still casts) a long shadow over public understanding of the case.

The book's title – *Who Killed Hanratty?* – was polemically provocative and reminiscent of the wording of the poster which John Lennon positioned in the background when he was photographed lending his support to the campaign. It may even have owed something to Karl Marx. Paul Foot's personal transformation from middle of the road supporter of the Liberal Party to ardent revolutionary socialist involved in what would become Britain's leading Trotskyist organisation gelled perfectly with his encounter with the Hanratty case.

In the year of the A6 murder the 24-year-old Foot encountered Yigael Glückstein, a charismatic Jewish Trotskyist twenty years older than himself. The bond that developed between them may have been strengthened by the discovery that they had each been born in Palestine during the years of British military occupation. Both men grew up to become bitter opponents of British foreign and domestic policy. Glückstein, who had emigrated to England and adopted the pseudonym "Tony Cliff", recruited Foot as an early member of his tiny "International Socialists" group. In due course it metamorphosed into the Socialist Workers Party, which in its heyday may have had as many as 10,000 members. The Party attracted socialists disillusioned with the Labour Party and held a particular appeal for students and intellectuals, including academics, writers and actors. During its history a number of public figures passed through its ranks including the journalist Peter Hitchens, the comedian Mark Steel and the fantasy novelist China Miéville.

Who Killed Hanratty?, as a rhetorical challenge, was in the same tradition as Marx's sarcastic retort to Bakunin's *Philosophy of Poverty*, entitled *The Poverty of Philosophy*. In fact the class aspect of the A6 murder case was kept largely as a sub-text in Foot's book, emerging only rarely, as in his reference to "a rasping duel between the brains of Mr Swanwick, trained at Winchester, University College, Oxford and the Inner Temple, and the untrained wits of James Hanratty. No one can say that Swanwick came off best." To Foot, Hanratty was a working-class hero, bravely standing up to a suffocating and sometimes corrupt elite. Not all observers saw it like that. Louis Blom-Cooper, like others, believed Hanratty to be "excruciatingly cocky". Unlike

Paul Foot, he had attended the trial and observed the prisoner at first hand. He thought that what he described as "Hanratty's insolence" must have left "a firm impression upon the jury". He was not alone in this. Many years later John Kerr recalled that Hanratty created a poor impression in the witness box. Kerr regarded him as cocky and arrogant.

Foot's belligerent title pointed an accusing finger at the Establishment. An innocent man had gone to the gallows – it was really nothing more than state murder – and many individuals and institutions were responsible for this appalling injustice. Foot blamed the police and Detective Superintendent Acott in particular. He blamed the judicial establishment, including Graham Swanwick QC and the other prosecution lawyers. He pointed a finger at Sir Anthony Hawke, Recorder at the Old Bailey, who had re-committed the case back to the Bedford Assizes, where Hanratty's defenders felt he would get less of a fair trial, on the grounds that there was a strong local feeling about the case, which might well influence a jury comprised entirely of men from Bedford. The Home Office and the Home Secretary were also culpable. In Marxist terms, the core message of Foot's book was quite straightforward. The capitalist state had ruthlessly executed a wholly innocent, uneducated, inarticulate young working-class man. Poor Jimmy Hanratty had never stood a chance.

But there was much more than this. At a human level Foot was bowled over by the decency and sincerity of James Hanratty's parents. They were working class; they were Catholics; Mr Hanratty was Irish. Foot found them "warm, gentle, determined people". They were "unlikely parents" of someone who had shot a man dead at point-blank range and then raped his girlfriend in the presence of the corpse. That man had been a psychopath and a monster, yet James Hanratty's parents were self-evidently kind, caring people and devout believers in their son's innocence. They were in possession of a clutch of letters which the condemned man had written to family members in the days before his execution. Letter after letter insisted on his innocence and asked them, after he was dead, to go on fighting to clear his name. That is precisely what they did do – assisted by Jean Justice, Jeremy Fox, Paul Foot, and various figures in the media.

In his book Foot brought to the subject not only the special knowledge imparted to him by Jean Justice but also his formidable skills and resources as a professional news reporter and also as a polemical writer on political topics. *Who Killed Hanratty?* remains the raciest and most readable of all the books on the A6 case, with Foot foregrounding himself as an investigator in the best Sherlock Holmes tradition. The description of his encounter with Louise Anderson, whom he found to be "living on her own in the most appalling conditions" is vivid, disturbing and compassionate.

Foot supplied important new background material on the central figures in the affair. Moreover, since he was a professional journalist he had ready access to a press cuttings library and was able to provide the first substantial account of the unfolding contemporary newspaper coverage of the murder and the police hunt, first for Alphon and then Hanratty. *Who Killed Hanratty?*, read on its own, is highly persuasive. It appears both comprehensive and plausible. If your only knowledge of the case is derived from this book then you will surely be persuaded of Hanratty's innocence.

Foot visited the scene of the Gregsten/Storie abduction on a later anniversary, to see what the light was like at 9.45pm. He interviewed everyone involved in the case who was willing to speak to him (many were not, including Valerie Storie and Detective Superintendent Bob Acott). At the time of publication *Who Killed Hanratty?* supplied by far the most detailed account of the crime, the trial and the aftermath to have yet appeared.

The book is divided into four parts. The first section provides an account of the crime and the subsequent police hunt for the gunman, which focused first on Peter Alphon and then, after Valerie Storie had failed to identify him as her attacker, on James Hanratty. The second section is devoted to a blistering critique of the prosecution case, arguing that the eye-witness evidence is every bit as questionable as the circumstantial evidence. The third section argues that James Hanratty was telling the truth when he said he had caught a train to Liverpool on the day of the abduction, and then spent two nights at a boarding house in Rhyl in Wales. Foot buttressed this alibi with a mass of new eye-witness evidence in its support. The final section is devoted to Peter Alphon and his confessions of involvement. Foot concluded that Alphon probably was the killer but acknowledged that conclusive proof remained lacking.

Thus, for the first time in any book published in Britain, Peter Alphon was identified as being almost certainly the true killer. Paul Foot also introduced two new names into the narrative of James Hanratty's innocence: the murdered man's widow, Janet Gregsten, and her brother-in-law, William Ewer. Foot drew attention to a strange story which had appeared in *The Daily Sketch* on 19 February 1962, shortly after Hanratty's conviction. This described how the pair had seen Hanratty in the street shortly after the murder and how Mrs Gregsten had an "amazing intuition" that he was the killer.

Although never overtly articulated, just beneath the surface of Foot's book lies the theory that Janet Gregsten and her brother-in-law William Ewer were instrumental in sending a gunman to the cornfield on a mission to frighten the lovers and make them end their relationship, so that Michael would return to his wife and small children. Foot later admitted that at the time of writing his book he was quite convinced that Janet Gregsten was a "jealous demon". But in his conclusion Foot restricted himself to the general argument that the crime was not a random one but pre-planned – the result of a plot to frighten Michael Gregsten into ending his affair with Valerie Storie. Hanratty was merely the fall-guy. Charles France was part of the conspiracy. It was Charles France who had placed the damning cartridge cases in the Hotel Vienna bedroom. Again, it was Charles France who had hidden the murder weapon and the spare cartridges under the upstairs back seat of a 36A bus. Peter Alphon had been hired to terrify the lovers by threatening them with a gun, but in choosing an unstable individual like Alphon the plot had gone disastrously wrong.

Foot did not explicitly identify who was behind the plot but anyone reading between the lines of the book could have guessed who they were. There were two very obvious candidates. One was Michael Gregsten's widow. The other was her brother-in-law, William Ewer. That the pair had attempted to draw attention to James Hanratty as a suspect long before the police were interested in him was explosive evidence of their sinister and central involvement in the case. Foot concluded that he was "as sure as it is possible to be that James Hanratty did not commit the A6 murder".

Who Killed Hanratty? enjoyed a very wide readership. Prior to publication in book form it was serialised in ten parts in *The Sun* newspaper (which half a century ago was in format, content and politics a very different newspaper to the tabloid of today). The hardback first edition of *Who Killed Hanratty?* was published by Jonathan Cape, which was both a mainstream publisher and, at the time, a cutting-edge one. "Most people working in publishing would concede that from the late sixties to the early eighties Cape was the greatest literary publishing house in England. We had the best authors, we produced the best promotions, and our production was the best." Tom Maschler's boast was close to the truth, and this ensured that *Who Killed Hanratty?* had an innate credibility and received maximum publicity.

It was enthusiastically received and generated widespread interest, with two debates in the House of Commons and calls for a new inquiry. To Foot's delight, Louis Blom-Cooper ate humble pie and wrote that *Who Killed Hanratty?* had convinced him that in his own book on the A6 murder he had been "rash" in some of his judgements and "overlooked countervailing arguments". Blom-Cooper now believed that his former conclusion that Hanratty was guilty was "based on all too slender a review of the accumulated material" and he supported calls for an inquiry. So did an editorial in *The Sunday Times*, although in the same issue (9 May 1971) it ran a hostile review of Foot's book by Dick Taverne QC, a Labour MP who had been involved in rejecting similar calls four years earlier.

"Despite the eloquent and generally, though not invariably, careful analysis by Paul Foot, there are no convincing grounds, in my view, for believing that Hanratty did not kill Michael Gregsten." Taverne revealed among other things that fresh evidence showed that Hanratty's sweetshop alibi was probably based on an incident in Liverpool in October 1961, where he was between Saturday 7th and Wednesday 11th, shortly before his arrest.

There were other sceptics. Giles Playfair in *The Financial Times* briskly dismissed the book: "The title is a nonsense, of course. There isn't any question about who killed Hanratty. The hangman did it on our behalf." In *The Sunday Telegraph*, Peter Gladstone Smith was also unpersuaded: "I have read everything Mr Foot has to say and remain unconvinced that there has been any miscarriage of justice." He added tartly, "a never-ending campaign to establish Hanratty's innocence *can* be unfair to other people". That Valerie Storie was implicitly among those who killed Hanratty and that the surviving and severely disabled victim of the crime bore some guilt did not perturb Foot's admirers. Tony Palmer in *The Spectator* gushed that it was "brilliant", "devastating" and "a powerful indictment" which could "leave no one in any doubt that a public enquiry is both essential and desirable". John Ezard in the *Guardian* agreed: "Mr Foot's outstanding narrative reconstruction of the alibi remains the strongest part of what is now an overwhelming case for a new and rigorous inquiry." Geoffrey Smith in *The Times* concurred: "he presents such a powerful argument for Hanratty's innocence that there is now to my mind a strong case for a public inquiry". But in spite of all the media pressure the Home Secretary firmly rejected a new investigation.

The following year *Who Killed Hanratty?* was offered at a reduced price as a title in "The *Private Eye* Book Club", with a free copy of Foot's Penguin Special paperback about the controversial Conservative politician Enoch Powell.

The A6 murder case was kept in the public eye when there was a debate about the case in the House of Lords. The film about the campaign financed by John Lennon also premiered. This documentary was titled *Did Britain Murder Hanratty?* It is not clear what kind of audience it ever had. Presumably it was shown at small public meetings organised by the campaign. The film was too amateurish in format ever to be shown on television, with much of it consisting of footage of a public meeting, with guest speakers who included Jean Justice and Paul Foot.

"We know how this murder was done because Alphon's told us how it was done," Foot insisted. "The murder was arranged." Peter Alphon had explained how it had happened, and to Foot is all made perfect sense. With gross exaggeration he told his audience that "everyone in the area knew that Gregsten and Valerie Storie used to go to that cornfield in that car, night after night, night after night". This last claim was utterly false.

The documentary also featured an interview with Hanratty's father. His son, he said, had assured him he was innocent. Mary Hanratty read out a prison letter from her son, in which he repeated that he hadn't done it. "We're going to write books and go on until this man's name is cleared" said Paul Foot, adding "until the rotten corruption which went into the framing of James Hanratty … is sewn up once and for all".

A questioner in the audience asked why Detective Superintendent Acott would want to frame Hanratty for the crime and what possible motive could there be for a gargantuan official cover-up? Foot replied that "the rigging" stemmed from the police desire to appear efficient. The crime required someone to be charged.

Who Killed Hanratty? was republished two years later as a mass market Panther paperback, with a lengthy postscript bringing the story up to date. One of the enigmas of the A6 case was the suicide of Charles France on 15 March 1962, not long before Hanratty's execution on 4 April. France was the criminal associate who told the police that the condemned man had shown him how under the back seat of a bus was a good place to dispose of unwanted stolen goods. He had appeared as a witness for the prosecution. Alphon had claimed that France had supplied him with the gun with which he had shot Gregsten, and had then framed Hanratty by hiding it on the bus and planting the cartridge cases at the Hotel Vienna.

In the wake of the publication of *Who Killed Hanratty?* *The Sunday Times* printed in full a letter which France had written to his wife shortly before killing himself. Foot reproduced it in his postscript, seeing it as further evidence of France's involvement in a criminal conspiracy. The letter was a smokescreen, Foot suggested. It was written, Foot argued, "to shelter his family from an association with the crime which he could not live with".

Foot's lengthy postscript described how two new eye-witnesses had been found in Rhyl who substantiated Hanratty's alibi – Pearl Hughes and Gerald Murray. All this publicity produced another dramatic development. Mary Lanz, proprietess of the Old Station Inn at Taplow, contacted Hanratty's parents to say she had new information about the case. She revealed that on the night that Michael Gregsten and Valerie Storie were having their last drink there, prior to their fatal trip to the cornfield, a man she now knew to be Peter Alphon was also present in the bar. She had seen him in her pub on a number of previous occasions. He was with a blonde woman in her early thirties. The implication was obvious. The woman was Janet Gregsten disguised under a blonde wig, and she was there to point out her husband and his lover to the gunman who had been hired to threaten and frighten them. The couple had left half an hour after

Gregsten and Storie.

Among other matters, Foot described the growing clamour in Parliament for a fresh look at the case. The Labour Party's then Shadow Home Secretary, Shirley Williams, supported a public inquiry, finding the evidence set out in *Who Killed Hanratty?* "disturbing". She promised to set one up if she became Home Secretary after the next General Election.

The same year that *Who Killed Hanratty?* came out in paperback there was a by-election in Lincoln. Jean Justice stood against the incumbent, Dick Taverne, presenting himself as "The A6 Murder candidate", in protest at Taverne's alleged role in blocking a pardon. He persuaded the Hanratty family to come to Lincoln to support him and to Taverne's embarrassment the MP found himself having to meet the parents of the hanged man. Many years later he confided that

> At the trial Valerie Storie's evidence had included a remark that what struck her in the brief glimpse she had of the killer were his staring blue eyes. I had not based my conclusion of guilt on identification but what was most striking about Hanratty's father were his staring blue eyes!

The Labour Party won the 1974 election but, sadly for Foot and his fellow campaigners, Shirley Williams was appointed Secretary of State for Prices and Consumer Protection. The new Home Secretary was Roy Jenkins, who agreed to set up an inquiry. However this was not held in public but behind closed doors. The person chosen to head this new inquiry was Cyril Lewis Hawser QC, described by Dick Taverne as "a prominent left-wing and anti-establishment lawyer". On the face of it this sounded like someone who would be sympathetic to the submissions of the A6 murder committee. In 1975 the conclusions of his investigation were published by Her Majesty's Stationery Office – in itself a sign that the government was aware of public interest in the case.

However, *The Case of James Hanratty: Report of Mr. C. Lewis Hawser QC of His Assessment of the Representations Put Forward in the Case of James Hanratty and of Other Relevant Material: Presented to Parliament by the Secretary of State for the Home Department* did not supply the A6 murder campaign with what it wanted – the exoneration of the hanged man. On the contrary, Hawser concluded that the case against Hanratty was "overwhelming". He asserted that all the new evidence presented by campaigners was devoid of real substance and "does not really cast any real doubt upon the jury's verdict".

Paul Foot wrote a blistering, anonymous critique of *The Case of James Hanratty* in *Private Eye* (18 April 1975) but despite his best efforts the Hawser report effectively marked the end of the first long phase of the campaign to clear Hanratty's name. Three years later, on 31 August 1978, Hanratty's father died. The A6 murder committee was shut down. The campaign had fizzled out and seemed to be at an end.

For almost a decade little happened and the crime began to fade as a topical issue. Then, in 1987, against a growing background of public unease about dubious convictions regarding individuals accused of involvement in IRA bombing campaigns in England – the Guildford Four, the Maguire family, Judith Ward, the Birmingham Six – a freelance journalist named Bob Woffinden published *Miscarriages of Justice*. This lengthy and well received book concentrated on eight classic criminal cases from postwar English history, together with the major IRA bombing cases of the 1970s. Woffinden argued that not only was the judicial system highly fallible and riddled with blatant miscarriages of justice but that the appeals system was seriously flawed, inadequate and unfair.

Two chapters of *Miscarriages of Justice* dealt with the A6 murder. Heavily influenced by Jean Justice's *Murder vs. Murder* and by Foot's *Who Killed Hanratty?* Woffinden prefaced his account of the case with a ringing declaration:

The whole story is so bizarre and complex that virtually the only absolutely safe conclusion is that the man convicted of the crime, James Hanratty, had nothing whatever to do with it.

In the first place, Woffinden asserted, Hanratty's alibi was rock solid. There was evidence he was in Liverpool on the afternoon of the day that Gregsten and Storie were abducted. From Liverpool the accused man said he had travelled to Rhyl and spent two nights there. This claim was supported by eye-witnesses, including the landlady of a boarding house which fitted Hanratty's description of the place where he had stayed. Since he was in Rhyl, Hanratty could not therefore have been the A6 gunman. The killer had been a poor driver, who needed the gears of a Morris Minor explaining to him. But Hanratty was an accomplished car thief.

Hanratty, Woffinden argued, was not only entirely innocent of the crime, he was also framed. The cartridge cases had been placed at the Hotel Vienna deliberately, to incriminate him. Likewise the murder weapon had been disposed of on a bus, where it was bound to be quickly discovered. If Hanratty had really been the killer surely all he needed to do was throw the gun into the Thames? Woffinden thought he knew who was responsible for this. It was Hanratty's friend and criminal associate, the late Charles France.

Finally, Hanratty was innocent because the prosecution had never been able to establish a motive. He had no convictions for violence or sexual offences and he had never been known to own a gun. The prosecution was unable to say how he was supposed to have acquired a gun, or what he was doing on the day of the abduction, or how he had suddenly appeared in a cornfield in a remote rural location well away from his usual urban haunts, or what he was doing in the days after the murder. The crime had been seen by many as the work of a madman, but psychiatrists who examined the prisoner all agreed he was perfectly sane.

Woffinden took the opportunity to refute the 1975 Hawser report. Hawser had decided that where the evidence of a visit to a Liverpool sweetshop was concerned Hanratty had deployed "the classical false-alibi trick of relating a true incident but putting it one day later than it actually occurred". Woffinden found this "preposterous" since there was evidence from a variety of sources that Hanratty had been in London on the day Hawser put him in Liverpool. Hawser had also given short shrift to the theory that the man responsible for the A6 murder could also have been the man who had threatened Audrey Willis with a gun in Hertfordshire on 24 August 1961 and again on 2 April 1962 (two days before Hanratty's execution) or who had assaulted Meike Dalal in Richmond on 7 September 1961. In each case the man had said he was the A6 killer but Hawser did not take such claims seriously. Woffinden, who believed otherwise, commented: "The vision of a pack of pseudo-A6 killers wandering around the country petrifying housewives is farcical."

He found it ironic that the year after his dismissive report Lewis Hawser QC had successfully defended the Liberal politician and activist Peter Hain from the charge of bank robbery. Hain had heaped praise on Hawser, calling him "one of the country's top barristers":

> ... bit by bit, he teased out the inconsistencies and downright contradictions in the prosecution case ... his whole performance in the trial was as emotionally moving to me as it was gripping. He worked with the precision of a surgeon ... As the trial continued he captivated the courtroom in his quiet and unassuming way that one sensed even the judge felt his authority threatened.

Woffinden was scandalised by this testimonial to Hawser's skill. He found it "strange" that where James Hanratty was concerned "he seemed temporarily bereft of his outstanding forensic abilities".

But if Hanratty was innocent, who was the real killer? Bob Woffinden devoted a chapter to the theory that it was Peter Alphon. Apart from his many confessions, Alphon had indicated that there had been a conspiracy. He had been hired by a man to frighten Gregsten into returning to his wife. The murder had only occurred when Gregsten's resolve to remain with Valerie Storie proved unshakeable.

Alphon had later retracted his confessions and Woffenden acknowledged that it was an open question whether or not he was really the killer. He had, however, supplied a plausible explanation of the crime: "Nobody had previously been able to provide that", least of all the prosecution. The conspiracy theory made perfect sense. It explained the enigma of the gunman's sudden appearance in the cornfield, the protracted nature of the abduction, and how events had slid out of control, resulting in murder and rape. Peter Alphon was all too patently a deeply narcissistic, volatile, unstable individual, fond of threatening and harassing people, and far more likely to have been the A6 gunman than a small-time crook from a decent family who had plainly respected his parents.

Woffinden's two chapters on the case contained nothing new but provided readers with an eloquent summary of the arguments previously put forward by Jean Justice and Paul Foot. *Miscarriages of Justice* received glowing reviews. Among those who admired the book, praising the author for his "great skill and scrupulousness" was one Paul Foot.

The year after Bob Woffinden's book was published, and against a background of widespread disquiet about convictions relating to the IRA bombing campaign, the third and final edition of *Who Killed Hanratty?* appeared. It was reissued as a paperback in the Penguin Books "True Crime" series, probably reaching its biggest readership ever and introducing the A6 murder to generations too young to have remembered the case.

In a new postscript dated April 1988, Foot once again brought the story up to date. He described Valerie Storie's new statement, which had emerged into the public domain only after the previous Panther edition of his book, some fifteen years earlier. This revealed that she had told police on the morning of 23 August 1961 that Michael Gregsten had split up with his wife a week earlier and had taken lodgings in Maidenhead. He planned to divorce Janet and marry Valerie. To Foot this revelation reinforced his belief that the crime was pre-planned, "part of a madcap scheme to frighten the lovers apart and weld together the Gregsten marriage".

Valerie Storie had also told Detective Sergeant Douglas Rees and Detective Constable Gwendolyn Rutland that in the conversation between them after the shooting of Michael Gregsten the gunman had said his name was Jim "but I don't think that was his real name". Storie's statement, Foot complained, "was deliberately withheld from Hanratty's defence lawyers".

Foot also took the opportunity to attack once again Hawser's 1975 report upholding Hanratty's conviction. He described it as "another victory for the legal establishment but no victory at all for truth or justice". It was, Foot asserted, "flawed from start to finish," marred by "a series of quite blatant errors and innuendos, all of which overstated the case against Hanratty or understated the case for him". The Hawser report was at its weakest, Foot argued, when it dismissed Hanratty's Liverpool and Rhyl alibis. Hawser's belief that Hanratty travelled to Liverpool on the day before the abduction was unsustainable. It contradicted the evidence of the three France family members as well as the woman at the Rehearsal Club. It also made no sense for Hanratty to have gone all the way to Liverpool purely for the purpose of creating an alibi for a crime which the prosecution had argued was not premeditated.

As for the Rhyl alibi, Hawser said that Margaret Walker, who recalled a man resembling Hanratty enquiring about a room, had said this person had no luggage. Therefore it could not have been Hanratty, because he had a case. But, Foot argued, a statement the condemned man had given to his lawyers indicated that he had left his case at "Ingledene" while he looked for better accommodation. Every part of the Rhyl alibi fitted what Hanratty had said. Moreover, it was "backed up by fourteen independent witnesses with no axe to grind".

Foot reported Mary Hanratty's belated discovery, in 1980, of her eldest son's blood donor card from Maidstone Prison. It showed that his blood group was in the rare category of O group, rhesus negative. The murderer had also had O group blood, as was revealed by his semen. "For a brief, delirious moment we all felt we might be able to prove his innocence once and for all." But Foot's hopes were dashed when it emerged that semen cannot show whether a blood group is rhesus negative or rhesus positive.

Lastly, pondering the possibility that there were three more bullets fired at Deadman's Hill than there were cartridge cases deposited there, and believing that two had afterwards been used to frame Hanratty, Foot invited Peter Alphon to get in touch with him. "If he wants to send me that third cartridge case, I would like to see it." Even the legal establishment couldn't explain something as tangible as that away. Needless to say, Foot was to be disappointed. No such cartridge case was ever mailed to him, or ever subsequently located.

Although he never ceased writing about the case, *Who Killed Hanratty?* was to remain the most substantial of Foot's attempts to expand on the fringe theories of Jean Justice and to assert that James Hanratty was blameless. The campaign in the form of an organised body was over. The stuffing had been knocked out of it by the Hawser report and by the death of Hanratty's father. Foot described still receiving letters from readers asking about the case and enquiring if the guilty verdict continued to be upheld by the Home Office. "I have to answer yes," he wrote. "I have to say that very little has come to light in the last thirteen years to force the case once more into the limelight." But all this was about to change.

Two years after the publication of the Penguin edition of *Who Killed Hanratty?* Jean Justice died. Before he did so, however, he gave a last interview to Bob Woffinden. By this time Woffinden had become a documentaries producer for Yorkshire Television. He was commissioned by Channel 4 to produce a documentary on the A6 case for its "True Stories" series. *Hanratty – The Mystery of Deadman's Hill* was transmitted for the first time on 2 April 1992, again in 1994, and again the following year. Theories which had once been restricted to an obscure paperback published in Paris in 1964 were now, some thirty years later, reaching millions of TV viewers. *Hanratty – The Mystery of Deadman's Hill* was, in the technical sense, a high-quality production. Its thesis was simple: Hanratty was innocent; Alphon was the murderer and rapist. A major miscarriage of justice had occurred. At the climax of the documentary the narrator emphasized that the judicial establishment, which had covered-up the truth for so long, was even obstructing *scientific* proof of Hanratty's innocence: "The police ... hold exhibits from which today's DNA scientists could finally establish guilt or innocence. That, too, is withheld."

In 1994 a submission on the case, written by Bob Woffinden in collaboration with the eminent barrister Geoffrey Bindman, who represented the Hanratty family, was sent to the Home Office. It was duly passed on for investigation to one of Scotland Yard's most senior officers, Detective Chief Superintendent Roger Matthews. The following year there was another exciting development for campaigners like Foot and Woffinden. The Metropolitan Police's laboratory in Lambeth confirmed that material from the A6 case was still held on file, including pieces of Valerie Storie's underwear with semen stains on them. Better still, the police now agreed to DNA profiling to establish conclusively whether or not there was a match with James Hanratty. Scientific proof of Hanratty's innocence now seemed to be within reach. However, as Woffinden subsequently explained, "initial work failed to produce a clear DNA profile. At that point we requested that tests be suspended, as we did not wish to use up all the available material, which was obviously a finite amount."

In 1996, according to subsequent leaks to the press, Detective Chief Superintendent Roger Matthews' report into the A6 case had concluded that there had been "a grave miscarriage of justice" resulting from "discrepancies, fabricated evidence and suppressed facts". The fullest account was published in *The Independent* (27 January 1997):

> James Hanratty, hanged for one of the most notorious crimes this century, is about to be cleared 35 years after his execution for the A6 murder ... Home Office officials are understood to have concluded that Hanratty was innocent. This follows an unpublished police enquiry which concluded last year that he was the victim of a miscarriage of justice and that the murder was probably part of a wider conspiracy.
>
> The reappraisal of the case follows more than three decades of campaigning by members of Hanratty's family and his supporters. Many of the campaigners believe the real killer was Peter Alphon, who is alleged to have admitted to the crime on numerous occasions. There is also a string of evidence that links Mr Alphon to the murder, though in an interview with *The Independent* he protested his innocence.
>
> One of the most implausible aspects of the case was the acceptance that Hanratty, a city dweller, should by chance come across a couple in a cornfield and carry out a random killing.
>
> It emerged after his execution that Hanratty also had a good alibi. Fourteen witnesses came forward to back up his claim that he was in Rhyl, North Wales – 250 miles from the scene of the crime.

Bob Woffinden's consuming interest in the crime emerged in a new form later that year when his book *Hanratty: The Final Verdict* was published. Almost 500 pages long, it was the sixth and by far the most comprehensive account of the A6 murder. Although deeply indebted to the work of Jean Justice, Paul Foot and others, it nevertheless contained a great deal of new information, about the crime, the police investigation, the trial, and the long campaign to clear Hanratty. It also supplied much new biographical information about some of the leading figures in the story.

The book was essentially a polemic. Woffinden now provided a refined version of the conspiracy theory first articulated over thirty years earlier by Jean Justice. According to Woffinden the crime had been commissioned by a man close to Janet Gregsten, who lusted after her. He wanted to break up her marriage so that she became available to him. In order to avoid a libel action, which would have required him to supply evidence of his allegation, Woffinden was careful not to name the man. However, anyone who had read Justice's second book or Foot's *Who Killed Hanratty?* would have been able to read between the lines and understand that he meant Janet Gregsten's brother-in-law, William Ewer. According to this interpretation of the crime, which rooted it in the Gregstens's collapsing marriage, it was "a malicious jape that went disastrously wrong" because the man, William Ewer, "fatally failed to understand Alphon's psychopathic personality". Hanratty was deliberately framed in order to shield Alphon. William Nudds willingly helped Peter Alphon establish his alibi. Charles ""Dixie"" France gave Alphon the spare ammunition, which he hid together with the murder weapon on the bus.

Campaigners like Woffinden had believed that the Home Office would forward its file on the case directly to the Court of Appeal, so that Hanratty's conviction could at last be quashed. This did not happen. Instead the material was sent for consideration to the newly established Criminal Cases Review

Commission (CCRC) set up in the wake of glaring miscarriages of justice involving Irish people and others who had been falsely linked to the IRA bombing campaign. Woffinden believed this was yet another delaying tactic, which he attributed to "the intransigence of the Home Secretary himself, Michael Howard".

But as his book went to press Woffinden felt full of confidence. He still found it "baffling that there is a residue of opinion which seemingly believes that Hanratty was guilty as charged" even though "In the years since his trial and execution, every fragment of information to come to light has only strengthened the case for his innocence." But things were looking much more hopeful. Hanratty's family had provided blood samples for use in DNA profiling and future improvements in this scientific technique of the surviving crime-scene material promised to provide the final objective proof of James Hanratty's innocence: "The material is in proper storage and with techniques in DNA technology improving all the time, a definitive result could be obtained at some point in the near future."

In a rare moment of dispassionate objectivity Paul Foot described the conspiracy scenario set out by Woffinden in *Hanrattty: The Final Verdict* as "tempting, but far from conclusive". (Ironically, although Foot's book and Woffinden's TV documentary had persuaded me of Hanratty's innocence it was this book which first alerted me to the probability of Hanratty's guilt – it contained a number of new and astonishing revelations the significance of which had evidently entirely passed its author by.)

Having received the Matthews report and other material relating to the case from the Home Office, the CCRC proceeded to set up its own inquiry, led by Baden Henry Skitt, formerly Chief Constable of Hertfordshire. In March 1999 the Commission reported that the Hanratty case had been referred to the Court of Appeal because of the suppression of vital information by senior police officers, a lack of disclosure of information to the defence, and a flawed process of identification. "The amount of information not disclosed by the prosecution is very substantial," alleged the Hanrattys' legal representative, Geoffrey Bindman. He went on to argue: "If that material had been disclosed, James Hanratty would not have been convicted."

Among the undisclosed material examined by the CCRC was evidence that Michael Gregsten had kept a strict record of the Morris Minor's mileage. It indicated that although the most direct route between Deadman's Hill and the London location where the car was abandoned was a little over 48 miles, there were a further 61 miles on the milometer unaccounted for. In other words, assuming Gregsten's mileage figures were accurate, the killer had apparently driven the car for around 109 miles to get from Bedfordshire to Ilford. Departing at 3am and arriving at 7am indicated an average speed of 27mph.

A variety of witnesses testified that they had seen the Morris Minor at a variety of different locations, at different times, casting doubt on the assumption that the killer had dumped the car in north-east London early in the morning. This information had never been passed to Hanratty's defence team. Having come to the attention of Bob Woffinden, it was used in the 1999 paperback edition of *Hanrattty: The Final Verdict* to refine his conspiracy theory. By June 1999 further DNA testing had produced only "equivocal" results but Woffinden was convinced that he at last understood the crime and its aftermath. He now argued that Peter Alphon had driven from Deadman's Hill to central London, parked it there "discreetly" or "hidden during the day", later moving it in the evening rush-hour to Redbridge. Woffinden now believed that William Nudds had been centrally involved in the conspiracy, quite possibly even supplying the gun and ammunition. He may well have also planted the cartridges in the room at the Hotel Vienna in order to divert attention from Alphon to Hanratty.

The year after Woffinden's revised edition of *Hanrattty: The Final Verdict*, Jeremy Fox died, aged 72. He had parted company with Jean Justice long before his former partner's death a decade earlier. "It is a great sadness that he will not be here for the final dénouement in the Hanratty case," Bob Woffinden commented in his obituary of Fox in *The Guardian* (31 May 2000). But on what seemed to be the brink of that final dénouement, with Hanratty being proclaimed innocent, there was a sensational and shattering development which brought dismay and shock to Woffinden and fellow believers. New improved DNA testing indicated strong similarities between the traces on the crime scene material and the DNA of the blood samples supplied by Mary and Michael Hanratty. It indicated that Hanratty had, all along, been the mystery gunman and rapist.

If this was so then what about the supposed culpability of Peter Alphon, the supposed solidity of Hanratty's Liverpool and Rhyl alibis, and the supposed conspiracy involving a number of individuals hired to frighten off Michael Gregsten? Sceptical scrutiny shows the extent to which Jean Justice, Paul Foot, Bob Woffinden and others built houses out of straw. Although the crime seemed mysterious and at times inexplicable it became clear that it could, after all, be explained in the light of James Hanratty's character and past, and by his behaviour in the period between the crime and his eventual arrest.

4   The Curious Case of Peter Alphon

"My difficulty is I'm a wanderer and nobody knows me."
Peter Alphon during his interview with Detective
Superintendent Acott, 24 September 1961

Peter Alphon was the man first suspected of the crime by the police. The case against him collapsed when Valerie Storie failed to pick him out on an identification parade. Later, after Hanratty's execution for the crime, Alphon made his first veiled confession of guilt. Subsequently, his confessions to having been the A6 murderer became increasingly vocal.

Even Paul Foot was at first uncertain as to whether or not Peter Alphon genuinely was the killer and rapist or was simply an unbalanced publicity-seeker and fantasist. Getting to the heart of the enigma that was Peter Alphon requires critical scrutiny of Alphon's first police interrogation, his night at the Hotel Vienna and how the cartridges came to be discovered in Room 24, his second interrogation, his later confessions, and his character.

The police were faced by two critical problems in connection with the case. One was the complete absence of any obvious motive for either the bizarre car ride or the crime. The second was the absence of any evidence to tie the crime to a particular individual. The initial assumption seems to have been that the perpetrator was some kind of deranged maniac.

In the days following the crime the newspapers published appeals from the police to the proprietors of boarding houses. Did they have a lodger who had gone out on the night of the murder and not returned, or who had returned the next day and behaved in an agitated manner? Did they have a lodger who had not stirred out for the past few days? As the police at that time had no real leads they were desperate for information.

Someone who matched one of these descriptions was "Frederick Durrant" who was staying at the Alexandra Court Hotel in Seven Sisters Road, London N4. "Durrant" had booked into the hotel on in the early evening of 23 August – the same day that Michael Gregsten had been shot dead in Bedfordshire in the early hours by a gunman who had then driven off in the Morris Minor and left it parked in north-east London. This guest had given his address as 7 Hurst Avenue, Horsham, Sussex. He had not appeared for any meals at the hotel and had drawn attention to himself by disturbing the person in the next room, who complained that he noisily paced up and down, talked to himself, and made strange rattling and banging noises.

On 27 August, after complaints from other guests, the hotel manager telephoned the local police station with his suspicions. A check with Sussex police revealed that the address was false. Detective Sergeant Arthur Kilner and a constable went to the Alexandra Court, where Frederick Durrant insisted his name and address were genuine. They therefore took him away for further questioning. At Blackstock Road police station the suspect admitted that his real name was Peter Louis Alphon. He was aged thirty (in fact he was just days away from his thirty-first birthday, on 30 August). He gave his true address as 142 Gleneagle Road, London SW16, which was in reality his parents' address. Ironically his father was a clerk at the Metropolitan Police headquarters at Scotland Yard. Peter Alphon also, it emerged, had a criminal record – almost eight years earlier he had been found guilty of taking and driving away a motor car.

Alphon cheerfully explained that the real reason he had used a bogus name and address was because he sometimes left hotels and boarding houses without paying the bill. Questioned about his employment he said he said that he sold *Old Moore's Almanac* door to door (this was a popular annual publication which, in the pre-internet age, combined useful information on a variety of subjects with colourful predictions of future events ranging from good and bad weather, the world of politics, and international affairs). The police searched Alphon's suitcase and found personal papers, a notebook, dirty underclothes and racist and fascist literature. At the very bottom of the case was a recent issue of *The Daily Express* with headlines about the A6 murder and a large photograph of the lay-by where the murder and rape had been committed.

Questioned about his movements over the period of the murder, Alphon said that at about 8pm on 22 August he had gone to the Broadway House Hotel in Dorset Square, Marylebone. They were full up but booked a room for him at one of the other hotels in the group, the Hotel Vienna in Maida Vale. He had then gone to meet his mother in Streatham, after which he had gone to Victoria Station to collect something from the left luggage office. He had then gone to the Hotel Vienna, arriving just after 11pm. He had stayed overnight in Room 6. He left the hotel the next morning at around 11.45am. He went back to Victoria Station, saw his mother again, and then went to cash a cheque at the Westminster Bank in Upper Richmond Road.

Alphon had been taken to Blackstock Road police station shortly after 7pm and was released at around 10pm after giving a statement. It was plain that he was an oddball and a drifter. He occasionally sold almanacs, sponged off his mother, and was an enthusiastic gambler who was a regular at London's greyhound stadiums. He held extreme right-wing views and was also interested in theosophy. In some respects but not all he matched the description of the wanted man. There were no bloodstained clothes in his possession but his case did contain a copy of a newspaper which prominently featured the A6 murder. When it was confirmed that he had, as he had said, stayed at the Hotel Vienna on the night of the abduction, there seemed no reason not to let him go. However, he was instructed to return to the Alexandra Court Hotel and re-register under his real name and address. He was also required to come back to Blackstock

Road police station at 7pm the next day. Alphon did as he was told. After this, he ceased to be a person of interest in connection with the case. Attention refocused on Peter Alphon only a fortnight later, with the finding of two cartridge cases from the A6 murder weapon.

They were discovered at the Hotel Vienna, where Alphon had stayed on the night of the murder. On Monday 11 September 1961 Robert Crocker, the manager of four central London hotels, was called to the Hotel Vienna, which was located at 158 Sutherland Avenue, London W9. He was there because £5 had disappeared from the till. The staff here consisted of four people. The first was a man calling himself "Jack Glickberg" (real name William Nudds, with a string of criminal convictions). His "wife", Mrs Glickberg, was actually a woman called Florence Snell, who also had a criminal record. They had been employed for only a week and worked under the hotel's manageress, Juliana Galves, just 22, and her husband, who were Spanish. On his arrival Crocker at once sacked the Glickbergs, telling them to get out immediately. (When they begged to stay one last night he relented.) Accompanied by Juliana Galves, Crocker then went to inspect the hotel bedrooms, perhaps to see if anything else from the hotel was missing, apart from cash.

In the basement of the hotel was Room 24. This was used only intermittently, even during the popular holiday month of August. It was a cramped room, evidently only dimly illuminated by the light leaking down from a window below street level. It contained one double bed and two singles, as well as an alcove containing a single bed with a dark brown upholstered chair at its foot, partly concealed by a partition. Despite its cosmopolitan name, the Hotel Vienna was cheap and at the less salubrious end of the London hotel spectrum. Room 24 was for families or where strangers were invited to share their accommodation during busy periods. But it would soon emerge that only one guest had occupied this room overnight in the preceding weeks. The date was 21 August 1961 – the night before the day of the hold-up in the cornfield.

As he surveyed the room Crocker spotted a piece of material dangling from the chair half-hidden in the gloomy alcove. He reached down to deal with it, repositioning the chair to make the defect less obvious. As he did so something rolled off and fell on to the floor. It was a .38 cartridge case. Juliana Galves ran her hand over the seat and discovered a second cartridge at the back of the chair. Crocker, who had served in the army during the Second World War, had experience of firearms and recognised what the objects were. He considered throwing the cartridge cases away and in the normal course of events would probably have done just that. However, two weeks earlier the police had telephoned to check the alibi of a man who had told them he had stayed at the Hotel Vienna on the night of the notorious abduction of Michael Gregsten and Valerie Storie. Crocker therefore decided to telephone Highbury police station and report his discovery.

Forensic analysis of the cartridge cases swiftly revealed that they had come from the murder weapon. This was a sensational development. The police investigation had, so far, been floundering. There were, as yet, no plausible suspects. The case was baffling and the motives behind the abduction and the strange journey insisted upon by the mystery gunman were opaque. Now, suddenly, the murder weapon was tied to a very specific London location – one, moreover, which involved a register of the individuals who had passed through it. Detective Superintendent Acott promptly switched his base from Bedford to London and began a new line of investigation.

Juliana Galves mistakenly informed Acott that no one had stayed in Room 24 between 16 August – six days before the abduction – and the discovery of the cartridges. However, among the guests staying at the Hotel Vienna on the night of the abduction was one "F. Durrant, 7 Hurst Avenue, Horsham, Sussex." Once the investigation team had checked their files on the case it emerged that a man using that alias and the same fake address had already been questioned as a person of possible interest in connection with the A6 murder.

In his statement to police Robert Crocker testified that the cartridge cases "may have some connection" to the man who had booked into the hotel on the night of the murder, using the name "Durrant". Perhaps Crocker was simply remembering the earlier police enquiry about this case or perhaps he was obligingly reiterating a suggestion put to him by an officer during the course of his interview with the police. The basic problem in linking Alphon to the cartridge cases is that he had no access to basement room 24, having stayed in a single room three floors above. Crocker, of course, did not work at the Hotel Vienna and was not there at the time of the murder.

In fact Durrant/Alphon seemed to have a cast-iron alibi. In her first statement to the police Juliana Galves said that the man had telephoned to say he would be late arriving. "[We] waited up for him. He arrived at about 11.30pm and said he was the man who had phoned up in the morning for a room in the name of Durrant. He was shown to his room and in the morning he declined breakfast and left about 12.10pm." She remembered him as wearing a dark suit with a white shirt and looking "unshaven and grubby". But in a second statement given on 13 September she changed her story. She now said: "The only time I saw the man about whom I have already been asked by the police, was about 11.45am on the day he left ... I did not see Durrant on his arrival." In her second statement Mrs Galves also reiterated that Room 24 had been empty since 16 August, but now added the qualification that here had been a period of five minutes when an Indian guest, Vigan Rapur from Delhi, has been put there before being transferred to a more suitable single room which had just fallen vacant.

As the murder suspect was a white male with a distinctive East End accent and vocabulary it was obvious that Rapur could safely be disregarded as a suspect. Examination of the hotel register however indicated that Juliana Galves was not an entirely reliable source of information when it came to accounting for occupation of the room. Far from being empty since 16 August, Room 24 had in fact been used by a guest for one night on Monday 21 August – the night before the abduction of Gregsten and Storie. This guest was a single man who had signed in as "J. Ryan, 72 Wood Lane, Kingsbury".

This additional information regarding "J. Ryan" seems to have been regarded at this stage as being equally as irrelevant as the revelation of the Indian guest who had briefly had access to Room 24. Cartridge cases are either ejected from a gun when it is fired or removed afterwards in order for it to be reloaded with fresh cartridges. It would seem the assumption made by the investigators at this time was that the gun was brought to the Hotel Vienna *after* the murder. The killer had gone to the Vienna and reloaded his weapon in Room 24 before having second thoughts about keeping it. It was then disposed of, together with all the leftover ammunition, under the upstairs back seat of a number 36 double-decker bus, which followed a route that took it close to this hotel. The possibility that the gun had been test-fired in the basement room and then reloaded was evidently discounted. The question of who had stayed in the room *before* the murder was therefore of no immediate interest.

The fact that Peter Alphon, previously questioned about his odd behaviour after the murder, was now known to have reserved a room at the Vienna on the night of the abduction seemed highly incriminating. Moreover, according to Juliana Galves' revised statement, he had not taken breakfast the next morning and not been seen on the hotel premises until almost mid-day. But if Alphon *was* the A6 murderer there were two immediate difficulties. Firstly, his mother, interviewed by Detective Superintendent Acott on 13 September, confirmed his alibi. She agreed that she had met her son at Streatham between 9.15pm and 10pm on the night of the abduction, when she had given him a suitcase. Secondly, his room at the Vienna was number 6 on the second floor, not number 24 in the basement.

Alphon's evident innocence of the crime was reinforced when William Nudds made a statement to the police on 15 September. He testified that the guest who called himself Durrant had checked into the Vienna very late ("I think about 11.30pm to midnight") on the night of the crime, and that Florence Snell had been present. She had taken this guest to his room.

With no other leads, Acott seems to have decided that Alphon was the only viable suspect. His team visited the Alexandra Court Hotel to take statements from the staff and guests. They were plainly seeking incriminating material. As a consequence William Nudds was called back to Scotland Yard on 21 September. After a day of ferocious interrogation he obligingly changed his tune. He now retracted his first statement, claiming to have been "confused". In its place he made a second statement which was helpfully packed with details that pointed to Alphon's guilt. In this new version of events Alphon was allocated the bed in Room 24 at the foot of which the two cartridge cases had been found. He expressed dissatisfaction with the room, later going out at night. By 2am he had not returned. A note was left telling him that Room 6 was now vacant and he could switch rooms. Alphon did not come down for breakfast. Nudds went to Room 6 at 9.50am and found Alphon in a dishevelled and agitated state. There was a curious postscript to this second statement: "I did not know until this moment when you mentioned it that two empty cartridge cases had been found by other members of staff in Room 24." This was presumably intended to underline Nudds's shining impartiality as a witness. It seems on the face of it unlikely. After being sacked, the couple were allowed to stay one more night and did not leave the hotel until the next day. If there was police activity at the Vienna at this time it seems unlikely that Nudds and Snell were unaware of it, or of what it was all about.

Unfortunately it is far from clear when the police did first pounce on the Hotel Vienna and its staff. The discovery of the cartridge cases was made some time between 8am and 9am on 11 September. Crocker phoned the police and a constable collected them ten minutes later. Scotland Yard's forensic sciences laboratory took only a few hours to establish that the cases had come from the .38 Enfield revolver used by the A6 killer. According to Paul Foot, "As soon as Superintendent Acott was told about the cartridge cases, he descended with his staff on the Hotel Vienna". But when was that? Acott was surely given the results of the forensic analysis immediately, on that Monday. Yet according to *The Daily Telegraph* (Thursday 14 September 1961) he returned from Bedford on Wednesday "on a surprise visit to London to take personal charge of the inquiry". This was the day that Juliana Galves first gave a statement about Room 24 and its occupants and about "Frederick Durrant". William Nudds did not give his first statement until two days later, on Friday 15 September. On this occasion he was surely telling the truth. He did not know what angle the police were pursuing, so was in no position to massage his testimony in order to assist them with a case against a particular individual.

Over the weekend of Saturday 16 September and Sunday 17 September, Detective Superintendent Acott seems to have concluded that Alphon was indeed the A6 killer. Paul Foot speculated that "The police may have received casual information on the underworld network. They may have been impressed by psychologists' advice after close study of Valerie Storie's description of her killer."

An underworld tip seems unlikely, in so far as Alphon was not a member of any criminal network. He did not mix with criminals. His only criminal conviction was for the theft of a motor car some eight years earlier. Psychological profiling may provide an explanation. This was a methodology which fell into disrepute after the debacle of the Metropolitan Police's bungled investigation into the murder of Rachel Nickell in 1992. On that occasion an entirely innocent man, Colin Stagg, was regarded as the prime suspect by the Met, simply because he was something of an oddball who happened to be in the area at the time of the crime. Peter Alphon fitted the widespread policing prejudice against single men who did not seem "normal". He was a loner and a drifter. Some nights he slept rough. He had no regular employment or income and moved around the London area on a haphazard basis. He had an interest in fringe supernatural philosophies and extreme right-wing politics. Peter Alphon was, in short, a bit weird.

The police were also under pressure. At the time, the A6 murder had the highest profile of any crime in Britain. By the weekend of September 16/17 almost a month had elapsed since the crime, with no arrest. This did not look good. And as far as Alphon was concerned there were two damning links to the crime. Firstly, there was his suspicious behaviour immediately after the murder, which first drew police attention to him. Secondly, there was the extraordinary fact that he had a room booked at the Hotel Vienna on the night of the murder – the very hotel to which the killer had apparently returned after the crime, where he had reloaded his gun.

But Alphon appeared to have an alibi. He had met his mother on the evening of the abduction, a meeting she had confirmed. Secondly, William Nudds's statement to the police (15 September) testified that the guest who called himself Durrant had checked into the Vienna between 11.30pm and midnight and that Florence Snell had taken this guest to his room on the second floor.

On 21 September, Nudds was interviewed for a second time by the police. He now retracted his original statement and claimed that Alphon had been allocated Room 24 on Tuesday 24 August and had gone out, but that a single room had then become available and a note had been left for him on his return telling him to use Room 6. Nudds further stated that the next morning Alphon appeared dishevelled and agitated. This was damning testimony.

Next day Alphon's mother was again questioned by Detective Superintendent Acott. What happened was leaked to the press: Mrs Alphon collapsed in shock at being informed her son was the chief suspect in the A6 case. His alibi was, it seemed, false. "Alphon's mother," reported *The Daily Sketch* (23 September) "told detectives that he last visited their home in Gleneagle Road, Streatham, two months ago."

Paul Foot asserts that "The alibi ... was smashed." But was it? Alphon in fact never said he had gone to his parents' home. As he explained in his first statement to the police, he did not get on with his father and had actually met his mother in the street – on the corner of Gleneagle Road. Acott, however, seems to have been in no doubt that he had his man. Shortly after the interview with Mrs Alphon on Friday 22 September he held a press conference and made an urgent appeal for assistance in tracing his number one suspect. A6 MURDER: THE POLICE SEEK A MAN'S HELP screamed the headline in London's mass circulation *Evening News*. Acott repeated his call for assistance in an interview on BBC television's evening news programme. Few could doubt that the police were finally on the trail of the infamous A6 gunman.

It came as a considerable surprise to everyone when, later that night, Alphon turned up at Scotland Yard and surrendered himself. For Bob Woffinden this was an example of Alphon's diabolical cunning. By arriving at the Metropolitan Police headquarters at midnight "Alphon shrewdly maximized his own advantages in his confrontation with the police. Under such conditions he was mentally sharp, and easily a match for Acott." This interpretation of Alphon's action is absurd. Alphon himself described "the exact moment when my world crashed". He had been selling almanacs at Wembley and was travelling back into London on a Bakerloo line tube train when he opened his evening paper.

> There was my name splashed across the front page. It was half past ten at night. I became quite cool – strangely calm, if you like. I knew I was innocent. Like any other citizen, I knew there was only one thing to do – go

immediately to Scotland Yard ... I telephoned the *Daily Express*. I wanted the whole world to know that I – an innocent man – was going to Scotland Yard of my own free will.

In fact Alphon (who later sold his story to the *Express*) also phoned *The Daily Mirror*, which recorded his call as having occurred at 10.57pm that night. Shortly after that he gave himself up to the police. This was what one might expect of an innocent person with nothing to hide, and his behaviour was very different to Hanratty's. Once Hanratty heard he was a suspect he went on the run and continued to evade the police until the moment he was spotted in Blackpool and arrested.

At first the police were sceptical that Peter Alphon was who he said he was but after half an hour they were finally persuaded that he was indeed their wanted man. He was then taken into custody to await interrogation by Acott. The Detective Superintendent rushed to the building and began interviewing his suspect at 2.15am. He asked Alphon if he thought he could help with the A6 murder. "No, I don't think I can," Alphon replied, adding coolly, "I'm not particularly interested in your case."

Questioned about his income Alphon explained that he was a gambler: "I depend on the dogs for my money. I go nearly every day, and I am pretty successful." He also grudgingly admitted to sponging off his mother. Asked about previous employment, Alphon retorted: "I'm not going to tell you ... It's got nothing to do with the murder ... I'm not prepared to discuss my private affairs with you, it's a political thing ... I am a fascist and we can't talk to policemen."

If Alphon was the A6 murderer his attitude was astonishingly insouciant and self-assured, at times even sarcastic. It suggested the bullish attitude of someone who is confident of their innocence. At one point he remarked: "I don't want my private papers scrutinised. They are political. How do you think that's going to help? Do you think I've got bloodstained shirts?"

Alphon's demeanour was the opposite of Hanratty's. Under interrogation, Hanratty repeatedly had to stop to think about his answers. The pauses were often long ones. He was obsequious, whereas Alphon was impudent. When it came to the matter of an alibi Hanratty blustered and equivocated.

Acott quizzed Alphon about his night at the Hotel Vienna and put it to him that he had changed his bedroom that night. "That's quite wrong," Alphon replied. "I only had one room at that hotel." Acott said he had two witnesses (i.e. William Nudds and Florence Snell) who were prepared to testify in court that he had booked in at mid-day, been given a basement room, and had not returned by 2am. Alphon responded that any such witnesses "must be lying. It couldn't possibly be a mistake. I only had one room in that hotel and that was number six." Acott asked why these witnesses would bother to lie and Alphon replied, "It's beyond me. I can't fathom it out at all." Questioned about Deadman's Hill, Alphon said he didn't know Bedfordshire at all.

A long extract from this interview is printed in Woffinden's book. Woffinden's version is on occasion very misleading, however. For example, Acott asked if Alphon had other clothes anywhere else.

> ALPHON. Yes, but they're in hotels and pawnbrokers and I'm not telling you where they are.
> ACOTT: I shall have every pawnbroker visited and I shall probably find them … Have you got any bags or cases?
> ALPHON: No.

Woffinden's ellipses are not innocent. Alphon in fact answered the Detective Superintendent's question. Responding to the comment that every pawnbroker would be visited, Alphon replied: "All right, I've a pair of trousers in Thompson's in the Uxbridge Road." By omitting Alphon's reply Woffinden succeeds in making him appear suspiciously devious and uncooperative.

The interview lasted all night and Woffinden's theory that a quick-witted Alphon ran rings around an exhausted and bumbling Acott is unsustainable. The police in fact tried to break Alphon by subjecting him to a barrage of questions about every aspect of his life and his activities on the night of the abduction. For almost seven hours Alphon was battered with questions. Every thirty minutes Acott and his colleague Detective Sergeant Oxford would leave the room and a plainclothes officer would enter and urge Alphon to cooperate. Then Acott and Oxford would return with more questions. Then, after half an hour, they once again left the room and a different plainclothes officer entered and spoke to Alphon. Then the senior detectives returned with yet more questions.

This relentless interrogation lasted all night and continued until 9am. "I can tell you it was an ordeal," Alphon later told *The Daily Express* (4 October 1961). He described how at the end of it he felt "utterly exhausted and defeated". Acott later gave a different version, suggesting a much shorter and milder interview, but there can be little doubt that Alphon's is the more reliable account of what occurred.

Following his long interrogation, Alphon volunteered blood samples and specimens of pubic hair and his clothing was examined. In the afternoon he was placed on two identity parades. The first one involved two of the eye-witnesses who claimed to have seen the driver of the stolen Morris Minor in Redbridge early on the morning of the murder. Edward Blackhall picked out another man; James Trower could identify no one.

The second parade was scrutinised by a 23-year-old Swedish woman, Mrs Meike Dalal. On 7 September she had been showing a man a room she had to let in her house on Upper Richmond Road when he had suddenly shut the door. He then hit her on the head, tied her hands with flex, and cried, "Listen! I am the A6 murderer and I want some money." He hit her twice more on the head, gagged her mouth, tied her ankles and lifted up her skirt. She managed to wriggle free and screamed for help. The man ran off and escaped.

She attended the ID parade in a condition described by the police inspector in charge as "distressed and trembling". She refused to tap anyone on the shoulder, as convention required, but said "I think it's the second on the left … I think it is him." This man was Alphon. However, Alphon said that at the time of the assault he had an alibi. He was collecting a supply of almanacs from the distributors in central London. At a later ID parade two men from the distributors positively identified Alphon and confirmed his alibi. The case against him was dropped. No one was ever charged in connection with the assault on Meike Dalal but whoever the attacker was he plainly was not the A6 gunman, merely someone pretending to be in order to intimidate and to deceive his victim.

The most important identification parade of all was held next day at Guy's Hospital. Alphon and nine other men were placed in a line and each given a numbered card to hold. The screens were then removed around Valerie Storie's bed and she gazed at the men standing in front of her. After about five minutes she said "Number four is the man". Number four was one of the men randomly collected for the parade. Peter Alphon was number ten. Valerie Storie had failed to pick him out as the person who had shot Michael Gregsten and then raped her. The case against him melted into thin air. Later, also cleared of any involvement in the assault on Meike Dalal, he was released and became a free man again. He sold his story to *The Daily Express* and returned to his lonely, wandering life of greyhound racing, gambling and rooms in cheap hotels and boarding houses. Peter Alphon would probably have disappeared completely from view and remained nothing more than a very minor footnote in twentieth-century criminology if it had not been for the intervention of Jean Justice.

According to Woffinden, Justice became interested in the A6 case only on 22 November 1961, when he glimpsed the newspaper placards about the start of committal proceedings at

Ampthill against Hanratty. "He bought an *Evening News* and started reading. The more he read, the more fascinated he became." Foot, however, dates the origins of Justice's interest to shortly after his return from a European trip in October 1961.

These claims are contradicted by Jean Justice's comment that "Anyone who saw Superintendent Acott making his appeal on the television screen will agree with me that his expression betrayed his inner certainty that Alphon was the A6 murderer." Justice was referring to Acott's BBC TV interview with Peter Woods transmitted on the evening news on 22 September 1961. This was exactly two months before committal proceedings began against James Hanratty at Ampthill. It should be remembered that this was the pre-internet, pre-digital age. Even video recorders did not yet exist in the 1960s. Moreover, Justice was writing prior to July 1964, at a time when no TV documentaries on the A6 case had been made. In short, contrary to what Paul Foot and Bob Woffinden believed, *Jean Justice's interest in the A6 case and awareness of Peter Alphon clearly existed long before James Hanratty ever became a suspect.*

Justice's knowledge of the A6 case seems to have been defective from the beginning, even though he had attended both the committal proceedings and the trial. In *Murder vs. Murder* he wrote that "The first man the police pulled in for questioning was Peter Louis Alphon ... [He] came within an ace of being identified by Miss Storie who, after what appears to have been a period of uncertainty, finally picked out a man from the line-up."

All three assertions are either dubious or demonstrably false. It seems highly unlikely that Peter Alphon was either the first or the only early suspect hauled in for questioning. In the early days of the investigation, with no immediately obvious suspect and no apparent motive, the police cast their net wide. Alphon was probably only one of scores of oddballs, misfits or convicted criminals called in for questioning. The case against him was so obviously flimsy that he was never passed on to the murder team for further interrogation. His name was only reconnected to the case as a result of the astonishing coincidence that he stayed at the Hotel Vienna on the night of the abduction, one day after James Hanratty. Ironically, it was because the police had checked out his whereabouts that Robert Crocker remembered police coming to the Hotel Vienna and decided that the discovery of the two cartridge cases there was worth reporting. Had the police never gone to the Vienna then Crocker might well have thrown the cases away. Had that happened it seems highly probable that the crime would never have been solved and James Hanratty would have got away with it.

Justice was also wrong to assert that Valerie Storie took some time to make up her mind. She picked out a man within five minutes. Later, when Hanratty appeared before her in a line-up, she took just over ten minutes to decide. The idea that Alphon "came within an ace of being identified" is absurd. Storie failed to recognise him as her attacker. The fact that she picked out an innocent man certainly raises doubts about the validity of her eye-witness testimony, although this needs to be tempered with the recognition that she must have believed that the police had got their man, who was standing there in front of her. The pressure on her to choose *someone* was enormous.

Students of the case have forever since been tormented by the lack of knowledge of what this wrongly chosen individual looked like. If he resembled Alphon this raises the question as to why Storie didn't pick out the real Alphon as opposed to the man who looked a bit like him. But of course Storie may simply have picked out the man who most resembled James Hanratty. This is one of the enduring enigmas of the case which it seems will never be resoved.

Justice claimed that after the murder Alphon had "shut himself in his room for five days". This is plainly not true. The copy of *The Daily Express* in his suitcase was bought the day *after* his arrival. When the police first came to question Alphon he was out. When they came a second time he was once again out. When he returned to the boarding house he found that that the door had been unlocked and the police were searching his room.

Alphon had no reason to know that anyone suspected him of being the A6 killer and therefore he had no reason to conceal anything suspicious which might have connected him to the crime. But in fact the police, on a surpise visit, found absolutely nothing to link him to the crime – unless you regard as significant Alphon's copy of a national newspaper mentioning it. Nor was Alphon's regular absence from breakfast a sign of him deliberately avoiding other guests. Peter Alphon was, quite literally, a layabout. He lived a lifestyle which some people experience when they are students – late nights, and long mornings in bed. Ironically, when Woffinden tracked him down in 1991 and went to visit him he found Alphon still living a nomadic existence in small, cheap hotels – and just getting dressed in the middle of the afternoon on a sunny summer's day.

Murder vs. Murder is basically a book about two unbalanced men and their mutual obsession. Jean Justice was fascinated by Alphon:

> He was so different from what I had expected. Even then I could sense his aching loneliness, as though some essential part of him was reaching out to me.

Though claiming that homosexuals disgusted and repelled him, Alphon was clearly thrilled by Justice's passionate interest in him. Revealingly, Alphon's former Pimlico landlady remembered him as someone who seemed to her not masculine but curiously feminine: he was, she said, "rather effeminate and liked gossiping as women do".

Alphon was a shabby, solitary, friendless man but now, suddenly, there was someone in his life who found him fascinating. It was like discovering that someone was in love with him. Jean Justice, born on 6 October 1930, was almost exactly the same age as Alphon (born 30 August 1930). Justice was wealthy, charming, sophisticated, debonair. He was an extrovert, with a network of affluent friends. He dined out at expensive restaurants and moved easily among the idle rich. Justice frankly confessed:

> I had certainly set out to pursue him, to flatter him perhaps, to introduce him to a sophisticated way of life that was completely alien to him. I had gone for walks with him and had often taken him to my flat.

Alphon became "infatuated" with Justice and before long was calling him his "little girl". In the traditional account of their relationship, Justice was interested in only one thing – the A6 murder and the possibility that Alphon was the true killer. The word for this is entrapment. Whether or not they ever went to bed together is an open question. Their relationship was volatile and highly charged. Alphon became adept at feeding Justice tantalising scraps, which whetted his appetite for more. Paul Foot had a similar experience (but without the smouldering sexual attraction). He discovered that "Alphon's aim was to maintain my interest", with hours of talk which led nowhere – or at least not to the conclusive evidence Foot was after.

One essential characteristic of Peter Alphon's lurid and interminable confessions is that they are littered with details which are either false or implausible. Take, for example, his claim that after the crime "I left the car at Redbridge and walked to Ilford station. I got the train there, changed at Stratford on to the tube … " (*The Sunday Times*, 14 May 1967). But the stolen Morris Minor was dumped in Avondale Crescent for the very obvious reason that it was by Redbridge tube station. It is inconceivable that the killer left it there and then walked to Ilford railway station. He surely wanted to get away from the car as quickly as possible. The London underground at the start of the rush hour offered immediate anonymity. There was, of course, no CCTV in 1961.

In one of his confessions Alphon said that the safety catch of the Enfield .38 was "on the handle". In fact the Enfield, in common with most revolvers, does not have a safety catch. Alphon may just conceivably have been trying deliberately to muddy the waters but the much greater probability is that he knew nothing at all about firearms.

Was there any other reason why Alphon should bother falsely to confess to the crime, apart from a lonely man's compulsive attention-seeking and his desire to perpetuate Justice's interest in him? There is one revealing aside in *Murder vs. Murder* which suggests that Alphon was still full of rage about the way in which Detective Superintendent Acott had publicly named him as the chief A6 suspect and then subjected him to a gruelling and humiliating interrogation and investigation. One of the first things Alphon ever said to Justice was, "We will get Acott together". In this ambition Peter Alphon was, in a sense, spectacularly successful. For the next four decades Acott was, for readers of books about the A6 murder, the man who had stitched-up and killed an innocent man. His career and retirement were henceforth overshadowed until his death by his association with the name Hanratty. If it had not been for Peter Alphon's willingness to feed Jean Justice's conspiracy theory that would never have happened.

Nowadays there is much greater awareness and knowledge of what is called "False Confession Syndrome". When the TV celebrity Jill Dando was murdered on her doorstep in April 1999 the police received calls from no less than 60 people confessing to the crime. An account of the phenomenon describes how, "One man in London has been confessing to every high profile murder for the past 20 years." In the years that followed, scores of men claimed to be the so-called "second gunman" alleged to have assassinated President Kennedy in Dallas in 1963. Russell Keys confessed to murdering five women and burying them on Blackpool Beach but police found no evidence to substantiate his claims. His wife shot him dead, claiming that he had threatened to strangle her, but prosecutors argued that she had persuaded her husband, who had mental health problems, to confess, with a view to selling the story to the press. She was convicted of his murder.

Even Paul Foot, although he never wavered in his conviction that Hanratty was innocent, grew to doubt the authenticity of Peter Alphon's confessions. After interviewing Janet Gregsten in 1994, Foot played Alphon a tape of their conversation. "It occurred to me, watching him carefully, that he didn't really know as much as he pretended."

Ironically, the essential truth about Peter Alphon appeared in a profile of him which appeared in the first edition of *The Daily Mail*, 23 September 1961. His old school chemistry teacher remembered him well. "He seemed lonely and always wanted to draw attention to himself."

"Miscarriages of justice, in the first instance, frequently seem to be the result of a shared delusion on the part of the police. They simply convince themselves that they have caught the criminal(s)." Bob Woffinden's generalisation is undoubtedly correct but as far as the A6 case is concerned the conclusion which can be drawn is rather different to the one he came to believe. When the police had what seemed to them to be a plausible suspect – Peter Alphon – they excluded every other possibility.

Peter Hain, a former Labour MP and current member of the House of Lords, has written eloquently of what happens to an innocent person in this situation. In 1975 he was a prominent Young Liberal and a high-profile activist against the apartheid regime in South Africa. To his amazement he was arrested and accused of having carried out a bank robbery in Putney. The charge was quite fantastic to everyone who knew him. His face was famous and for him to have robbed a bank would have been an extraordinarily reckless and irrational action. The case against him rested on some very dubious eye-witness evidence. Astonishingly – it is hard not to feel that this was a malicious prosecution, designed vindictively to punish Hain for his political activism – it went to trial. The jury found Hain not guilty.

As Hain was horrified to discover from his own experience, "The first consideration of the police is ... to lay their hands on a viable suspect as soon as possible. The second is to obtain as much incriminating evidence against that suspect as possible; they are rather less interested in evidence favourable to the suspect for the very good reason (given their approach) that too much of it could lead to the need to find another suspect and more evidence."

The problem, especially during this era of policing, is that if incriminating evidence was lacking some officers were perfectly happy to fabricate it. It was known as being "bent for the job" and in the eyes of these officers it made perfect sense. If they *knew* a suspect was guilty, why should lack of evidence spoil a good case? The difficulty was that this privileged knowledge all too often amounted to nothing more than stereotyping and prejudice. It was an aspect of a police culture which was pervasive and self-perpetuating. In the words of one critic, "officers are quickly implicated into marginal or off the books or downright illegal pactices. That process is a very important one in understanding how the police achieve solidarity of outlook."

Alphon first came to police attention because of his odd behaviour at the Alexandra Court Hotel. What Acott perhaps failed to appreciate was that this was not the abnormal behaviour of a guilty, agitated murderer but was in fact entirely characteristic of the suspect. Alphon was an oddball and a loner who exhibited signs of instability from his late teens. At the age of nineteen he was allowed to quit his compulsory national service and leave the RAF because of a "mental or nervous disorder". His aunt described him as an incommunicative person who sometimes cried and who had talked of killing himself. His landlady in Pimlico, where Alphon lodged for a year until February 1961, said she had had complaints from other residents "about a tapping noise from his room".

When the cartridge cases were found at the Hotel Vienna, Chief Superintendent Acott seems to have jumped to the conclusion that the murderer had gone there *after* the crime and reloaded the murder weapon in the basement room, before dumping it on the bus. As Alphon had a room booked there on the night of the abduction and was already in the A6 case files he became the number one suspect, even though his room was not the one where the cartridge cases were found. Interestingly, he had a criminal record which seemed not unconnected to the A6 case. He had been convicted in October 1953 for taking and driving away a motor car. Even more significantly, he was a rootless drifter – just the kind of man to fit the popular image of the wandering psychopath or "moon maniac". All these aspects condensed marvellously to match the notion that the murderer was a vagrant and a madman.

There was just one problem. The staff at the Hotel Vienna confirmed Alphon's assertion that he had turned up at the hotel at 11pm and had not gone out again. If he was in Maida Vale at 11pm he could not possibly have been the gunman in the cornfield. This little local difficulty was disposed of after William Nudds was treated to a ferocious interrogation at Scotland Yard. Nudds, himself a career criminal, was only too happy to change his story and provide incriminating "evidence" against Alphon. Presumably his perjured testimony derived from the fear that the police might seek to incriminate him in some way in a serious crime in which he had absolutely no involvement. Possibly he was also leaned on – bullied, threatened – to supply the kind of material which would help the investigators to clinch their case against Alphon. Wiliam Nudds could not afford to risk the possibility that the police might think he was protecting Alphon in some way.

By the standards of the police conduct of the era the pressure put upon Nudds was probably relatively mild. As James Morton puts it, this was an era when allegations against the police of "lies, brutality, planting, and the fabrication and suppression of evidence" were widespread and plausible, resulting in the introduction of the Police and Criminal Evidence Act 1984.

If Valerie Storie had picked Alphon out as her assailant there seems little doubt that he would have gone to the gallows instead of James Hanratty – accompanied by vast publicity about the shy, timid loner who had turned into a vicious killer and rapist. But the fact remains that, one month after the murder and rape, from a line-up of ten men, Valerie Storie did *not* pick out Alphon. That may well be because her glimpse of her attacker was so brief – the merest glimpse of his face in the lights of a passing car at dead of night – that she simply could not recognise him. Her memory, too, was inevitably fading and changing. Memory is not fixed like a photograph but something which evolves and becomes subject to constant reinvention. That said, it should be remembered that Valerie Storie always insisted that the A6 gunman had staring eyes – "icy-blue large saucer-like eyes". Alphon had hazel eyes. His eyes were not deep-set or staring or especially unusual or noticeable.

The A6 killer also had a very distinctive, uneducated, working-class London accent. He said "fink" instead of "think" and "fings" instead of "things". But Alphon was, in the words of the *Evening News* when it first reported the police desire to question him (22 September 1961), "well-spoken". A woman who knew Alphon as a child remembered how "Peter spoke beautifully. He was always telling me off, politely, for not speaking properly. He would often correct me and remind me when I dropped an 'h'." This impression of Alphon's voice is reinforced by his various TV interviews. His voice is drawling, clear, not distinctively accented – in short, nothing at all like the voice of the man whom Valerie Storie described to the police.

Not true, argued campaigners like Woffinden. Jean Justice tape-recorded Alphon speaking in an uneducated, working-class accent. "The same recordings also demonstrate that in moments of great excitability Alphon pronounces 'th' as 'f'." There was, however a quite simple explanation for this, as acknowledged by Justice himself: "Alphon happens to be an excellent mimic. It would have been easy for him to have played the role of an uneducated person. He gives precisely such an imitation on one of the tape recordings in my possession." In other words, the more Jean Justice became obsessed with Alphon and the notion that he was the A6 killer, the more Alphon fed his obsession, even using his skills as a mimic to play the part of the killer.

The idea that Peter Alphon threatened Michael Gregsten and Valerie Storie with a gun, using a fake accent, and then sustained his mimicry over the next five hours, even during a sudden, violent murder and a rape, is surely self-evidently preposterous. The killer was not someone exercising icy control but, on the contrary, was indecisive, badly spoken and dull-witted. This was quite unlike Alphon, who was both highly articulate and at times quite blunt. Although living a life on the margins he seemed intelligent, and his understanding of Jean Justice and Paul Foot was shrewd enough to encourage and outwit both men by leading them ever-onwards through an endless labyrinth.

There are two other substantial objections to the idea that Peter Alphon could have been the A6 killer. Firstly, the gunman was someone who knew a lot about life in prison, and used prison slang which was incomprehensible to Valerie Storie. Alphon, of course, was neither a career criminal nor a jailbird. He did not associate with the criminal underclass. In fact he had no friends at all and knew nothing about prison life.

Secondly, Alphon had no access to firearms. He had no links with any criminal network or ordinary criminals. Obtaining a gun from an underworld gun dealer is not the easiest of matters for an ordinary person. It is hardly a question of turning up at a pub or club and telling people you want to buy a gun and asking for help. A stranger doing such a thing is likely to be regarded with great suspicion. They would be suspected of being either an undercover police officer or a prospectively murderous amateur who is well worth informing on.

There was one man, however, who matched many aspects of the suspect. He had unusually deep-set staring blue eyes. Unlike Peter Alphon, whom one police officer distinctly remembered as "a weak, insignificant man ... looking very small, crumpled, shabby", he was always well turned-out, a snappy dresser who always wore a tie. He had a distinctive, uneducated, working-class London accent. He pronounced "th" as "f". He was a career criminal, who although only twenty-four-years-old had already spent much of his early life in prison. When he was released from his latest incarceration on 24 March 1961, some five months before the A6 murder, he told one of his criminal associates that he was interested in getting a gun. Before long he was back in Soho, mixing with the criminal underclass and committing burglaries.

His name, of course, was James Hanratty.

> We can now be certain that Hanratty was innocent. In
> the first place his alibi stood up to examination ... His
> alibi was watertight.
>
> Bob Woffinden, *Miscarriages of Justice* (1987)

"Let me get this clear, Jimmy. Are you telling me that these three friends of yours in Liverpool can clear you of murder by giving you an alibi?"

"Yes, but they don't want to know."

"Listen to me carefully, Jimmy. My duty is to investigate this murder and find out the truth. If you are innocent it is my job to try and prove you are innocent. It is not my job just to charge you and get you convicted. If I can help you I will do my best for you. Is that clear, Jimmy?"

"Yes, I understand Mr Acott, but there's nothing you can do for me."

> Telephone conversation between Detective
> Superintendent Acott and James Hanratty,
> 7 October 1961

After the discovery of the two spent cartridge cases in Room 24 of the Hotel Vienna on Monday, 11 September 1961, the police were originally led to believe that this basement room had been empty between 16 August and that date. Two days later this was qualified by the revelation that a visitor from India had very briefly had access to the room many days after the murder. This, clearly, had no bearing whatsoever on the case. The killer was a white man, not an Indian.

The fact that a man calling himself "J. Ryan" had stayed in Room 24 overnight on Monday 21 August did not seem to emerge until towards the end of the first week of the police investigation at the hotel. It had obviously become known by 15 September, when Nudds made his first statement, mentioning both "Ryan" (Hanratty) and "Durrant" (Alphon). By this time police attention was firmly focused on Alphon, to the exclusion of everything else. This, in fact, is a textbook example of how miscarriages of justice occur. By jumping to conclusions and assuming that Peter Alphon must be the prime suspect the police investigators abandoned even the most rudimentary exploration of other possibilities. Their minds were made up. They were not interested in the "J. Ryan" who had stayed in Room 24 the night before the abduction in the cornfield. There wasn't even a simple check to see if the man's name and address were genuine. The assumption was that the gunman had reloaded his gun only at the hotel *after* the murder, not *before*. It was a false deduction which could easily have resulted in the wrong man being convicted, while the real killer evaded justice.

On Monday 25 September Acott held fresh interviews with the hotel staff. By now he seems to have discovered the true identity of "Jack Glickberg" and the third statement by this now ex-employee was at last signed in his real name: William George Richard Nudds.

Incredibly, Acott made no attempt to track down "J. Ryan" until *after* the collapse of the case against Alphon on Sunday 24 September. Now he was obliged to consider other lines of enquiry. On Tuesday 26 September 1961 Acott and Detective Sergeant Kenneth Oxford went to the address which Ryan" had written in the hotel register: 72 Wood Lane, Kingsbury. Significantly, Wood Lane, London NW9, was very close to the Hanratty family home at 12 Sycamore Grove. The householder at number 72, George Pratt, explained that he had lived at the property for 25 years. He said no one called Ryan had ever lived there during this time. He had however recently received an envelope addressed to a man of that name, which had been mailed in Ireland. Acott opened it and discovered it contained documentation regarding a car which "Ryan" had recently rented in Dublin.

That afternoon Acott and Oxford visited the Hanratty family home and questioned his parents about their oldest son's whereabouts. In order not to alert their suspect that he was wanted for murder they blandly explained that he was wanted for questioning regarding stolen cars. Hanratty's parents had no idea where their son was and the officers duly departed.

One of a number of enduring mysteries about the A6 case is how by the afternoon of 26 September the two top police investigators had connected "J. Ryan" to James Hanratty. The answer seems to lie with Hanratty's friend and criminal associate Charles France. He evidently had his own reasons for suspecting that Hanratty might be the A6 killer. France seems to have quelled his suspicions up to this point, but with the collapse of the case against Alphon these suspicions were now revived with a vengeance. Chief among them must have been the knowledge that Hanratty had actually shown him how the cavity under the back seat on the top floor of a London double-decker bus made a good place to dump unwanted stolen property. That, of course, was precisely where the murder weapon and the unused ammunition had been dumped. But he had one, perhaps two other reasons, for believing that Hanratty might be the A6 killer, and he knew his associate's character well (probably much better than Hanratty's parents or brothers, who were always keen to believe that the personality he displayed towards his family was his essential self). On Monday, 25 September, it seems Charles France went to Scotland Yard with his suspicions. He took with him a postcard which his friend, using the pseudonym "Ryan", had sent him from Ireland earlier that month. France did not know where Hanratty was and had not seen him since he had called at his house just over a week earlier, on 16 September.

Acott decided Hanratty must still be in Ireland and flew

there on 29 September. He was still there on 3 October when Hanratty's father received a birthday card from his son, postmarked London. Two days later Acott returned from Ireland and promised the press a description of the new prime suspect. By now James Hanratty was well aware that the police wished to interview him regarding the A6 case. On 6 October he telephoned Detective Superintendent Acott twice. He denied being the A6 killer but said he couldn't give himself up because he had only recently come out of prison and knew he would get at least five years more inside for his latest burglaries. Five days later Hanratty was spotted in Blackpool and arrested. On 13 October he was put on an identity parade in Bedford. Two of the witnesses who said they had seen the driver of the stolen Morris identified Hanratty. The next day he took part in an identity parade before Valerie Storie. After scrutinising the men in the line-up and hearing them each say "Be quiet will you, I'm thinking," she picked out Hanratty. He was taken to Ampthill police station and charged with the murder of Michael Gregsten. Asked "Have you anything to say?" Hanratty replied: "No."

When questioned, Hanratty insisted that he had an alibi for the crucial period 22-24 August 1961. He said he had left the Hotel Vienna on the morning of Tuesday 22 August and walked to Paddington Station. He did so claiming to have forgotten that this was not the station for trains to Liverpool. When he realised his mistake he took a taxi from Paddington to Euston station, where he caught a morning train to Liverpool. Having arrived in that city he went looking for a dealer in stolen property he knew about, in order to sell him some jewellery and a gold watch. He went into a sweetshop to ask directions and spoke to the woman at the counter. Next, having still failed to locate the dealer, he had tried to sell a watch to a man on the steps of a billiard hall. He then spent the next two nights in Liverpool with some men whom he refused to name, on the grounds that they had told him they didn't wish to be involved in confirming his alibi.

Hanratty was confident that the crime could never be

pinned on him. He therefore claimed that although he had an alibi he could manage without it. In his typically cocky way he told Detective Superintendent Acott, "I am a very good gambler ... I have gambled all my life. I am going to gamble now. I am not going to name the three men. I can get out of this without them."

His self-confidence started to crack once his trial started. He was warned by his defence team that the judge might instruct him to be taken to Liverpool to identify the flat where he said he had stayed. Since his bogus alibi could not be sustained he abandoned it and came up with a new one. He now admitted that he had not spent two nights in Liverpool. Instead, he claimed that although the first part of his Liverpool story was true he had then left the city, catching a bus to Rhyl. This seaside resort on the Welsh coast was some 50 miles to the south-west. Hanratty said he had arrived at nightfall and spent two nights at a guest house near the railway station. On Thursday 24 August he had returned to Liverpool and caught the night train to London. But if he was really an innocent man, why on earth lie about this? Why pretend he spent two nights in Liverpool, if all along he was in a guest house in Rhyl?

Paul Foot argued that there was "a mountain of evidence" to support Hanratty's alibi in its various aspects. But was that really so? A critical scrutiny of Hanratty's alibi suggests a very different story.

The Journey to Liverpool

Hanratty said that he walked to Paddington Station carrying his pigskin suitcase. When he reached Paddington he suddenly remembered that it was the wrong station for trains to Liverpool. This claim does not ring true, as Hanratty had travelled between Euston and Liverpool on at least five occasions during the previous five years. He had last travelled between the two stations less than a month earlier, on 26 July. Hanratty was a Londoner, and any Londoner would know that the four stations for long-distance travel to northern destinations are King's Cross, St Pancras, Euston and Liverpool Street. Paddington, something of an isolated station quite some distance from the West End and the Soho where Hanratty used to hang out, is a station for destinations to the west. It is also the station for trains to, Maidenhead, Taplow and Slough – in other words, the neighbourhood of the cornfield where the abduction was to occur later that day.

"I do not know why I made this mistake," Hanratty said. "Perhaps I was excited by the jewellery and the deal I was going to do." Having supposedly realised he had gone to the wrong station, Hanratty then claimed that he had taken a taxi to Euston station. No taxi driver was ever identified who could have confirmed this journey. Hanratty then said he caught either the 10.55am or 11.55am train from Euston to Liverpool but was unable to remember which one it was. In fact there were no trains at these times. Originally Hanratty told police that he had been on a train which arrived at Liverpool "at about 3.30pm". That timing fitted the 10.35am train from Euston which arrived at 3.25pm. Attempting to make sense of Hanratty's vagueness (which, from a sceptical perspective, was plainly strategic), Paul Foot concluded that he must have caught one of the mid-morning trains. "It is hard to see how, on his own timings, he could have missed the 10.20 and the 10.35 and been forced to wait nearly two hours for the 12.15," he decided.

Of the two options Foot preferred the 10.20am train. But Bob Woffinden, trying to make sense of the contradictions in Hanratty's testimony in a different way, breezily asserted that Hanratty "would probably have arrived at [Euston] at about 10.45". Woffinden's mathematical gymnastics were designed to support Hanratty's later revision of his alibi. During his trial, Hanratty changed his story and said that his train had arrived some time between 4pm and 5pm. In order to accommodate this change of alibi, Woffinden conveniently concluded that Hanratty must have caught the 11.30am train.

Hanratty described in some detail the people he claimed sat near him in his carriage. Among them he particularly remembered a "clerky gent" who was very smartly dressed, smoked a black pipe and had initialled gold cufflinks marked with the letter "E". But despite being in Hanratty's company for five hours neither this man nor any of the other passengers ever came forward to confirm this aspect of his alibi. None of the campaigners for Hanratty's innocence ever seem to have noticed that on 12 August 1961, just ten days before the cornfield abduction, he carried out a burglary in the Harrow area. Among the articles stolen were "six sets of gold cuff-links with the initial 'E' on them". His bogus alibi plainly drew on this memory. It is also very noticeable that in constructing a false narrative of his whereabouts on 22-23 August 1961, Hanratty offered up very specific localized detail when it suited him but was strategically vague about train times, geography and even the interior of the room he claimed he had stayed in.

Another curiosity is that after his arrest Hanratty was "apprehensive about the prospect of photographs of himself appearing in the press". But surely an innocent man facing a very serious charge, who knew he was very publicly elsewhere over the crucial two days during which the crime occurred and the car and murder weapon were dumped, would have welcomed such publicity. If he was genuinely innocent then when his photograph appeared on television and in the newspapers there was the possibility of memories being jogged and numerous individuals coming forward to confirm his alibi and to testify they had seen him on the train, in Liverpool, and in Rhyl.

Liverpool Lime Street Station

Having supposedly arrived at Liverpool Lime Street station on the afternoon of 22 August, Hanratty claimed that he went to smarten himself up in the toilets under the station buffet. He said he exchanged a few words about horse racing with the attendant. He then had a cup of tea in the buffet and afterwards took his case to the left luggage office. A man with a withered hand took his case at about 5pm. The man asked his name and Hanratty said it was Ryan.

Two men who worked at the left luggage office had disabilities. One, Peter Usher, had two fingers missing from his left hand. The other, Peter Stringer, had an artificial arm. But on 22 August, Usher had worked the 6am-2pm shift, so could not have been the man mentioned by Hanratty. Stringer, who was on duty in the afternoon, had no memory of Hanratty. Moreover his artificial arm was always covered. The defence employed a former Liverpool police officer, Joe Gillbanks, to check out the alibi. Usher said he thought he remembered a man asking for the name of "Ratty" to be put on the left luggage ticket, which he declined to do because the ticket already had its own individual number. But even if this memory was true it cannot have been James Hanratty, as he always hid behind a pseudonym, usually "Ryan". Usher further remembered that the man was wearing a cap (which Hanratty never did) and that the incident had happened between 11am and 12.30pm. None of this fitted the defendant's account. The fact that Usher remembered the name "Ratty" suggests that he was aware of the context of the questioning, which had coloured his response. The defence decided not to call Usher on the grounds that his account did not match Hanratty's and because he displayed a troubling enthusiasm to "get in" on the trial. There was therefore no one to confirm this part of Hanratty's alibi and indeed the facts on this particular day contradicted it.

The probability is that Hanratty was drawing on a hazy memory of having used this facility on a separate occasion. But his gamble failed because the man with the overt disability (which in any case did not involve a *withered* hand) was not on duty at the time.

During his first police interrogation Hanratty described an alibi in Liverpool. But according to Acott he did not mention the sweetshop in this original account. The implication is that Hanratty invented this episode in the days following his arrest in order to add some detail to what was a vague account involving three men he said he didn't want to name. The Detective Superintendent said the first he heard about the sweetshop was from Hanratty's defence counsel, not the defendant himself. As soon as he was informed about this new aspect of the claimed alibi he contacted Liverpool CID on 16 October, asking them to investigate.

Hanratty had told his defence counsel that he knew a Liverpool fence named Aspinall he could sell his stolen jewellery to but he couldn't quite remember the name of the street the man lived on. He thought it was Carlton Avenue or Tarlton Avenue. He wandered out of the station and began asking people if they knew where Carlton Avenue was. He said a woman told him it was a twopenny bus ride away, along Scotland Road. He asked two or three other people, then got on a bus. He got off the bus and went into a sweetshop on Scotland Road to make enquiries.

> Went into sweetshop and tobacconist. I asked for Carlton Avenue or Tarlton Avenue. She said no Carlton Road (*sic*) around here. Woman and young girl. I had pin-striped suit on. Woman came to the door of the shop and showed me the bus stop which was near it. The sweet shop in the Scotland Road, opposite a picture house. A woman and young girl there. I asked them the way to Talbot Road (*sic*), then said Carlton Road. The woman said "This is Bank Hall, and you have to get a bus and go into town." Bank Hall joins Scotland Road. I did not get to Carlton Road. I could not find the street.

Hanratty's alibi was throughout composed of a kind of strategic vagueness dotted with enticing details to give it a veneer of credibility. Scotland Road is a very long street in Liverpool which today bears very little resemblance to how it looked over sixty years ago. At the time of Hanratty's arrest there were no less than twenty-nine sweetshops on Scotland Road. But by August 1961 there were no cinemas left on this street. By introducing a "picture house" into his alibi Hanratty was probably drawing on a memory of a previous visit to Scotland Road. The advent of television was accelerating the slow collapse of the golden age of cinema and regular, weekly, mass attendance. The two cinemas which had once existed on Scotland Road, the Gaiety and the Derby, both closed on 4 May 1960. This was something Hanratty cannot have known, since between 26 March 1958 and 24 March 1961 he was in prison.

Investigation revealed that at a sweetshop on Scotland Road, at number 408, a woman named Olive Dinwoodie had been helping out on 21 and 22 August 1961. She said she did remember a man coming in and asking for directions "to Carlton or Tarleton Road, or something of the kind". But this cannot have been the sweetshop described by Hanratty, since it was not opposite a cinema. The derelict Gaiety Cinema was much further up the street, at 41-45 Scotland Road. The derelict Derby Cinema was on the same side as the sweetshop, at 318a-322 Scotland Road.

There was another problem. Mrs Dinwoodie believed she had given directions to the man on Monday 21st August between 3.30pm and 4pm. This was because Hanratty was insistent that a little girl was with the woman in the sweetshop and Mrs Dinwoodie had been helped by her grand-daughter Barbara Ford on the Monday. However, it emerged that the next day Barbara had called into the sweetshop with a friend named Linda Walton at about 4.45pm and stayed for half an hour. Linda confirmed this but said she thought they had been in the shop between 4pm and 5pm. But even if the timescale for Hanratty's movements is treated elastically to make it fit, it then encounters another obstacle. Hanratty mentioned a woman and a young girl, not a woman and *two* young girls.

There is a more substantial difficulty in treating this episode as persuasive evidence of Hanratty's alibi. Mrs Dinwoodie did not supply her evidence fresh to the police. She first heard about the story of the man who had asked for directions to Talbot or Tarleton Road (*sic*), from the shop's owner, Stella Cowley. Detective Constable Pugh, who had earlier spoken to Mrs Cowley, returned later to the shop to take a statement from Mrs Dinwoodie. He made the elementary mistake of showing her just one photograph – that of James Hanratty – and asking if that was the man. Mrs Dinwoodie said that it was. D.C. Pugh should, of course, have shown her photographs of a number of different men and invited her to say if she recognised any of them. In retrospect it is clear that Mrs Dinwoodie's statement was coloured by information which D.C. Pugh had given her. She said, "It was definitely the Monday, because I was alone on the Tuesday, my grand-daughter was only with me on the Monday." Mrs Dinwoodie evidently knew from the officer that Hanratty said he had spoken to a woman with a young girl with her, which framed her statement.

Plainly someone called at the sweetshop and asked for directions. But it was on the Monday and it wasn't James Hanratty (who was in London that day). Mrs Dinwoodie, understandably, had only a hazy recall of the name of the street which the man had been enquiring after. However, what she was very firm about was the time when the man came in. She said it was "just gone four o'clock, the *Echos* [i.e. copies of the *Liverpool Echo* newspaper] had just arrived." If Hanratty had caught the 10.35am train that arrived at 3.25pm he could not possibly have been in the sweetshop on Scotland Road forty minutes later – not if, as he insisted, he had gone for a wash and brush up, had a cup of tea in the buffet, checked in his case at the left luggage office at around 5pm and then sauntered off in search of Carlton or

Tarlton Avenue (*sic*), before catching a bus and getting of "a few stops from the Scotland Road".

Another difficulty is that Olive Dunwoodie's account of what happened in the sweetshop bears no relation to Hanratty's version of an encounter in a sweetshop. Hanratty said that the woman was helpful, came to the door with him, pointed at a nearby bus stop, and advised him to catch a bus there back into Liverpool city centre. But Mrs Dinwoodie remembered she was busy serving a man with cigarettes when the man entered and asked for directions.

> I could hardly understand him when he asked for directions to Tarleton Road. I told him I did not know that road, only Tarleton Street. Several others, customers, came into the shop and I said perhaps they could help him out and I went on serving and I did not even notice him go out. He was hard to understand, I thought he was Scots or Welsh ...

Could this barely comprehensible figure have been Hanratty? Hanratty's father was Irish and his English mother, from Durham, had a strong regional accent, but when the suspect was examined by a leading expert on speech and phonetics he reported that while it would have been possible for this family background to have resulted in "dialectical traits" he had not been able to detect any. According to Michael Sherrard, Hanratty had "a normal and average young Londoner's voice".

Hanratty was plainly not the man who had gone into the sweetshop and asked Olive Dinwoodie for directions. Every aspect of this part of the alibi was contradicted by the facts. The location was wrong, the day was wrong, the timing was wrong, and what occurred inside the sweetshop was wrong. Finally, Mrs Dinwoodie's description of the man she spoke to bore no resemblance at all to James Hanratty. Her memories of the episode were surely coloured by knowledge of the context of her evidence. It is doubtful if this barely comprehensible individual, who interrupted her during a busy period, was even asking for "Tarleton Road" at all, but somewhere else. Mrs Dinwoodie's knowledge of Hanratty's alibi quite probably coloured this aspect of her testimony, producing a classic false memory. Her first response to questioning is likely to have been the most accurate one. She couldn't remember the name of the street: it was "Carlton or Tarleton Road, *or something of the kind.*" Michael Sherrard QC, who defended Hanratty at his trial, later appeared on Bob Woffinden's 1992 television documentary *Hanratty – The Mystery of Deadman's Hill*, insisting that the sweetshop alibi "was supported by [Olive Dinwoodie] in material particulars". On the contrary, her testimony contradicted Hanratty's, the sweetshop was not the one described by him, and this aspect of his alibi is a giant red herring.

A fence named Aspinall

Hanratty claimed he went to Liverpool to sell jewellery to a dealer in stolen goods named Aspinall. This raises the obvious question as to why he needed to go all the way to Liverpool to sell stolen goods when there were people in London only too happy to buy them off him.

This man Aspinall was supposed to live on a street called Carlton Avenue, or perhaps Tarlton Avenue, or perhaps Talbot Road, or perhaps Carlton Road. Detective Superintendent Acott later learned that Hanratty had allegedly gone into a sweetshop and asked for directions to a street which approximated to one of these names. He did not initially know what the purpose of Hanratty's supposed quest was. Once he did know it seems he was no wiser. The Liverpool police surely had a good idea of who the well established dealers in stolen goods were and where they lived. It seems that there was no such person living on any street the name of which approximated to the one Hanratty claimed to be looking for. "Aspinall" did not exist.

There is no Carlton Road or Carlton Avenue or Talbot Road in Liverpool. There is however a Carlton Street, just off the waterfront, west of and within walking distance of Scotland Road. There is also a Tarleton Street very close to Lime Street station. Hanratty claimed that he was directed to a Carlton Avenue by a woman who told him it was a twopenny bus ride away, along Scotland Road. As there is no such street this seems unlikely. The overwhelming probability is that, alone in his prison cell and desperate to concoct an alibi, Haratty recalled that street near the station and made use of it.

Hanratty's alibi is also in glaring contradiction to his usual behaviour when travelling alone in cities. When he arrived at Paddington on the morning of 22 August and allegedly realised that this was not the station for trains to Liverpool he said he then took a taxi to Euston. He could have easily (and much more cheaply) made the trip by underground train or bus, but taxis were his preferred mode of travel. For example, on the evening of 21 August Hanratty took a taxi from Hendon greyhound racing stadium to Leicester Square. He later took a taxi from Soho to the Broadway House Hotel, Dorset Square. They had no rooms but fixed Hanratty up with one at the Hotel Vienna, advising him to take a cab. Bob Woffinden avuncularly comments: "Hanratty, of course, would have considered nothing less." He duly took a taxi to Sutherland Avenue.

In other words, Hanratty, who knew London well, commonly used taxis, even for quite short distances. Yet having gone all the way to Liverpool to sell a man named Aspinall a case full of expensive jewellery, he didn't do the obvious thing and go straight to the taxi rank at Lime Street Station. Instead he said he wandered aimlessly around asking for directions, then got on a bus, then asked for more directions, then returned to the city centre. A taxi driver, of course, would have possessed an intimate knowledge of the city's streets. He could have taken Hanratty to Tarleton Street and Carlton Street and waited while Hanratty checked to see if Aspinall lived there. Hanratty didn't even bother to go to the station bookstall and buy a Liverpool street map. Instead he claimed that he just drifted aimlessly around, getting nowhere.

It is also worth noting what occurred on 25 July 1961, when he broke into a house and stole some items of silver. When he arrived in nearby Liverpool he went straight to a jeweller and sold them for twenty-five shillings. If Hanratty had rings to sell and couldn't find "Aspinall" he had other outlets available.

The man outside the billiard hall

Hanratty said that after leaving the sweetshop he decided not to take his hunt for Aspinall any further. Instead of going to the bus stop he walked back to Lime Street Station. When he was nearly there he saw the manager standing outside a billiard hall and asked him if he would like to buy a gold watch. The man, Robert Kempt, declined. He realised Hanratty was selling stolen goods and told him he did not want him on his property. However, he did allow Hanratty to go inside and use the toilet.

Kempt confirmed that such an episode had occurred. However he said that "I have no idea of the day, date or month, except that it was in the evening time". He also said that he regularly stood on the steps of his billiard hall on summer evenings "any time between 6.00 and 7.30pm". But this conflicted with the next stage of Hanratty's alibi, which involved him catching the 6pm bus to Rhyl.

This episode underlines a fundamental problem with Hanratty's Liverpool alibi. He was in the city in July 1961, on 24 August, and again in October. The man standing outside the billiard hall was a regular sight. Hanratty knew that he was the manager. As he explained to his defence counsel, this individual "is always there in Lime Street, he stands on [the] steps". Kempt went off on holiday on 26 August, so his encounter with Hanratty could have occurred at almost any time. It seems more than likely that it occurred on the evening of 24 August, when Hanratty very definitely *was* in the vicinity of Lime Street station.

Hanratty's whereabouts in the weeks before and after the A6 murder are largely unknown. After the killing he had all the time in the world to fine-tune aspects of an alibi which featured Liverpool. When he returned to the city on 7 October he said he had no difficulty in establishing contact with criminal acquaintances. He offered them £250 (in those days quite a substantial sum) if they would provide him with an alibi. They told him to get lost. "You can't blame them," Hanratty explained to Detective Superintendent Acott, "because they're fences – you know what I mean – they receive jewellery." These acquaintances were probably as fictional as the rest of Hanratty's alibi – but if they were not it represents a glaring contradiction to his story of how hard it was to find the man who would buy his stolen jewellery.

Two nights in Rhyl

James Hanratty lied to Detective Superintendent Acott about his whereabouts on the critical nights of 22 and 23 August 1961. In his telephone call to Acott on 7 October he claimed he had been in Liverpool between 22-24 August, staying with three criminal acquaintances he was not prepared to name, in order to protect them. He told his defence counsel a similar story.

Hanratty maintained this fictional alibi throughout the committal proceedings at Ampthill during November and December 1961. It was only later, at the end of the first week of his trial at Bedford, that he told his defence team that his story of staying with three men in Liverpool was false. He now presented them with a new alibi, claiming that he had travelled from Liverpool to Rhyl on the evening of 22 August and spent two nights at a boarding house there, returning to Liverpool on 24

August. But he couldn't remember which street it was on, or the street number, or the name of the people living there.

What is remarkable is that when Hanratty returned to London on 25 August he said nothing at all to his closest associates and friends about visiting Rhyl. At this point in time no one suspected him of being the A6 murderer. If he was an innocent man and had really spent two nights staying in Rhyl, why on earth bother to lie about it? Likewise, if Hanratty had really been in Rhyl on the night of the abduction, why bother lying to the police and pretending he had been in Liverpool?

Bob Woffinden, ever eager to exonerate Hanratty, puts a brave face on this difficulty. He says that Hanratty had told Charlotte France that he was going to Liverpool to visit an aunt "so he could hardly have admitted on his return that he'd been somewhere else altogether". This reasoning seems both specious and preposterous. If Hanratty was really concerned about social niceties he could simply have pretended to have seen his aunt and said he had gone on to Rhyl afterwards to visit a friend.

Charles France's nickname was "'Dixie'". On Sydenham Avenue in Rhyl there was a café popularly known as Dixie's, where Hanratty claimed he ate. He might have been expected to remark on this amusing conicidence when he met up with "Dixie" and his family at the end of that week. Instead Hanratty said nothing at all about visiting Rhyl or eating at that café. When Hanratty had last seen the France family on Monday 21 August he had told them he was going to Liverpool. "Send us a postcard," Charlotte France said. Hanratty did send postcards to his friends when he was away. He sent both the France family and Louise Anderson cards from Ireland. Neither received cards from the seaside resort of Rhyl, even though Hanratty claimed he spent his time there just idly drifting around.

Woffinden believed Hanratty must have "felt awkward" that his trip north to sell jewellery had been unsuccessful and that he was too embarrassed to admit it. This, too, was preposterous reasoning. A compulsive liar like Hanratty could have told any tale he chose to. He could, for example, have said he had sold it when he hadn't. But of course the story of going north to sell jewellery was false. On the day in question he didn't travel north to Liverpool but west from Paddington. The Liverpool/Rhyl alibi was a fiction concocted out of scraps of memory of previous visits he had made to those two locations.

There is a very simple explanation as to why Hanratty discarded one bogus alibi and dreamed up a second one. He had no choice. Hanratty was something of a cocky, self-confident individual, as is obvious from his sarcastic exchanges with the prosecutor at his trial. He seems to have believed that his swagger would see him through, and that the evidence against him was too weak to secure a conviction. But as the trial proceeded reality collided with complacency. Or as Bob Woffinden put it: "The opening days of the trial must have been a shattering experience for Hanratty. From the dock he must have followed proceedings with, at first, perplexity and, then, increasing perplexity." During the first week of the trial three witnesses had positively identified him as the A6 killer. His closest associates and friends were cooperating with the prosecution and testifying against him. But there was an even bigger problem. His Liverpool alibi was starting to disintegrate in a spectacular fashion.

Prior to his trial Hanratty had eventually supplied more details of his original, very vague alibi. He divulged the name of one of the three men he said he had stayed with in Liverpool at the time of the crime. This was a man named Terence McNally, whom he had known when they were both in Walton Prison. He had stayed with McNally at a flat "in the Bull Ring off Scotland Road". A man called John lived there with a woman named Lil, and two children, a boy and a girl. One of the men had a warrant against him for an unpaid debt to do with a rented television. But his alibi quickly came unstuck. Hanratty's reference seems to have been to St Andrew's Gardens, a large circular block of council housing in Liverpool L3, popularly known as "the bullring". If this was what Hanratty meant it was not "off Scotland Road" but some distance away, to the east. The police checked every apartment and were unable to find anyone matching Hanratty's description.

Hanratty refined his story for his defence barrister, Michael Sherrard. He now said that the flat was exactly opposite a flower shop in the Scotland Road.

> There is a red phone box opposite the flower shop on the right hand side. The flat is between the flower shop and the Post Office on the opposite side of the road. It's on the second floor with a green door.

Joe Gillbanks, the investigator working for the defence checked no less than twenty-three tenement blocks in the area and had the same lack of success. He advised the defence team that Hanratty should be taken under guard to Liverpool to locate the flat himself. Interviewed again by Sherrard, Hanratty seems to have agreed to this.

> I can go right there. Two bedrooms and a little kitchenette and living room. I slept in the living room. John took the jewellery the first evening, the Tuesday. McNally and John went out to get rid of the stuff.

But then, in mid-January, McNally was traced and served with a subpoena to give evidence. A furious McNally said he had not seen Hanratty since leaving Lewes Prison four years earlier. Moreover, he said he did not frequent the Scotland Road area of Liverpool, he had no relatives or associates there, did not sleep away from home, and had been going straight. During the week of the crime he was working at Dunlop Rubber in Speke, on the 7am to 3pm shift. He had no time off during that week.

When the trial began, Hanratty was still stoutly insisting that he had spent his time in Liverpool. In the final version put together by his defence team he asserted:

129

During the three days I was in Liverpool I stayed with McNally in a block of flats known as the Bull Ring or the Gardens in Scotland Road, or a road just off it, Skellone Road. McNally lives there with a married couple. It is a second floor flat, and I think there is an entrance in the Scotland Road ... It has a balcony with a green door.

There is no "Skellone Road" in Liverpool.

Hanratty said that on the Tuesday evening – the time of the abduction in the cornfield – he had gone alone to see *The Guns of Navarone* at a local cinema. On Wednesday he had hung around waiting for McNally to sell the stolen jewellery. On Thursday he had gone to a fun fair in New Brighton, and had tried to get into a boxing title fight involving a black man. On Thursday evening McNally sold the jewellery and Hanratty left the flat and caught the night train back to London.

By the end of the first week of his trial Hanratty seems to have realised that his Liverpool alibi was fooling no one. He was also warned that the judge might order him to be taken to Liverpool to identify the flat where he claimed he had stayed on the night of the abduction and murder. If he refused to go or was unable to locate it, Sherrard told him, "you will be lost".

Hanratty now came up with a new version of events. He claimed it was true what he had said about going to Liverpool on 22 August, about going to the sweetshop, and about talking to the man outside the billiard hall. But after that he had caught a bus to Rhyl. He arrived at the seaside resort as it was getting dark. He had gone in search of accommodation, asking five or six times if there was a vacancy. But it was the peak summer season and everywhere was full. Eventually he found a boarding house near the station, which put him up for two nights. The reason he had gone to Rhyl was in search of a man named John. He knew John from a previous trip to this seaside resort in July. On that occasion he had stayed at the man's house. John had told him he knew people locally who might be able to get rid of stolen goods.

Hanratty said he spent the next day searching for John without success. The next day he returned to Liverpool at around mid-day.

The phenomenon of the new alibi produced without warning in the course of a trial was well known to the courts. It was a trick known as an "ambush alibi". It was a technique which threw the prosecution off-balance because it meant there was no time thoroughly to check the new alibi and establish that it was false. The use of "ambush alibis" had become so widespread and frequent that legislation was introduced to make them inadmissible. If his trial had occurred five years later Hanratty's switch of alibi would not have been allowed and the jury would never have known of his new claim that he had been on the Welsh coast at the time of the crime. The 1967 Criminal Justice Act put an end to that kind of manoeuvre.

What this last-minute change of alibi meant was that the first attempts to verify it were not made by the police but by agents acting for the defence. Gillbanks and a retired police officer who lived in Rhyl quickly located "John", who turned out to be a local man called Terry Evans. Evans evidently volunteered to help Gillbanks look for the boarding house which Hanratty had described. The accused said there was a green bath in the top part of the house, "I would say the attic". He could also hear trains from his room. A boarding house named "Ingledene" on Kinmel Street seemed to match Hanratty's description. It was near the station and it had a green bath in an attic room with a bed. Gillbanks had a photograph of Hanratty which he showed to the owner, Mrs Grace Jones. The investigator recorded that "She has a feeling that she does know the young man." This seemed like solid support for Hanratty's second alibi. Or was it?

Ingledene

Hanratty said that the woman who ran the guesthouse was "Middle-aged, about fifty, average build. She wore glasses and had greyish hair." This was a description which must have fitted many guesthouse owners, in Rhyl or any other seaside resort. In fact Grace Jones had fair hair, not greyish. She did not normally wear glasses. In the photograph of her standing outside the court in Bedford used in Paul Foot's book (Plate 23) she is not wearing glasses. She was not of average build but actually "rather small. No more than 5' 2'"". Therefore Hanratty's description did not fit Mrs Jones.

Grace Jones was shown just one photograph – that of James Hanratty. That of course was no way objectively to determine if she really remembered seeing the face in the photograph. If she had been shown a collection of ten or more faces and had picked his out then that would have been much more credible in establishing if she actually remembered him. As it is, once she had been shown his image and given his name her credibility and value as a witness was diminished.

In fact Mrs Jones was not at first very sure about James Hanratty's visit to her guesthouse. "She can't be certain where, and in which room, Hanratty stayed," the defence investigator reported. During the latter part of August her establishment had been filled with guests. She believed "H[anratty] *might* have been one of them" (my italics). She had "a feeling" that she knew the man in the photograph. During the course of the trial Terry Evans asked if she recognised the man in the dock and she replied that she was "*almost* sure" (my italics). When Graham Swanwick QC said, "It would not be quite right, would it, to say that when you were shown the photograph, you recognized it?" the hapless Mrs Jones replied, "Well, no." When Swanwick challenged Mrs Jones to explain why she claimed she had said she recognised the man in the photograph "when in fact what happened was that you said you could not remember the person or not", she replied, "No, I got muddled – the hair. He had not got that coloured hair when he was in our house."

At this point Paul Foot draws the conclusion that she was an impressive witness because Hanratty's hair was indeed a different colour in August 1961 to how it appeared in February 1962. But in fact it was Terry Evans who suggested to Grace Jones that the reason she might not have recognised the prisoner in the dock was because of the colour of his hair. Once again her supposed memories had been shaped in advance by a third party. Instead of testifying along the lines of "well, I think I recognise him but the colour of his hair seems different now" she at first confidently identified Hanratty as the man in the photograph she had been shown. That in itself involved a circular, self-verifying line of evidence. But under cross examination she admitted that at first she hadn't recognised the man in the photo. Then, changing her story again, she said she was in a muddle because of the colour of Hanratty's hair. But until Terry Evans mentioned this to her she had said nothing at all about Hanratty's hair colour. The same campaigners who regard as unreliable the three eye-witnesses who unequivocally identified Hanratty in ID parades simultaneously treat Grace Jones, whose evidence was filled with hesitations and uncertainties, as a witness who supplied formidable proof of his innocence.

Hanratty's strategic vagueness came into play again when it came to describing the interior of the boarding house. He said he remembered a coat rack with a mirror in the hall, which was a traditional feature of hallways, whether in private homes or guesthouses. He said he also recalled "a green plant in a bowl in the hall". But according to Gillbanks there was not a bowl but a vase in the hall. It contained not a green plant but artificial flowers. Once again, Hanratty's description did not fit the supposed reality. It may have been that he was actually creatively using memories of the one place where he really *had* stayed in Rhyl: the home of Terry Evans, whose mother matched Hanratty's description of the landlady, and where the hallway's interior also resembled his description of the boarding house.

There was one other feature of "Ingledene" which Hanratty said he remembered and which has become a legendary feature of the case. This was the famous green bath. Hanratty was careful to keep his options open in describing the location of another common feature of guesthouses. At his trial he said it was "In the top part of the house, I would say the attic" but in the next breath he also said, "It might not be the attic."

When at his trial Hanratty was asked how many flights of stairs he went up at "Ingledene" to get to his room, he replied: "I am not quite sure because I have been in so many boarding houses and you get confused with – I do not want to make such a serious…". His lapse into incoherence and silence was characteristic. He was vague about times, vague about places, vague about people. When he offered precision, as in the case of the flat in Liverpool and the people who lived there, his account turned out to be false in every aspect. Vagueness was a safer option. For the campaigners this was very useful as it allowed them great flexibility in attempting to construct a plausible narrative.

To people like Paul Foot and Bob Woffinden, Hanratty's reference to a green bath upstairs in an attic (but which might not have been an attic) was conclusive evidence that the accused was telling the truth. But baths are usually found upstairs. In the nineteen-sixties most baths were white or green. In any case Hanratty's account was contradicted in numerous ways. He said he remembered that his room had curtains and a small sink. But the attic room with a green bath had no curtains and no sink.

Hanratty could be studiously vague when it suited him, yet on other occasions his memory could be quite sharp. (As Nick Russell-Pavier commented about another 1960s criminal wriggling under interrogation: "He knew as well as anyone that lies are often more convincing when they contain an element of truth.") James Hanratty said he could remember quite clearly his room at the Hotel Vienna: "It was a very big room with three or four beds. I slept in a small bed against the wall." Yet, the following night, when he claimed he was at "Ingledene", he had no memory of the most striking feature of the room with the green bath: it contained not a single but a double bed, squeezed in (against local authority boarding house regulations) beside the bath. However, Hanratty did not claim to have slept in this room. But if this was so he could not have known about the existence of the green bath, because it was hidden away in a room marked PRIVATE. The green bath could not be seen, even when the door was open. The reason for all this secrecy was because Grace Jones was on the fiddle. She was banned from using this bathroom for accommodation but was prepared to use it for exactly this purpose during the busy month of August. Any unbooked person or couple seeking accommodation would be shown it and given the option of taking it or going off into Rhyl to look for something better. This is precisely the room Hanratty would have been offered had he been telling the truth. However, in Hanratty's version he slept in a different room, at the back. The problem here is that all rooms at "Ingledene" were occupied on the night of Tuesday 22 August 1961. The room which best fitted Hanratty's description contained the Sayle family.

Paul Foot attempted to get around the glaring contradictions present in Hanratty's second alibi by arguing that perhaps he spent one night on a sofa and then moved to Room 1, which had curtains and a sink and was at the back, on the second night, or perhaps he spent both nights in Room 5, the room of the proprietor's daughter Brenda Harris, who herself moved into the attic room to create a vacancy for Hanratty. Or perhaps he spent both nights in the attic room. Bob Woffinden arrived at the opposite conclusion. He believed Hanratty spent the first night in the room with the green bath and the second in Room 1. But Room 1 was on the first floor and Hanratty said his room was on the second floor. Room 5 was a family room and Brenda Harris had no memory of moving out to make way for Hanratty. Finally, the attic room was inconsistent with Hanratty's description of curtains and a small sink. He would also surely have remembered the double bed, wedged alongside the bath. In any case, Hanratty never said he had to change rooms at the guesthouse. The dizzying permutations which Foot and Woffinden indulged in displayed a desperately threadbare line of reasoning. The logic of their arguments is less plausible than the obvious reality that Hanratty never once set foot inside "Ingledene".

Hanratty said that there was a small courtyard at the back of the guesthouse. He said he had eaten breakfast in a general room with two tables. The breakfast room at "Ingledene" had five tables. Campaigners argued that he must have eaten his breakfast in the family's own room at the back, which had two tables. But this could hardly be described as a "general room". On the contrary it was a private family lounge, with a settee, armchairs and a television set.

Hanratty's second alibi, like his earlier discarded one, drew on his personal knowledge of Liverpool and Rhyl. The implausibility, holes and glaring contradictions of his twin alibis were because he had not been in those places on Tuesday 22 August and the following morning and afternoon, nor had he met there any of the people he claimed to have encountered on those two days. Hanratty was in Rhyl on 25 July 1961 – exactly one month before the A6 crime, even on the same day of the week.

Another oddity of Hanratty's "Ingledene" alibi is what he *didn't* remember. He said he remembered that the guesthouse was somewhere near the station. But as the first investigator to check out the Rhyl alibi noted in some exasperation, there were "Hundreds of bed and breakfast houses which back on [the] railway station which have no front gardens". Though he allegedly spent two nights at "Ingledene" he never noticed that it was across the road from the Windsor Hotel. Nor did he notice that it was just a few doors down from a betting shop. Yet Hanratty enjoyed greyhound racing and gambling. "He loved gambling," Michael Hanratty told Bob Woffinden. A little flutter in Rhyl would have been in character. But Hanratty, even though by his own admission he was at a loose end, never noticed the betting shop or patronised it.

There is one final point to bear in mind when considering the legendary green bath. "Green" is an adjective which occurs elsewhere in Hanratty's two alibis. He claimed there was a green plant in the hall of the guesthouse, though in fact at "Ingledene" there was only a vase of artificial flowers (presumably with bright primary colours). In Liverpool he initially claimed to have stayed in a flat off the Scotland Road: "It's on the second floor, with a green door." In another version he said that the flat had "a balcony with a green door".

The problem for Hanratty when he concocted his bogus two-nights-in-Liverpool alibi as that he provided too many precise details about this flat. This enabled both the police and the defence investigators to establish that no such flat existed and that the individual Hanratty named as a witness to his stay there denied having seen him for four years and was able to prove he was at work at a time when he was supposed to be out trying to sell the stolen jewellery. In constructing a second alibi, this time in Rhyl, Hanratty made the same mistake. The individual details were enticing but they could not be fitted together. Lurking inside the Rhyl alibi is just another version of the Liverpool alibi: an aimless, inconclusive hunt for Aspinall (Liverpool), an aimless, inconclusive hunt for Terry Evans (Rhyl); a second-floor flat (Liverpool), a second-floor room (Rhyl); a green door (Liverpool), a green bath (Rhyl).

When DNA testing indicated that Hanratty had raped Valerie Storie and disposed of the murder weapon, Paul Foot insisted that the analysis must in some way be defective. As far as he was concerned the science was wrong because of the Rhyl alibi: "Hanratty's detailed description of the boarding house exactly fitted Ingledene, then at 19 Kinmel Street, Rhyl. There was a green bath in the attic, as he alleged, and the landlady confirmed that a young Londoner looking like Hanratty had stayed two nights there."

This was wishful thinking on Foot's part. Hanratty's description of the boarding house did not fit "Ingledene" but differed from it in significant and substantial ways. The landlady herself was initially confused and uncertain as to whether or not

Hanratty had stayed with her. And she never once said anything about her supposed guest being "a young Londoner". Hanratty couldn't even remember which street he had stayed on, which is odd, since Rhyl is a small place and Kinmel Street is very close to the railway station. Perhaps most tellingly of all, none of the other guests at "Ingledene" during the time Hanratty said he was staying there had any memory of seeing him at all.

The credibility of landlady Grace Jones was further undermined by the stark proof of her personal dishonesty which emerged during the trial. She was exposed as someone on the fiddle. Local authority regulations did not permit guests to be boarded in bathrooms. This was hardly a major misdemeanour but it did show that she was prepared to bend the rules to maximise her income. Since anyone who took the attic room was not officially a guest she presumably did not declare the revenue as income to the tax authorities.

Of rather more significance was her flouting of court rules. During the course of giving her evidence Mrs Jones had been explicitly instructed by the judge not to talk to anyone about the case. She promptly went out and had a conversation with another Rhyl witness, Terry Evans. It was a juror who spotted this and raised it with the judge, asking to know "whether in fact she had discussed anything with relevance to the case". It turned out that she had and it was something of direct relevance to her role as a witness for the defence. But when she was called back into court and questioned by Mr Justice Gorman, she replied: "We were just talking about lunch, that is all."

That was a lie and it was exposed as such when Terry Evans was called. He breezily explained that they had been discussing Hanratty's appearance and the change in the colour of his hair. Grace Jones was later caught out in another piece of dishonesty. She was asked how many visitors' books she kept. Two, she replied. In fact there was a third one. It was only discovered when the police raided "Ingledene" and searched it. Mrs Jones had a list of all her guests. James Hanratty (or even

"Jim Ryan") was not there. Every guest listed during the relevant days was tracked down and questioned. None had seen Hanratty at "Ingledene".

The defence was clutching at straws when it produced Grace Jones. Curiously, when she was first asked about a possible visit by Hanratty to her establishment, it was noted that she said "She will be as helpful as she can because she wants justice done." This was revealing phrasing. It indicated that Mrs Jones was not a detached witness but someone already passionately committed to a particular point of view. She can hardly have been unaware of the A6 murder trial, since it was the major news story of the time. The trial started on 22 January and it was not until February 6 that Grace Jones first spoke to the defence investigator. On February 7 the national press carried prominent reports of Hanratty's new alibi and the hunt for potential witnesses in Rhyl. This was the worst possible kind of context in which to locate genuine witnesses.

It is worth recalling the case of the man at Lime Street station left luggage office. The defence decided not to use him because he displayed a worrying eagerness to "get in" on the trial action. By the end of the first week of the trial these scruples had vanished. The defence was desperate. But after Grace Jones's credibility was shredded under cross-examination the old caution returned.

Other witnesses in Rhyl

In the wake of publicity in the national press apparently no less than nineteen people came forward to say they though they had seen James Hanratty in Rhyl. The police took statements and passed their identities on to the defence.

Mrs Margaret Walker was one such witness. She lived in South Kinmel Street, round the corner from Mrs Jones. On the evening of 7 February 1962 she saw a small crowd gathered in

Kinmel Street. The fact that Grace Jones was going off to Bedford the next day to give evidence in the famous A6 murder trial had transformed her into an instant local celebrity. Mrs Walker then suddenly remembered that she, too, might have seen the accused in Rhyl. The next day she went to Rhyl police station and made a statement.

She said a man aged 24-27 had come to her front gate at about 7.30pm on the evening of 22 August 1961. He was neatly dressed in a dark suit and his hair was brushed back, though there was something "streaky or tacky" about it. A neighbour, Ivy Vincent, backed up Mrs Walker's account. She said she remembered seeing Mrs Walker talking to a young man at her gate "about the third week in August". He wanted bed and breakfast for two nights. Mrs Walker had told him to go further up, and then try the houses in Kinmel Street.

Margaret Walker had plainly followed the trial and knew all about the accused man's hair having been dyed, then re-dyed, then later bleached. She added: "I have seen photographs of James Hanratty in the weekend papers and they are very much like the young man, but I don't want to commit myself. The photographs you have shown me are very like the man who called here, but the hair was dark. Mind, I couldn't swear it was him." She was equally unsure when this incident had happened. When defence investigator Frank Evans questioned her he recalled that "she was not completely clear about the date of the man's visit".

It seems obvious that Margaret Walker's testimony was coloured by the existing published material on the case and the excitement in Rhyl that there might be a connection with Britain's top news story. The same applies to Ivy Vincent's testimony. In any case, when Hanratty arrived in Rhyl, why would he have asked for *two* night's bed and breakfast? His purpose in travelling there was to sell stolen jewellery. Having accomplished this he had no reason to stay a second night. It's another glaring anomaly of the kind that never bothered the campaigners for Hanratty's innocence.

There was also one rather stark fact that destroyed the value of both women's testimony. Margaret Walker said her encounter with the Hanratty-like young man had occurred at around 7.30pm. But the bus which Hanratty said he had caught in Liverpool did not arrive in Rhyl until 8.19pm.

The day after Margaret Walker went to the police station, Friday 9 February, a man named Trevor Dutton contacted the police, as did half a dozen others in Rhyl. Plainly the excitement had reached fever pitch.

Dutton said that on 23 August a young man had tried to sell him a gold watch in Rhyl High Street. "I am afraid that I cannot describe this man. However, I can say he was not an old man, but was probably in the twenty-five to thirty-five year age group, but seemed a little bit older than he probably actually was."

The problem with these kinds of testimony is that they were generated at a time of massive media publicity. Trevor Dutton, for example, came forward when "one of my customers read part of a newspaper report to me and mentioned that Hanratty claimed he had tried to sell a watch in Rhyl." In fact Hanratty never made any such claim. There was clearly confusion with the story of Hanratty trying to sell a watch to a man in Liverpool. He had never said he had done this in Rhyl. Had he claimed to have done so in High Street, Rhyl, to a man of Dutton's appearance, this would have lent impressive support to his alibi. But he made no such claim.

Press publicity had very obviously shaped Dutton's memory of the incident. Hanratty had an Irish name and an Irish father, and Dutton recalled that the man had an accent which he couldn't place: "more like a dialect … possibly Irish or cockney or a mixture of the two." This is the kind of accent which James Hanratty might well have been expected to have but in reality he had been born and grew up in England and had not the slightest trace of an Irish accent. In an attempt to bolster Dutton's credibility Paul Foot asserted that this witness was "most anxious to avoid publicity". This was an odd claim to make about a man who was happy to be photographed and named alongside the Hanratty family, Jean Justice and other members of the "A6 Committee's delegation to Rhyl", as shown in Plate 30 of *Who Killed Hanratty?*

The identities of these potential new witnesses were given to the defence. Investigator Frank Evans, a retired police officer who lived locally, went to interview them. They apparently included the landlord of a pub, three girls in a café, an old woman who lived on River Street and various landladies. Evidently much of this material, once subject to critical scrutiny by an experienced police officer, was of zero importance.

On 12 February Christopher Larman made a statement to the police. He said he believed he might have met Hanratty in Rhyl the previous August. On 21 February he made a statement to the defence saying that, having seen photographs of Hanratty in the national newspapers, he "immediately remembered" that he had seen him before. He had, he said, met a smartly dressed young man on 22 August at about 7.30pm at the junction of Kinmel Street and Bodfor Street, Rhyl. The man had a London accent and hair that was bronze and dark in parts. Larman said he directed the young man to the guesthouse opposite the Windsor Hotel, which was, of course, "Ingledene". Plainly this individual was James Hanratty – or what Larman knew about the suspect from the press. But once again the timing was wrong. According to Hanratty he was still on the bus at this time and some fifty minutes away from Rhyl.

Paul Foot decided that Mrs Walker must have muddled her timing and, because she stated "it was getting dark and the street lamps were lit" when she said 7.30pm, she really meant 8.30pm. Evidently Christopher Larman made the same remarkable error in remembering the time. In reality both witnesses were tailoring their accounts to what had been published and they did not know that their statements did not fit with the timetable of the bus Hanratty claimed to be on. If there really was a young man asking for accommodation in the manner described he very plainly was not James Hanratty.

There are other probems associated with Hanratty's Rhyl alibi. Firstly, when precisely did he leave Liverpool and travel to Rhyl? Hanratty was asked this in court and replied "about half past seven". But, as usual, he was keen to qualify a precise detail with a framework of vagueness. "It might not be the exact time." It wasn't. Hanratty was *an hour and a half out.* He was making a wild guess about bus times because, of course, he wasn't in Liverpool, and he didn't travel to Rhyl on a bus. At the time in question he was probably in Maidenhead, some 162 miles away.

In concocting his second false alibi Hanratty was obviously unaware that there was only one bus from Liverpool to Rhyl in the evening and that it left at 6pm and arrived in Rhyl at 8.19pm. What is both remarkable and revealing is that Hanratty had actually travelled on this bus service on Tuesday 25 July 1961, but since he said he arrived some time after 6pm he had obviously caught an earlier bus. His second alibi was, like the first, a version of a real experience but displaced to a later time and based on imperfect knowledge.

The trial judge, Mr Justice Swanwick, who appeared to some observers to be deeply sympathetic to the defendant, tried to pin Hanratty down as to the approximate time of his arrival in Rhyl. Hanratty replied, "I am not sure." He did however concede that "it got dark towards the evening" – a masterpiece of banality which revealed nothing. Hanratty's bluster and equivocation was rooted in the fact that his second alibi was as bogus as his original discarded one. Sunset in Rhyl on that date was shortly after 8.30pm. It was therefore not dark when Hanratty supposedly arrived in this Welsh seaside resort.

After the trial

After the trial was over Robert H. Fish came forward and made a statement to the police. He said he remembered helping a man in

August 1961 who was standing on the corner of River Street and Aquarium Street looking for lodgings. When he saw Hanratty's photograph in a newspaper he became convinced this was the man he had spoken to.

The campaigners' high profile visit to Rhyl in 1968, where a public meeting was held, produced what Paul Foot and others regarded as exciting new evidence in support of the second alibi. Mrs Betty Davies remembered that a young man had come to her house at 21 Kinmel Street one evening in late August 1961. He was looking for bed and breakfast. She turned him away because she did not like the look of him and he had no luggage. But Hanratty said he had traipsed around the town looking for accommodation while carrying a case containing stolen jewellery. Paul Foot believed that this contradiction could be explained by Hanratty having left his case at "Ingledene", after being shown the attic room with the green bath and then gone off on the basis that he would look for a better room elsewhere and only take it if one could not be found.

The problem with this ingenious explanation is that Hanratty never did stay in the attic room but in a room which had curtains and a basin. In any case, Hanratty does not come across as someone who was choosy about the accommodation which was on offer. A double bed beside a bath was positive luxury to someone who had spent much of his adolescence and early adult life in prison cells sleeping on thin, stained, frequently malodorous and notoriously uncomfortable prison mattresses. Finally, if Hanratty had left his valuable jewellery behind at "Ingledene" and gone off into the night to search for a superior room he would surely have taken note of the name of the guesthouse and the street on which it was located. His attention span was evidently extraordinarily brief and his memory for streets and house numbers very poor. He would hardly have risked losing his way back to "Ingledene".

Because Hanratty's Rhyl alibi was never mentioned until his trial was underway it meant that it received massive publicity.

144

Any potential witnesses in the town were saturated in details of the crime, the defendant and his sudden explanation that all along he had been in Rhyl. This inevitably coloured memories of supposed encounters with the accused. The defence, acutely aware of holes or ambiguities in the accounts, chose not to use the majority of the witnesses from Rhyl. Statements given to a friendly defence investigator or a sympathetic journalist or, years later, in the highly charged atmosphere of a public meeting, in the presence of Hanratty's family, can turn out to be less impressive if they are subjected to hostile critical scrutiny in a court.

Terry Evans took a keen interest in the campaign to clear Hanratty's name. Hanratty claimed that the reason he went to Rhyl was to see if Evans could help him sell stolen jewellery. He had stayed with Evans just a month earlier but in constructing his Rhyl alibi he now claimed he was unable to remember where he lived. After two nights at a boarding house he had still not traced Evans so on Thursday he went back to Liverpool.

In *Who Killed Hanratty?* Foot described Evans as a scrap metal dealer. He did not mention, and perhaps was unaware, of Evans's criminal record. He had convictions for poaching, failing to stop after a collision, and driving without due care and attention. When Hanratty met up with him in July 1961 he was due in court, charged with theft.

Evans was keen to assist in the investigation of Hanratty's newly minted alibi. He said that when it was first publicised in the media two locals had told him that a man who greatly resembled Hanratty was looking for him the previous summer. One of these witnesses was Ernie Gordon, who ran Dixie's café near the fairground. The other was a newspaper seller named Charlie Jones. Ernie Gordon later denied this and declined to talk to A6 campaigners.

Charlie Jones said that the man who looked like Hanratty had got off a bus from Liverpool and asked him for help in finding a man who worked at the fairground. Jones had pointed him in the direction of the fairground and had watched him walk away towards it. But when Detective Superintendent Douglas Nimmo questioned this witness a rather different story emerged. Jones muttered, "I wish from the bottom of my heart I had never got into it ... It's that Evans made me do it ... The whole lot came from him, sir ... I didn't mean no harm at all. I never realised it would come to this. It was just that Evans said there might be some money in it and I was broke at the time."

In Bob Woffinden's 1992 television documentary *Hanratty – The Mystery of Deadman's Hill* the idea that Hanratty arrived in Rhyl and went first to the fair is presented as fact. The guest witness testifying to its veracity is none other than Terry Evans. But this added twist to the second alibi raises new difficulties. The bus arrived at 8.19pm. Hanratty supposedly walked to the fair. He then wandered around looking for a guesthouse with vacant accommodation. He was directed to "Ingledene". The only room was in the attic, containing a double bed beside a bath. He wandered around some more. He then went back to "Ingledene" and slept in the attic room.

This scenario was constructed by the campaigners in an effort to make sense of the multiple contradictions inherent in eye-witness testimony produced against a background of feverish press publicity and speculation. Any story which seemed to fit was eagerly slotted in. In a postscript to the first paperback edition of his book, Paul Foot described how on 9 May 1971 "the Hanratty family and a large body of supporters" arrived in Rhyl for a public meeting about the case. The hall was packed with some 300 people. After the speeches a Rhyl resident, Mrs Pearl Hughes, stood up. She had new information to impart.

She said that she remembered in the summer of 1961 being approached by a young man who asked her to help him find a friend. "He did not know the friend's name but remembered that he was swarthy and had a mark on his forehead." After a short conversation she realised the friend must be Terry Evans, who lived very close to where they were standing. "The man then asked her to knock on the 'friend's' door, while he waited in the road to see if he could identify him." Mrs Hughes declined to do so as she was late for work and went on her way. But Mrs Hughes, Foot explained, "had very clearly identified Evans, Evans's features, Evans's house and Evans's wife." Mrs Hughes added, "to the amazement of the meeting", that the man she had talked to looked very much like Richard Hanratty, who was on the platform. "Of the three Hanratty brothers," Foot observed, "Richard most closely resembled James".

All this, to Foot, was further conclusive evidence that Hanratty's alibi stood up to examination. "The behaviour which Mrs Hughes described to us precisely fits that of a criminal on the run, who has forgotten the name and address of a possible fence." But on 22 August 1961, if Hanratty really was in Rhyl as Foot believed, he was *not* a criminal on the run. The first the Hanratty family knew that the police were searching for their errant son was on 27 August, when they were visited by Detective Sergeant Douglas Elliott of Ruislip police station. In any case the notion that Hanratty got as far as Evans's door and was then bashful about knocking on it was absurd. As a career burglar he was well used to seeing if someone was at home before he set about breaking in. Hanratty's second alibi purported to involve a two day hunt for the whereabouts of Terry Evans. He never said that he had found Evans's house but that no one ever answered the door.

Another odd aspect of Mrs Hughes's story is why she chose to reveal it a full decade after this supposed encounter with James Hanratty occurred, and why she did so in the feverish, highly charged atmosphere of a public meeting packed with Hanratty's supporters and his family. Pearl Hughes was a Rhyl resident and the A6 case had been a major local news story from the moment Hanratty first mentioned the town in February 1962. Mr and Mrs Hanratty had been making forlorn visits to Rhyl on a number of occasions during the 1960s, with adverts paced in the local press and the poignant appeal, "For the sake of justice, please come forward." Some did – but not Pearl Hughes.

Perhaps these glaring anomalies occurred to Foot's

number one fan, Bob Woffinden, because although his book *Hanratty: The Final Verdict* remains by far the fullest and most detailed account of the case it curiously makes no mention whatever of Pearl Hughes and her sensational story.

In the postscript to the Panther edition of his book Paul Foot mentioned one other exciting new local witness. "After a few hectic days in Rhyl [Mr and Mrs Hanratty] interviewed a barber, Mr Gerald Murray, who said he may have been the barber who shaved Hanratty in 1961." Hanratty did indeed claim to have had a shave at a barber's in Rhyl. But in fact this was not what Murray himself said. He believed he might have given the convicted man *a haircut*. Apart from the inconsistency there is again the fundamental problem of someone claiming to remember something which happened ten years earlier. There cannot have been all that many barbers in Rhyl in August 1961 but it seems the defence failed to locate one who could confirm Hanratty's story.

Amid the welter of detail about the Rhyl alibi it is easy to lose sight of the broader picture. Hanratty claimed that his sole purpose in going to Rhyl was to find Terry Evans and seek his help in disposing of stolen jewellery. But Evans was not a fence. If Hanratty couldn't find someone to buy it in Liverpool he was hardly likely to have better luck in a small Welsh seaside resort.

Where Evans actually lived in Rhyl is something neither Foot nor Woffinden bothered to reveal, even though the location is plainly pertinent to Hanratty's alleged quest. Evans was a well known local character, with a prominent star tattoo on his face (in an era when very few people apart from sailors had tattoos). Hanratty could very easily have gone to the fairground and asked for Evans there. Campaigners claim that he was too bashful to do this because, having got a casual job there the month before, he had promptly walked out. This was hardly something that can have much mattered, and the idea that it would have prevented him from trying to sell his jewellery is unconvincing. If we are to believe Pearl Hughes, Hanratty actually got as far as Terry Evans's house but was too timid to knock on the door. In the end we are

148

supposed to believe that Hanratty then went back to London carrying unsold stolen goods. When he got back to the capital he never mentioned Rhyl to any of his friends and criminal associates. This portrait of Hanratty as a shy, retiring delicate individual who deferred to social niceties is not remotely convincing.

In any case the idea that Hanratty would have been too bashful to call at the fair and ask for Evans but would not have been at all embarrassed about finding him rather overlooks the fact that when he had stayed with him in July Evans grumbled that after supplying him with accommodation Hanratty had scarpered without a word "and stole a pair of shoes". Hanratty would hardly have been a welcome guest had he returned.

When Paul Foot spoke to Grace Jones in October 1966 she said she was "more certain now" that Hanratty had stayed at "Ingledene". But all this indicates is how easy it is for uncertainty and vague impressions to solidify into something absolute and unyielding. Memory is not like a photograph, fixed for all time, but is rather like a painting which is constantly being touched-up and restored. It has become something of a truism that the sincerity of an eye-witness is no guide whatever to his or her accuracy in making an identification. The objections made by campaigners to the eye-witness evidence which helped convict Hanratty apply with equal force to the rag-taggle collection of individuals from Rhyl who felt they might well have encountered the accused in their town.

There is a much-reproduced photograph of Hanratty's father stubbornly parading outside the House of Commons with a placard which reads *JAMES HANRATTY, murdered by the state for the A6 murder, ELEVEN WITNESSES SWEAR HE WAS IN RHYL, 200 MILES AWAY, WHEN THE CRIME WAS COMMITTED.* But this eye-witness evidence was in reality vague, brief, impressionistic and utterly inconclusive. That nineteen people made statements to the police in connection with Hanratty's second alibi sounds impressive, but as Bob Woffinden tersely conceded, "Some of the original statements ... are not helpful." The fundamental problem is that *all* the eye-witness testimony from Rhyl was generated during massive media publicity in the course of the trial, or immediately afterwards in the emotionally heated atmosphere of an impending execution, or in later years in the presence of the dead man's parents, or at highly charged public meetings where figures like Paul Foot raged against a monstrous injustice perpetrated by a corrupt and oppressive state, which had hanged a wholly innocent young man.

The only one of those nineteen witnesses to appear in court was Grace Jones, and her credibility was irretrievably damaged by her exposure as someone who was prepared to lie to the judge, and whose business affairs had a streak of dishonesty running through them. Her claim that Hanratty had stayed at "Ingledene" made her into a minor local celebrity, and benefited her establishment, as for many years afterwards true-crime fans and Hanratty supporters made pilgrimages to it. Yet Grace Jones was the best and only witness which the defence put into the box in support of the Rhyl alibi. Although others were prepared to appear in court the defence chose not to use them. Even when a representation was made to the Court of Appeal the defence preferred not to use those witnesses. Plainly there were doubts as to their value.

When, much later, some of this evidence was subjected to critical scrutiny by Detective Superintendent Douglas Nimmo, it had a tendency to crumble. Charlie Jones said he had been put up to it for mercenary reasons by Terry Evans. Ivy Vincent remembered that her sighting of the man resembling Hanratty had occurred when a couple named Barnett had been staying with her. When Nimmo contacted them he discovered that they had not been to Rhyl in 1961.

In the end there was not a single piece of hard evidence that James Hanratty was in Rhyl in the period 22-24 August 1961, and not a single witness who conclusively and unambiguously recalled seeing him there. By contrast, what is striking is who *didn't* remember seeing Hanratty. He is supposed to have spent two hours and nineteen minutes on the 6pm double-decker bus travelling from Liverpool to Rhyl. But no one remembered a smartly dressed young man travelling the entire route. (With glaring inconsistency campaigners claimed that Hanratty could not have left the murder weapon on a bus because no one remembered seeing him.) Hanratty claimed he did the reverse journey on the Thursday. Again, no one stepped forward to say they remembered seeing him. Hanratty claimed that on the Wednesday morning he had had a shave at a barber's but no Rhyl barber was ever found to confirm this. Hanratty said he had a mid-day meal at "Dixie"'s, but no one there remembered him. During the afternoon he is supposed to have spent some time in the amusement arcades and in Woolworth's department store. In the evening he went to the fairground and then returned to "Dixie"'s. No one stepped forward to verify his alibi.

On the Thursday morning Hanratty said he returned on the bus to Liverpool. Having failed to find Evans he might have been expected to have another look for Aspinall, the fence in Liverpool. He was still carrying around the stolen jewellery. Instead he claimed he went to the cinema and saw *The Guns of Navarone*.

What this all boils down to is that between early on the morning of Tuesday 22 August 1961 and the evening of Thursday 24 August, James Hanratty disappeared from view. He vanished from the circle of his usual acquaintances. He returned to London on Friday 25 August. He said nothing about having been in Rhyl, not even to his closest friends and criminal associates. On 5 October Hanratty discovered for the first time that he was now the prime suspect for the A6 murder and the police wanted to interview him. He fled from London and by 7 October was in Liverpool. He was still in the city by 10 October but by the evening of the next day he was in Blackpool, where he was arrested at 11.10pm.

In this period before he was taken into custody he had four full days in which, if he was as innocent as he claimed, to return to Rhyl. He could have tracked down the boarding house where he said he had stayed for two nights and asked if they had a written record of his stay, or remembered him. But, tellingly, Hanratty made no attempt to go to Rhyl. He was challenged on this point at his trial. His reply was a masterpiece of obfuscation: "when I went to Liverpool I didn't have the right bearings of Rhyl as I had only been there on two occasions". Rhyl is a tiny seaside resort and no one could possibly get lost there. But instead of going there to obtain confirmation of his supposed alibi he went to Blackpool.

In those final days of freedom James Hanratty drifted around. He tried to change his appearance by having his hair bleached. He offered large sums to criminal acquaintances if they would provide him with an alibi. They declined to get involved.

His actions were those of a man who was nowhere near Rhyl on the 22 and 23 August 1961. He behaved as if he were guilty. He behaved as if he had no alibi. And of course he didn't. He wasn't in Rhyl at all on those dates but much further south.

6   Conspiracy?

The desire to find a conspiracy in the Kennedy assassination will continue to be answered for years by more "confessions", witnesses who change their testimony to recall disturbing events, the appearance of papers of dubious authenticity, and by writers and researchers who present cases of guilt by association supported by rumour and innuendo. But for those seeking the truth, the facts are incontrovertible. They can be tested against credible testimony, documents, and the latest scientific advances.

Gerald Posner, *Case Closed* (1993)

Making sense of the A6 case is not easy. The first great mystery is what the gunman was doing in the cornfield late at night on a Tuesday in August. The second great mystery is why he sat there chatting to Michael Gregsten and Valerie Storie for quite some time, before forcing them on a lengthy car journey to a lay-by in faraway Bedfordshire, where Gregsten was shot dead and Storie was raped, repeatedly shot and left for dead.

Louis Blom-Cooper attended the trial in Bedford and was persuaded by the evidence that Hanratty was guilty as charged. But he was puzzled that it seemed to be "an apparently motiveless crime". What on earth was a smartly dressed Londoner like Hanratty, whose natural home was Soho, *doing* in a field in rural Buckinghamshire at that time of night? And what was the point of the hold-up? None of it seemed to make any sense. It was these aspects and the subsequent involvement of Peter Alphon which helped make the A6 case unusual and intriguing.

Since the two victims were an adulterous couple, Louis

Blom-Cooper wondered if this was where the clue to the enigma of the crime could be found. He wondered if Hanratty had been "sent to that remote spot in Buckinghamshire to scare Gregsten" and that he was there "at the behest of someone else".

The obvious candidate to hire a gunman to frighten off an erring husband involved with a younger woman would of course be the man's wife. But Blom-Cooper was careful not to hint that he had any particular individual in mind. On the contrary, he qualified his speculation as being nothing more than a wild hypothesis – just one fantastic possibility among other possible explanations for a motive. His target was not the conspirator or conspirators who might have hired James Hanratty to put the frighteners on Michael Gregsten but rather the criminal justice system itself. As far as Blom-Cooper was concerned the British method of investigation and prosecution was defective because it concerned itself exclusively with criminal responsibility. In his view this obscured the realities which lay behind a crime and left essential details open-ended, unsolved and teasingly mysterious.

The notion that elements of a criminal conspiracy lay behind the A6 case was first put forward in a very rudimentary form three years after the crime in Jean Justice's book *Murder vs. Murder*. At this time he believed that "the motive for the crime was not robbery but sex". Justice was convinced that Peter Alphon was the gunman and that he was a sexually repressed pervert and voyeur. Alphon told Jean Justice that "he pulled the trigger to prove his superiority to the frustrations that hedged him in on all sides".

Justice initially appears to have believed that Gregsten and Storie were accidental victims of a random attack by Alphon, who had in advance taken steps to cover his tracks by pretending to be Hanratty, and who afterwards had help from others in framing him. Justice was convinced both that Peter Alphon really was the A6 gunman and that he had a previous association with Hanratty. Both assumptions were entirely false but, consumed by his obsession, Justice asserted as fact that Alphon frequented the same Soho dives as Hanratty. He wrote that "*a reliable witness ... once saw them together on a Sunday morning*". Unsurprisingly, he did not give the name of this witness or say on what date this miraculous meeting had occurred. He went on to claim that Alphon was a regular at the Rehearsal Club and that he "*could have learned a great deal about Hanratty's movements from Charles France*". Alphon almost certainly never once went to the Rehearsal Club. He was a socially inept loner, whose primary occupation was attending greyhound races.

The attention-seeking Alphon helpfully supplied hints and clues to the conspiracy which supposedly enmeshed an innocent Hanratty. In his first lengthy written "confession" he said that he had obtained a gun, which involved a man named George. Alphon said he knew William Nudds and that there had been a frame-up at the Hotel Vienna which involved altering the register. These were fantasies which Alphon knew Justice would be unable to check out and verify.

He further claimed that the cartridge cases were planted in the room when Hanratty was out. He checked with Nudds that Hanratty had left. The crime itself was a chance one. There had been a "*Past attempt at cornfield*", by implication involving a different courting couple. On the night off 22 August "*Couple in car fitted my mood and my main plan.*" In this early version of Alphon's ever-changing conspiracy narrative, Gregsten and Storie were random victims. When it was all over Alphon said he went to Southend. The gun was disposed of.

On 18 March 1964 Alphon changed his story. He asserted that the confession notes which he had given Justice (and which take pride of place in *Murder vs. Murder*) were "a lot of rubbish". Alphon now said he had been commissioned by Janet Gregsten's brother-in-law, William Ewer. Ewer had paid him £5,000 to go to the cornfield and confront Gregsten and Storie. "Let's say the mission was to see that they were separated ... The mission was to see that the affair was finished."

When Paul Foot became involved with Alphon he was never able to extract from him definitive proof of his involvement in the crime. Alphon did however eventually allow Foot access to his bank accounts for the years 1961 and 1962. These revealed that after his discharge from Mortlake magistrates court on 3 October 1961 he opened a deposit account with a payment of £750. He proceeded to bank a total of £3,300 in a series of cash payments up to 24 November. Later the same month Alphon also opened a current account and in the following weeks £2,050 was paid into this account in cash and cheques. In December he paid in a further £1,800. Between October 1961 and June 1962 the grand total of £7,569 was paid into Alphon's two accounts. Where did this money come from? To conspiracy theorists the answer is obvious. Most of it – perhaps £5,000 – came from the person or persons who commissioned Alphon to threaten Gregsten and Storie with a gun. The problem is that Alphon deliberately withheld access to his bank account until the time (six years) that all bank records of cheque transactions were destroyed. There was therefore no proof at all of where the money came from.

Paul Foot calculated that Alphon may have earned as much as £2,500 from newspapers for his sensational story as the first chief suspect in the case. But that figure was speculation. He guessed that some of the rest may have come from "spectacular wins at the races". Foot felt that there must be a surplus of money which was unaccounted for and this reinforced the conclusion that Alphon had been paid for his involvement in the A6 murder. But this was also speculation. The two obvious sources for Alphon's income – press payment and gambling wins – could well have accounted for the sums involved. In his interview with Acott at Scotland Yard Alphon mentioned winning £1,000 on the dogs the previous month.

In May 1967, in a gesture which seemed designed to revive flagging interest in the case and keep himself in the spotlight, Alphon made his first public confession to the murder. However, he was careful to do so outside the jurisdiction of

English law. In Paris he said he had been paid £5,000 to carry out the crime. But soon afterwards he retracted his statement. He told *The People* newspaper that the money in his bank account "had nothing to do with the murder. It was paid to me for something quite different" (21 May 1967).

Jean Justice, of course, preferred to believe the confession rather than its retraction. Alphon's claim that the crime was planned in advance and that it had been commissioned by William Ewer formed the climax of *Le Crime de la Route A6*, published the following year. Chapter Twelve described Justice's own meetings with Ewer. He argued that what Ewer and Alphon had in common was extremist right-wing views. But whereas Alphon proudly described himself as a fascist, Ewer never did. Whatever his politics may have been he was against the death penalty and hanging, indicating that some of his views were liberal and progressive.

Le Crime de la Route A6 was also the first book to publicise the extraordinary story which appeared in *The Daily Sketch* two days after the Bedford trial ended. AMAZING STORY OF MRS GREGSTEN'S INTUITION was the headline, above the story of how Janet Gregsten had spotted Hanratty in an arcade of shops at Swiss Cottage Station on the London underground. At the time the police had absolutely no leads as to who the killer might be. "That's the man!" Mrs Gregsten cried out. "He fits the description. But it's more than that. I've got an overpowering feeling that it's him." She was with her brother-in-law, William Ewer, at the time. Ewer found out that the man was called "J. Ryan" and had given an address in St John's Wood. The next day Ewer saw the man again and called the police. A squad car came but by this time Hanratty had gone. They discovered, however, that the man had been into a florist's and ordered a dozen roses to be sent to a Mrs Hanratty at an address in Kingsbury. After that Ewer went out every day looking for the man. He visited the Greek Street shop of a business acquaintance, Mrs Louise Anderson. He did not know that Hanratty, who was an associate of hers, had been in her shop only that morning. Ewer later fund out that he had been in Petticoat Lane at the same time as Hanratty.

A similar story appeared in *The Daily Mail* on the same day. Mrs Gregsten had seen Hanratty's "blue, staring eyes" and had "a flash of intuitive recognition". In short it was, as *The Daily Sketch* put it, the "amazing intuition" of Janet Gregsten which had "helped to put James Hanratty on trial for his life".

To conspiracy theorists these press stories provided proof that either Janet Gregsten or William Ewer or both were directly involved in framing Hanratty for the A6 murder. In *Who Killed Hanratty?* Paul Foot made much of these press stories. It was all very suspicious. "Scotland Yard," he commented, "had Hanratty's name and his alias long before they started to hunt him as a murderer. The articles presented a series of coincidences which would strain the credulity of the most gullible mystic." Earlier, on the opening page of the first chapter of his book, Foot insinuated what he believed lay behind the crime. He wrote that Janet Gregsten was "irritated and depressed by her husband's affair with Miss Storie. She and her family did everything in their power to discourage the relationship." They had complained to the Director of the Road Research Laboratory. Gregsten's landlord had been advised not to let the flat to Gregsten as he was a married man.

Though Foot was careful not to spell out his conspiracy theory and risk a libel action, the inference was very clear. Janet Gregsten had commissioned the gunman, Peter Alphon, to frighten the adulterous couple and break up their relationship. Janet Gregsten was also the prime conspirator in seeking to frame Hanratty. When the police failed to connect Hanratty with the crime, despite all the clues Alphon had scattered to pin the crime on him, it became necessary for Gregsten to take decisive action. She therefore stepped forwards with a helpful "sighting" of a man who seemed to resemble the published identikit pictures of the suspect. The police were deliberately pointed in Hanratty's direction. Janet Gregsten also had an accomplice, who was part of the conspiracy. Foot was more circumspect in naming this person. He was simply identified as "Mr X". This un-named person was William Ewer and Foot's account of his role in the conspiracy was derived entirely from the confessions of Peter Alphon.

In *Hanratty: The Final Verdict*, Bob Woffinden provided another spin on the conspiracy theory. Woffinden pointed the finger of suspicion at a man who, he believed, secretly lusted after Janet Gregsten (who in photographs certainly appears to have been a very attractive woman). This man commissioned Peter Alphon to confront Gregsten and Storie in order to break up Gregsten's marriage so that Janet became available. Apart from Alphon being coached to pretend to be Hanratty, the plan was not precisely plotted, which confused Alphon. It all went horribly wrong because of Alphon's unstable personality. Woffinden never put a name to the man who he believed had commissioned the crime. Had he done so he would have risked a libel action, and Woffinden had no tangible evidence to support his conspiracy theory. The man was, of course, William Ewer. All Woffinden knew was that Ewer and Janet Gregsten had begun a relationship after the murder. On that flimsy foundation he built his tower of speculation.

According to Woffinden, Alphon followed Hanratty around, which is why he knew Hanratty had stayed at the Hotel Vienna and why he went to check himself in there. In his haste and anxiety after the murder Alphon accidentally dropped the two cartridge cases in Room 24. Nudds was asked by Alphon as a favour to provide him with an alibi, which Nudds was happy to do. Alphon then contacted "Dixie" France for assistance in dumping the gun in just the way that Hanratty might have done. Attempts to implicate Hanratty were a panic-stricken effort to cover up for Alphon rather than a deliberate plot.

In 1971 a reporter named Lewis Chester went to see Acott, who had now retired from the force. In a discussion of the A6 murder Acott is alleged to have said, "To us it always seemed a simple gas-meter case". By this, Acott would have meant an inside job, i.e. that the crime was pre-planned and involved people close to the victims. However, there is no evidence that the police ever believed that the murder was the result of a criminal conspiracy involving Janet Gregsten or William Ewer. If the police had really suspected these two of being murderous conspirators then they would surely have had them both in for the kind of long, tough interrogations to which Alphon and Nudds were subjected.

There is one rather obvious objection to every one of the A6 conspiracy theories, which is that there is not a scrap of evidence to support any of them. Jean Justice started the ball rolling in 1964 by suggesting that Hanratty and Alphon knew each other. They didn't. Nor is there the slightest scrap of evidence that Alphon knew Charles France. These were fantasies of the needy, attention-seeking Peter Alphon which the gullible Jean Justice eagerly lapped up. Justice in fact had little understanding of the man he became besotted with. Alphon had no "circle of friends". Alphon had no friends at all. He was not gregarious. He was a shy, timid loner. He shunned human company, apart from his mother's. There is no evidence whatever that Alphon was a regular at the Rehearsal Club or other Soho dives. He wasn't someone who passed his days in clubs, lingering over a drink and eyeing-up the women. Alphon's favourite venues were not Soho clubs but public libraries. He was an autodidact, an ersatz intellectual interested in theosophy and fascist politics. But even where these interests were concerned he did not join any groups or organisations. Peter Alphon was the quintessential fringe loner.

If Jean Justice's conspiracy theory rested on the fantasy of Alphon as a gregarious man who spent his time in clubs and pubs and was acquainted with Hanratty, Paul Foot's conspiracy theory depended on someone else. Foot believed that Janet Gregsten was a crazed woman consumed by jealousy who would stop at nothing to break up the relationship between her husband and his young mistress. This was a complete fantasy on Foot's part. He knew nothing about the marriage. Janet Gregsten

160

tolerated her husband's relationship with Valerie Storie. She wasn't happy about it but she accepted it and muddled along for the sake of their two young children. There must have been thousands of other wives in this situation in Britain at this time. The Gregsten marriage was hardly unique in being a rocky one. Nor was Janet Gregsten consumed by sexual jealousy. She later confided that relations with her husband had been sexually unsatisfying. She accepted that his sexual needs were met elsewhere, outside their marriage. Though she wanted him to stay with her, this was for the sake of their two small boys. Michael's desire to move out and live with Valerie was a cause for distress but it was not something that Janet planned violently to disrupt. The idea that she had hired a gunman – Peter Alphon – was a surreal fantasy on Foot's part. Not only was Alphon not a gunman but Janet Gregsten would have had no idea how to contact and commission a man familiar with handguns who was prepared to threaten strangers in return for money. Foot's conspiracy theory heaped absurdity upon absurdity.

Twenty-three years after *Who Killed Hanratty?* was published Paul Foot finally had the opportunity to sit down with Janet Gregsten and discuss the case with her. He found her an "impressive" woman and was discomfited to discover that she evidently knew nothing about the murder. She was not the jealousy-consumed woman of his imagination. He concluded, with a breathtaking blandness, that this was "a warning against jumping to hasty conclusions, in particular about Peter Alphon". This deflected attention away from his own lack of critical judgement over many years and his culpability in insinuating that Janet Gregsten bore responsibility for her husband's violent death. Nor had Foot ever stopped to consider what the two Gregsten boys might think and what effect it would have on them when they grew up and read a book which suggested that their mother had been involved in a murderous conspiracy.

Afterwards Paul Foot went to see Alphon again. He played him the tape of his interview with Janet Gregsten. Foot had the sudden insight that Alphon did not really know as much as he pretended to. "I started to wonder whether perhaps, if Alphon was the murderer, he had no idea who commissioned him; or even perhaps whether he had not done the murder himself, but had become involved in some other way." In other words, as the main foundation of *Who Killed Hanratty?* crumbled to dust, Foot began to shore up his ruins with fresh guesswork. But this seems to have been more or less his last word on the subject as far as trying to *explain* the crime was concerned. Still unwaveringly committed to the notion that James Hanratty was innocent, Foot was left floundering as he finally perceived Peter Alphon's unreliability and Janet Gregsten's ignorance of the crime. Fortunately for him Foot had a disciple who gave the old conspiracy theory a fresh twist.

Bob Woffinden revived the theory that Alphon knew William Ewer and Charles France, had help from Nudds at the Hotel Vienna, and set out to commit the crime having planned to pretend to be Hanratty. It was a preposterous scenario devoid of evidence but had the advantage of exonerating Hanratty. In the final edition of *Hanratty: The Final Verdict*, Woffinden expressed the view that the role played by Nudds now seemed "more central than had hitherto been supposed". He based this idea on the claim that three years earlier Nudds had owned a gun and because someone who had known Nudds in prison said he had been told by him that Hanratty was innocent. The gun claim was unsourced and evidently at best anecdotal. The name of the prisoner who had heard Nudds's testimony was not given.

This aspect of the conspiracy theory is spun out of thin air. Woffinden seems to be insinuating that Nudds supplied the gun. But Nudds did not know Peter Alphon, nor was he an associate of Charles France or William Ewer. He knew nothing about the A6 murder. If he did express the view that Hanratty was innocent (and this kind of vague anecdote is highly dubious) that cannot have been anything other than an opinion, not something based on direct knowledge of the A6 murder.

Why did Peter Alphon seek to implicate William Ewer? The answer seems obvious. Jean Justice, obsessed with meeting everyone involved in the case, had gone to Ewer's shop at Swiss Cottage in 1962 and struck up a conversation with him. Alphon apparently knew nothing of this. Unknown to Alphon, Justice and Ewer met often to drink and talk about the case. It seems that Alphon did not discover about the friendship between the two men until shortly before his phone call of 18 March 1964. In other words, Alphon's rambling, emotive, sensational new confession derived from a jealous rage that Justice had been seeing someone else about the A6 murder and that Justice had concealed this from him. In a child we call this kind of tantrum "attention seeking" and this, it is starkly obvious, is what the new confession was. In claiming that Ewer was the man who had commissioned the crime, Alphon was all too clearly trying to refocus the spotlight back on himself – the true killer, the man with sensational secrets which he was releasing in dribs and drabs. He was simultaneously trying to muddy the waters and make Justice mistrust Ewer. With luck he might even break up their friendship. If these were indeed Alphon's motives he enjoyed some success. Justice, gullible as ever, now began to construct a new pattern out of Alphon's fantasies.

Ewer, who had attended the trial, was convinced that Hanratty was indeed the killer. He also correctly perceived that Peter Alphon was a fabulist. Pestered by phone calls from Alphon, and aware of the latest allegation about himself, Ewer commented to Justice: "If a man's got an *idée fixe* that he's done something and he's a lunatic to this degree, it's only as near as you'll ever get to doing it or something similar. This man is simply linking everything together here. It's something which everyone is wishing to forget." Ewer's was the small voice of reason here. The delusion that Hanratty wasn't guilty and that what really lay behind the crime was a complex conspiracy simply perpetuated the pain for those who were closest to it and who had to live with the aftermath of a violent death and a rape. Ewer's exasperation with Alphon and his inventions was plain: "I've never seen this man. I've not got involved with this man. I know nothing about it. I've never met the man, and that's the great thing, I never have. And I've had no conversations with him." But none of this mattered to Paul Foot. *Who Killed Hanratty?* insinuated a conspiracy involving a jealous wife and her brother-in-law, William Ewer. If Hanratty was innocent then others must be guilty. Foot was convinced he knew who they were. He would reveal himself to be equally dogmatic when DNA analysis provided a conclusion which was not the one he was expecting.

What are we to make of "Mrs Gregsten's amazing intuition" reported in *The Daily Sketch* (19 February 1962)? The story was credited to Peter Duffy, the paper's chief crime reporter (and a man who, ironically, never for a moment doubted that Hanratty was guilty as charged). Its origins lay in a chance conversation in a Bedford pub between William Ewer and two journalists. These were George Hollingbery of the *Evening News* and Bernard Jordan of the *Daily Mail*. They did not take notes until later, after Ewer had gone. Jordan later passed the story on to Duffy, who checked it out in person.

According to Paul Foot, this news story contained "a series of coincidences which would strain the credulity of the most gullible mystic". But is this really true? On 31 August Janet Gregsten was at her brother-in-law's shop, one of a number in the arcade which then existed at Swiss Cottage underground station. She was trying to come to terms with her bereavement by doing something active – helping out in a shop. That same day Hanratty went into a different shop in this very same arcade. His trip to the shops was the result of the fact that he was staying nearby, with the France family. They lived on Boundary Road, just a short walk away.

It might seem a remarkable coincidence that the killer and his victim's widow should both have been in the same vicinity at the same time but that is all it was – a coincidence. Janet

Gregsten could not possibly have known in advance that Hanratty would have been in the neighbourhood. Nor did she know who he was. Why, then, did she identify him as the man the police were looking for? "That's the man," she is reported to have said. "He fits the description." When in 1966 a BBC TV *Panorama* reporter questioned Duffy about his report he was asked how Janet Gregsten could possibly have identified Hanratty "having only the identikit to go on, which doesn't really look much like [him]". Duffy agreed that the identikit looked "nothing like him" and said that this episode was "completely inexplicable".

This is inaccurate and untrue in a number of ways. For a start there were two identikit pictures of the suspect. They bore significant differences. When they were shown on television in the France household, when Hanratty was staying with the family, Charlotte France pointed at one of them and said to him, "Doesn't that look like you?" It surely did not occur to her then that he really was the killer, and her remark, blurted out on impulse, was presumably half-whimsical. But it indicates that to those who knew Hanratty well his face did indeed resemble one of those portrayed in the identikit pictures.

Arguments on this topic by Hanratty's defenders are in any case flawed by the fact that our knowledge of his appearance is based on a handful of black-and-white photographs. There is no motion film of his face, not even any colour photographs. What he looked like in the flesh and how accurate the identikit pictures were can now never be known. But the fact that Charlotte France noticed a similarity is damning.

The identikit pictures may also be a red herring. Janet Gregsten did not say "he looks like the man in that identikit picture" (or pictures), she said "He fits the description". And this, surely, was entirely accurate. The first police description of the wanted man, sent out on the morning of the murder, was of a man "aged about 25 years, smooth face, big eyes, smartly dressed in a dark grey or black suit". If Janet Gregsten registered anything about her husband's murderer on the day her world collapsed it would have been that – amended at 5.20pm to "Man aged about 30, height 5' 6", proportionate build, dark brown hair, clean-shaven, brown eyes, fairly pale face ... Wearing dark lounge suit and believed dark tie and shirt." This was later amended again to "deep-set brown eyes".

According to the *Sketch* report, Janet Gregsten's intuition was ignited by Hanratty's "blue staring eyes". This made Paul Foot deeply suspicious, as "up to that morning, August 31st, neither in her detailed conversations with policemen nor with the Identikit experts had Valerie Storie spoken of the killer's blue eyes ... In no newspaper, radio broadcast or television bulletin had blue eyes been mentioned as a characteristic of the A6 killer."

Foot was wrong about Valerie. In a statement given by her to police on 28 August she described her attacker as "aged between twenty-five and thirty, about 5 feet 6 inches, proportionately built, slender brown hair, clean-shaven, a very smooth, pale face, with icy-blue large saucer-like eyes". Valerie Storie had never once said that the killer had brown eyes. The erroneous "brown eyes" description seems to have originated in what Woffinen describes as "hastily scribbled and probably confusing [police] notes".

The new description of the suspect's "icy-blue large saucer-like eyes" appeared for the first time in the evening papers on 31 August. Janet Gregsten might in theory have seen an early edition ("evening" papers hit the news stands in the afternoon). Far more probable is that the police had already told her of the new, amended description of a staring, blue-eyed killer from three days earlier. Janet Gregsten was, after all, in a privileged position. She was the widow of the murdered man. The police would surely have kept her up to date about their suspect.

What, then, happened in the arcade at Swiss Cottage underground station? There is one aspect of this strange episode which neither Foot nor Woffinden mentions but which is surely very relevant to why she thought this stranger might be the killer.

Hanratty's deep-set staring blue eyes were a family feature which some people noticed in his father. This striking aspect of his appearance, together with his smart clothes, were surely what first drew Janet Gregsten's attention. In her emotionally fraught state it is easy to understand that her eyes roamed across everyone she saw, seeking out the mystery man who had slaughtered Michael. It was an irrational thing to do, as the chances of the murderer living close to where William Ewer had his shop would, you might think, be very slight. But the man was a Londoner and this was London and this, incredibly, is what occurred. Hanratty was staying with the France family a short distance away. And then this man, whose appearance was slightly unusual, and who fitted the description of the suspect, did something which must have magnified her suspicions tenfold. She saw him "walking into a Burtol cleaners shop". This was surely the moment of explosive revelation. The killer was believed to have blood on his clothes and here was this man going into a cleaners! Perhaps he was collecting an item or items of clothing which he had worn on the night of the murder. Perhaps he was taking in something bloodstained!

When she told Ewer he laughed it off. His response was the same as anyone's would have been: "I calmed her down and told her she was overwrought". But to humour her he went into Burtols (as a fellow shop-owner in the arcade he presumably knew the owner) and made enquiries. He was told that the man had given the name "J. Ryan", with a local address. And what did William Ewer do with this information? Precisely nothing. He did not contact the police and tell them that a man fitting the description of the killer had visited Burtols. William Ewer plainly didn't believe that this man was the mystery A6 murderer.

The next day the man appeared again at the arcade. William Ewer saw him and began to wonder if Janet Gregsten's suspicions were not as crazy as they had sounded. He watched the man go into one of the shops and then rang the police. By the time they arrived the man had gone. Ewer explained his suspicions. The police went into the shop – a flower shop – and learned that the man had placed an order for some roses, to be sent to a Mrs Hanratty in Kingsbury. Hanratty had given his address as 72 Boundary Road. This was the street "Dixie" France and his family lived on (although Hanratty, characteristically covering his tracks, gave a non-existent street number).

As far as the police were concerned there was nothing further to investigate. The suspicions of Janet Gregsten and William Ewer were at best tenuous. At this time the police were deluged with "sightings" of the A6 killer. There was nothing about Ewer's story to make them think that "J. Ryan" had anything to do with the crime. "Ryan" had taken his suit into the cleaners the day *before* the abduction in the cornfield. There was nothing here for the police to think that the matter was worth pursuing. It was a reasonable conclusion that Janet Gregsten and William Ewer were overwrought. The central claim of the *Sketch* story – that Janet Gregsten "helped to put James Hanratty on trial for his life" – is simply false. What, in the end, led the police to Hanratty was the two cartridge cases in the room at the Hotel Vienna. Janet and Ewer had no connection whatever with that establishment. Moreover, if the hotel chain manager had not had military experience and had not reported the find to the police, James Hanratty would probably never have been identified as the A6 gunman and the crime would have remained unsolved.

The *Sketch* further claimed that Ewer went to see Louise Anderson in Soho and also went looking for Hanratty in the West End, in the Elephant and Castle neighbourhood south of the River Thames, and on Petticoat Lane. Ewer denied this. He said he had never met Louise Anderson. His denials seem convincing. It is difficult to see what the point would have been in Ewer continuing to search in this way for "J. Ryan". If the police had wanted to know more about this individual they only had to go to see the woman to whom "Ryan" had sent the roses. They were simply not interested. Besides, the blue-eyed mystery man had been spotted two days running in the Swiss Cottage arcade. What would be the point in wandering around in those other neighbourhoods hoping to encounter him? It makes no sense at all.

Janet Gregsten later denied that the *Sketch* story was in any way accurate. None of the journalists involved in this murky episode ever spoke to her. The story was based on a conversation in a pub with William Ewer. No notes were taken at the time. Years later Ewer explained to *The Sunday Times* what had happened. He denied that Janet Gregsten had ever been involved. He said that in early September 1961 in a café near his shop he had seen a man with "quite unusually staring eyes. The eyes were as distinctive as if he had a carbuncle on his face." He telephoned the local police and let the matter rest. Much later, when it became public that the police were looking for a man named Ryan, he called in at the cleaning shop opposite his own and asked if anyone of that name had been there, and they confirmed that he had.

The truth of this matter is elusive. The foundations of the *Sketch* story are a boozy conversation in a pub. Even if every aspect was in fact true it amounted to little more than a storm in a teacup. But it is more probable that Ewer exaggerated for effect. It made a cracking good story. But also possible is that whatever Ewer said was garbled by his listeners. Anyone who has ever had any dealings with journalists, no matter how banal the subject, will surely know that sinking feeling when they see the topic written up and published. Simple statements end up horribly distorted, names get mis-spelled, remarks are misheard or garbled. Anyone who possesses in-depth knowledge of almost any news story will surely be aware that journalists, whether local or national, seem chronically incapable of transmitting any information with one-hundred per cent accuracy.

In any case, if Janet Gregsten and William Ewer were brilliant conspirators who had plotted the A6 murder and successfully framed James Hanratty, why on earth blurt out such a story to two journalists from the national press? The essence of a successful conspiracy is secrecy. Foot's conspiracy theory is also riddled with contradictions. If William Ewer was part of a plan to frame Hanratty why did he need to chase around London trying to find out who the smartly dressed man was *when he already knew*?

In 1971 Ewer sued both *The Sunday Times* and Jonathan Cape for libel. Cape settled out of court for £1,000 and *Who Killed Hanratty?* continued in print without amendment. *The Sunday Times* also settled out of court for what has been described as a "substantial" sum. What did the man regarded by Hanratty's defenders as the sinister brains behind the conspiracy do next? He invited Paul Foot to lunch at his home in Golders Green. He patiently explained to Foot why the stories in the *Sketch* and *Daily Mail* had been "a farrago of nonsense".

Fixated on his conspiracy theory, Paul Foot was instrumental in producing exciting new evidence of Peter Alphon's supposed involvement. This appeared in *The Sunday Times* (4 July 1971) and was repeated in the postscript to the Panther paperback edition of *Who Killed Hanratty?*

What happened was this. On 1 July 1971 Hanratty's parents received a phone call from Mary Lanz, who ran The Old Station Inn at Taplow, where Valerie Storie and Michael Gregsten had enjoyed a last drink together before heading off for the cornfield. Mrs Lanz told them that she felt disturbed by all the publicity surrounding the case and wanted to make a statement about something which had been troubling her for a long time.

This was communicated to Foot, who went off with a fellow reporter to interview her. Mary Lanz had a sensational tale to tell. On the night that Gregsten and Storie were at the Inn, she said, there was also present "a man who I now know to be Peter Louis Alphon". Alphon had been there on several previous occasions but on the night of 22 August 1961 he was accompanied by "a blonde woman who was, I would say, in her early thirties". Half an hour after Michael Gregsten and Valerie Storie left, Alphon also left. He was accompanied by the blonde woman.

The inference was clear. The mysterious blonde was Janet Gregsten, wearing a wig. She had commissioned the crime and she was present at The Old Station Inn to point out her husband and his mistress to Alphon. When they left she may even have been leading him to the cornfield.

The problem with Mary Lanz's sensational story is that she said no such thing at the time of the crime. Why wait ten years to come up with evidence of a conspiracy? When she made a statement to police on 24 August 1961 she was keen to help. On that occasion she said she remembered "two strange men" who left her establishment around the same time that Gregsten and Storie did.

Ten years later she had ceased to be a detached spectator of the A6 case. Even before Hanratty was executed, Jean Justice had taken Peter Alphon to The Old Station Inn and questioned Mary Lanz about him. Through Justice, Lanz was drawn into the saga. Although Paul Foot did not mention it, he knew Mary Lanz long before he went to interview her about what was supposedly a sensational new piece of evidence. When he first visited the Hanratty family home on Sycamore Grove in February 1966, after the reburial of Hanratty's remains at Carpenders Park cemetery, among the guests he encountered there was Mary Lanz. Lanz in fact knew all about the conspiracy theory and the idea that Alphon was the real killer. Why, then, did she wait until July 1971 to tell Mr and Mrs Hanratty about her new evidence, when she knew them and could have told them years earlier? The answer presumably lies in the feverish atmosphere created by the serialisation of *Who Killed Hanratty?* in *The Sun*, and its subsequent book publication to widespread acclaim.

In his May 1971 *Sunday Times* statement, William Ewer, exasperated by the publicity surrounding Alphon's fantasy that there was a vast conspiracy, responded to the insinuation that he was connected in any way with Charles France, William Nudds and Peter Alphon. He explained that he had met Charles France only once in his life. This was shortly after Hanratty's trial had ended. France, who lived nearby, visited Ewer's shop: "He came in to offer his apologies for Mr Gregsten's death. He said it had all been most regrettable."

Bob Woffinden worked himself up into a frenzy over this revelation, which he regarded as "amazing" and "astonishing". But was it? Charles France committed suicide on 15 March 1962, just weeks before Hanratty's execution. He was 42 (but looks considerably older in photographs). He had made an earlier suicide attempt on 18 January, just before the start of the trial. He was taken to Hammersmith Hospital, where he had to be restrained from jumping out of a window. He was subsequently taken to Horton Mental Hospital and subjected to ECT shock treatment. When he appeared in court at Bedford he was accompanied by two nurses from Horton.

The whole France family seemed stunned and distressed by the revelation that the man who had stayed in their home was a murderer and a rapist. Charlotte France was haunted by a conversation she had with Louise Anderson while waiting to give evidence at the committal proceedings at Ampthill on 28 November 1961. The two women had never met. Anderson, unaware of whom she was talking to, mentioned "those poor people" Hanratty had stayed with in St John's Wood. "They didn't know he had the gun, but I did."

Stunned, Charlotte asked her where the gun had been kept. She was told that Hanratty kept it in a cupboard at the top of the stairs, hidden in a carrier bag among the blankets. Anxious to verify this story, Charlotte asked for more details. She was told that the blankets were pink. "He used to keep the gun in a screwed-up carrier bag which had the name Tomkins or Timkins on it." Charlotte was appalled. Her butcher's name was Tomkins and every detail of the story fitted.

Bob Woffinden interpreted this episode as a deliberate provocation by Louise Anderson. He believed she knew who Charlotte France was. But there is no evidence to support this belief. Secondly, the kind of detailed information about the hiding place can only have come from Hanratty. But it was too damning and much of Louise Anderson's evidence against Hanratty was treated as inadmissible by the trial judge.

Whatever one chooses to make of this story, the point is that the France family firmly believed it. Charles France was plainly driven to the brink of madness by the knowledge that he had welcomed a murderer and a rapist into his home. France, who had a string of minor criminal convictions, first met Hanratty in 1955 when the latter was 18 or 19. He became a kind of godfather to the apprentice criminal. Once out of prison in March 1962, Hanratty eventually bumped into France at the Rehearsal Club in Soho. Soon he was staying on a regular if intermittent basis at the France family home on Boundary Road in St John's Wood. He was "Uncle Jim" to the children.

Charles France testified in court that Hanratty had shown him that under the upstairs back seat of a London double-decker bus was a good place to dump unwanted stolen goods. Hanratty did not deny it. This, of course, was precisely where the A6 murder weapon was found. Hanratty had also mentioned showing his Hotel Vienna receipt to Charles France. To conspiracy theorists this all adds up. France dumped the gun on the bus to incriminate Hanratty. He also placed the cartridge cases in the room at the Hotel Vienna to provide further evidence of his guilt. Then, tormented by what he had done to an innocent man, he killed himself.

But this kind of theorising turns reality on its head. The two criminal associates who knew Hanratty best both believed he was indeed the person responsible for abducting the couple in the cornfield, shooting Gregsten, and raping Storie. Charles France was suspicious of Hanratty after the murder precisely because of *where* the murder weapon had been found. Because of his suspicions he was keen to see verification of Hanratty's whereabouts at the time of the murder. Hanratty duly supplied him with the only evidence he had – his Hotel Vienna receipt.

When the erroneous "brown eyes" description was changed to "icy blue large saucer-like eyes" his suspicions must surely have deepened. Moreover, his own wife believed that there was a resemblance between one of the identikit pictures and Hanratty.

When the case against Alphon collapsed, Charles France could hold back no longer. He went of to Scotland Yard with his Irish postcard from Hanratty. In November, at the committal proceedings, he discovered to his horror that Hanratty had actually abused his hospitality by hiding the murder weapon in the France home. As a sociopath Hanratty was devoid of any feelings of gratitude – he repeatedly abused the generosity of people who had shown him only kindess. Apart from the France family, the list includes Hanratty's own father and Terry Evans.

Charles France plainly felt a crushing, overwhelming sense of personal responsibility for the crime. He, after all, had been Hanratty's mentor. He had even unwittingly sheltered him after the crime. And the murder weapon had even been hidden in his own home! It was in this agonized state of mind that he called in at William Ewer's shop to apologise for the murder. Ewer, quite reasonably, tried to calm him down and told him not to blame himself. But kind words could not provide the absolution Charles France needed. He was suffering from a form of survivor's guilt. It is now a well-known and well-understood phenomenon: the individual who survives a disaster or some other violent event in which many people have died often feels an irrational yet very powerful sense of personal responsibility for what occurred or debilitating guilt that they have survived when others did not. How much more acute must Charles France's sense of complicity have been in the light of his very tangible connections to Hanratty at the time of the crime.

Soon after apologising to Ewer, Charles France killed himself. Some insight into his mental torment was supplied by his suicide notes, one of which was reproduced some years later in *The Sunday Times* and again in the first paperback edition of *Who Killed Hanratty?* Charles France wrote: "They are going to crucifie (*sic*) us all". He said that he would rather die than suffer the stigma of "bearing the the (*sic*) fact that I have done what was honestly write (*sic*) but will be so twisted as to make it look as though I was an associate of this filthy act". Paul Foot believed these remarks offered dramatic support for the notion that France was part of a conspiracy. He argued that France's motive in writing his suicide notes was "to shelter his family from an association with the crime which he could not live with".

But that was a wildly speculative interpretation of words which are open to a much simpler analysis. France knew that the person who first put the police on Hanratty's trail was himself, by assisting Acott with his enquiries so that he connected the mysterious "J. Ryan" to the recidivist James Hanratty. France knew that in so doing he had himself committed a crime against the code of the underworld: he had grassed on a fellow criminal, who would now be hanged as a consequence. France had also apparently successfully concealed his own criminal past and existing activities from his children. Now all this risked exposure. Simultaneously he had become obsessed with the idea that the truth of what had occurred would be twisted to make it seem as if he had somehow been complicit in the crime. No one had been closer to Hanratty in August 1961, unless it was Louise Anderson. That such an anxiety was not irrational is illustrated by what happened to Janet Gregsten and William Ewer after the story in the *Sketch*. Even though they had no connection whatever with what occurred in the cornfield and after, they ended up being regarded as the evil brains behind a conspiracy to frame a wholly innocent man. Finally, in the days leading up to his death, Charles France received a barrage of threatening and abusive phone calls, which surely helped to unhinge him further. There can be little doubt that they came from Peter Alphon, himself an unstable individual, who, encouraged by Jean Justice, was now combining attention-seeking with a ferociously vindictive and obsessive pleasure in shredding the nerves and the patience of a number of people on the edges of the A6 tragedy. Alphon, a sad and lonely person, seems to have taken a malicious and deeply unpleasant delight in making others suffer for his own damaging experience of being considered the original prime suspect in the case.

Conspiracy theories are everywhere in modern society. They include the idea that an alien spacecraft crashed at Roswell, New Mexico, in 1947 and the US government has covered up the truth; that in 1963 President Kennedy was assassinated not by Lee Harvey Oswald acting alone but by the CIA, or the Mafia, or others; that the 1969 moon landing was faked; that the death of Princess Diana in 1997 was no accident; that 9/11 involved the US government or some other body, and that the twin towers were brought down by explosives planted inside the buildings. All these theories, it can safely be said, are complete nonsense.

This is not to say that politicians do not routinely lie, or that conspiracies never exist, or that governments do not attempt to conceal the truth about scandals in which they are complicit. But every case has to be assessed on its merits. Sometimes there are conspiracies but often there are none at all. And often a particular kind of person is attracted to conspiracy theories, because they make the complex and the ambiguous appear beautifully simple. As Robin Ramsay points out,

> People in the grip of theories find it difficult to change their minds: the human brain is adept at finding reasons why information which refutes our core beliefs can be ignored. It may also demonstrate that of all theories, conspiracy theories can be the most difficult to shed. For, by their nature, conspiracy theories have built into them strategies for accommodating information which apparently contradicts them.

When the foundations of *Who Killed Hanratty?* crumbled to dust – Janet Gregsten had not commissioned the crime, Peter Alphon was not the gunman – Paul Foot simply moulded the dust into a new pattern. He decided that Alphon must have been involved in some other way. And even if Alphon was a fantasist who had nothing at all to do with the crime, Foot, shameless and unabashed, drew the cheering conclusion that Alphon had nevertheless performed a service in establishing Hanratty's innocence by having "in his own macabre way, helped to keep the case alive all these years".

When improved, more sophisticated DNA analysis finally supplied a conclusive identification, Foot and Woffinden then adopted the circular logic that because they knew Hanratty was innocent then the DNA evidence must be, in some way, wrong.

Conspiracy theory is attractive because it smooths out all the ambiguities, mysteries and extraordinary coincidences which life sometimes throws up. A conspiracy theory joins all the loose endings and explains *everything*. As Paul Foot excitedly explained after getting involved with Peter Alphon, "All the bits and pieces of a confession at last became forged into a single, coherent story. Aspects of the A6 murder, which had been unexplained in the court at Bedford, were explained by Alphon." Alphon's confessions were replenished and adjusted until they explained everything – the motive, the long drive, the conversation in the car. For Bob Woffinden, Alphon was not simply the A6 killer. He also attacked Meike Dalal and threatened another woman, Audrey Willis, with a gun. Alphon not only found time to wave a gun at Mrs Willis at her home in Old Knebworth, Hertfordshire, at 11 o'clock on the morning of the abduction, but also returned on 2 April 1962 to wave a gun at her again. Mrs Willis was quite certain that the man was not Alphon but Woffinden, bending the evidence yet again to fit his own preconceived views, thought she was mistaken. Quite how and where Alphon managed to obtain not one but two guns Woffinden never explained.

Conspiracy theorists like Foot and Woffinden were deluded in three ways. Firstly, they believed that the crime was planned in advance. But no one could possibly have known that

Michael Gregsten and Valerie Storie would be in the cornfield on that evening at that time. The couple's visits to the cornfield were irregular and unpredictable.

Secondly, the conspiracy theorists believed that a gunman (who was not Hanratty) was commissioned to break up the relationship between Gregsten and Storie. Janet Gregsten seemed the obvious candidate. But neither Foot nor Woffinden knew anything about her personality or circumstances. She was not consumed with jealousy, she had a liberal and forgiving attitude to her husband's infidelity, she did not have the financial resources to hire a gunman, nor would she have had a clue as to how to go about finding a gun for hire. That scenario is the stuff of crime fiction, not the reality of a woman with two small children to look after, struggling to hold her life together.

Woffinden's adaptation of Foot's conspiracy theory to propose that a man commissioned Alphon to break up the marriage was equally absurd. (He meant William Ewer but, having no evidence to back up his theory, chose not to name him, thereby avoiding an action for libel.) Woffinden speculated that if the gunman in the cornfield had walked up to the Morris Minor and seen the couple having sex then Janet would have terminated the marriage. It is hard to see the logic of his argument, since she was all too well aware of the affair. Behind these feverish theories lay Foot and Woffinden's knowledge that Janet Gregsten and William Ewer had entered into a sexual relationship. But their affair happened in the aftermath of the crime, not before it. The idea that Ewer planned the crime so that Janet would become available is devoid of substance. Once Michael had moved out, as he was on the brink of doing, she would have become available anyway – an abandoned wife, in need of comfort and consolation.

The conspiracy was, Woffinden further argued, "a malicious jape that went disastrously wrong". Yet he also believed that the prank was commissioned for the price of £5,000 – a truly staggering sum for 1961. (You could buy a couple of houses with that money.) But since the gunman had exceeded his brief – he was supposed to terrify the couple, not kill Gregsten and rape his lover – why bother paying him afterwards? The gunman was hardly in a position to sue for breach of contract. Woffinden also believed that William Ewer lusted after his sister-in-law, Janet, and encouraged the crime in order to make her available. But this theory only made sense if murder was the purpose of the crime. Frightening Michael Gregsten, had it worked, would simply have sent him back into the arms of his wife.

The third objection is the most fundamental of all. The conspiracy theories all derived from the lurid fantasies of Peter Alphon. They assumed a connection between individuals – Peter Alphon, Charles France, William Ewer – who in fact had never met before the A6 murder, and there was not a scrap of evidence that they ever met afterwards, apart from a brief, inconsequential meeting in a shop between the latter two.

He would be like that for the rest of his life and that was
what his life was. You would never know how he got that
way because even if he told you it would not be the truth.
                          Raymond Chandler, *The Long Goodbye* (1953)

To make sense of the A6 murder it is necessary to understand
James Hanratty, which is by no means easy. In a case in which one
key aspect was eye-witness testimony, and another aspect was the
diction and accent of the killer, we have very little visual
information and no aural evidence at all about Hanratty.

There seems to be no film of him, other than a brief TV
shot of him being led out to a waiting police car, his face and head
concealed under a blanket, after his arrest in Blackpool. There is
apparently no home movie of him. His family were not well-off
and in any case home-movie cameras were only just coming on to
the market in the early 1960s. There seem to be no sound
recordings of his voice. It is not even clear if there are colour
photographs of him prior to his arrest.

What we are left with is a handful of black-and-white
photographs. There is even very little written material to draw on.
The only autobiographical material in the public domain takes
the form of letters from prison, including the sequence written
after his conviction, almost up to the hour of his execution. These,
it seems, were mediated by prison officers. Hanratty dictated his
thoughts and the officers wrote them down. None of this tells us
anything about his life in the formative years leading up to his
career as a petty criminal.

Hanratty was an enigma and much of his life is a mystery.
Even as an adult, once out of prison he lived below the radar and
off the grid. He covered his tracks, using pseudonyms and false

addresses wherever he went. Nowadays this would be very much harder to achieve. In the digital age anyone who owns a mobile phone or who uses a bank card leaves traces of their daily lives. Every journey through a town or city, every journey on public transport, is caught at some point on CCTV and recorded. But in 1961 it was possible to lead the Hanratty lifestyle, dropping from view and reappearing to friends and family when it suited him.

The first enduring mystery of the A6 case is how James Hanratty came to be in a cornfield in Buckinghamshire late on a Tuesday night in August, smartly dressed and carrying a gun. To his defenders this makes no sense at all. They argue that Soho was his natural habitat; that he was an urban criminal, not a rural wanderer. In reality everything about this episode is consistent with what we know about Hanratty's past.

The cornfield is often represented as a lonely, isolated place. I remember the first time I watched Bob Woffinden's TV documentary *Hanratty – The Mystery of Deadman's Hill* and its dramatized re-enactment of the crime, I took away the impression that the Morris Minor was parked in the countryside, in some distant farmer's field. Of course it *was* a farmer's field and it was sufficiently isolated to make it a popular location for courting couples but it was not exactly a long way from civilisation. It was about a mile from the A4 and from there it was less than two miles to Maidenhead and less than four miles to Slough. It was close to two residential areas, Dorney and Dorney Reach. To the north, within walking distance, were two railway stations on the Paddington to Maidenhead line.

In his book on the case Lord Russell of Liverpool acknowledged that "The cornfield, although remote, lay between a small village, where there had been house-breaking attempts previously, and the back of another estate of houses." Two white cottages overlooked the field at one side (the only photograph is in *Le Crime e la Route A6* – a book Bob Woffinden seems never to have looked at). It was August, which is an attractive month for burglars, as many people are away on holiday. This was particularly so in 1961, when English holidays were much more rigidly defined than today, when jobs are much more flexible and people can more easily go on vacation at any time. In August, before the era of cheap flights abroad, the English flocked to the seaside. When the gunman materialised out of the dusk and forced his way into the car one of Valerie Storie's first impressions was "I thought he was a burglar ... "

Hanratty, of course, was just that – a professional housebreaker. He was born on 4 October 1936 and first appeared in court at the age of seventeen, on 7 September 1954, charged with the theft of a motorcycle. He was placed on probation for a year. Eleven months later he was charged with housebreaking and remanded in custody, in August 1955. He was sentenced to two years in prison and released in February 1957. In July 1957 he was charged with stealing a car, as a result of which he served four months in Walton Prison, Liverpool. In March 1958 he was again convicted of car theft and given three years' corrective training (known in the prison world as "C.T.") He served his sentence in Wandsworth Prison, Maidstone Prison, Camp Hill on the Isle of Wight, Strangeways Prison in Manchester, Durham Prison, and then Strangeways Prison again. He was released from there on 24 March 1961.

Upon his release Hanratty travelled to London and contacted former associates. During the Easter weekend (31 March-3 April) he robbed a house in Wood Lane, leaving his fingerprints on a window frame. He then fled to Durham and worked for a week in an engineering factory. But regular salaried employment never suited Hanratty and he walked out of this job. He returned to the Hanratty family home and the company of his parents and brothers on 13 April, saying he wanted to settle down. For the next three months he lived at home.

In July 1961, not long before he appeared in the cornfield, Hanratty resumed his criminal career as a burglar. He targeted affluent neighbourhoods on the edge of London, breaking into homes in Harrow, Wembley, Stanmore, Edgeware,

Ruislip and Northwood. He chose houses where he hoped to find jewellery and cash and any other small, valuable objects he could carry on foot. In a revealing remark, he said: "I always work on my own. I often change my area. I usually do night jobs." That Hanratty should have been wandering around Dorney Reach and Dorney late at night is perfectly consistent with everything we know about his criminal activities. There was nothing at all unusual about him appearing late in the evening in that cornfield. All it indicates is that he had shifted his focus slightly further to the south and west than in the past.

Defenders of Hanratty say that there is no evidence that he was ever in the area from which Gregsten and Storie were abducted. This is perfectly true. But Hanratty's whereabouts from the moment he left prison on 24 March 1961 to the moment of his arrest in Blackpool on 11 October are often a mystery. Even when he was living with his parents he led a double life. He was, he claimed, a regular client of a Soho prostitute, visiting her two or three times a week for nearly two months in the period before the A6 murder. Paul Foot asserts that Hanratty "did not spend a night away from home" between 13 April and the first two weeks in July, but it is clear that even when he was ostensibly living a respectable life with his parents he was slipping away to the twilight world of Soho.

Hanratty moved between compartmentalised worlds. There was the domestic world of family life and his relationships in particular with his mother and his younger brother Michael. He also had a range of criminal associates, who remain shadowy and obscure figures in the narrative of Hanratty's short life. He had a fleeting, shadowy relationship with a girl named Gladys Deacon. Around the time of the A6 murder he had friendly relations with Charles France and his family, and a 48-year-old widow, Louise Anderson. She dealt in stolen property from her shop, Juna Antiques, on Greek Street in Soho. Hanratty stayed from time to time with the France family at their home on Boundary Road, St John's Wood. He also stayed with Louise

Anderson at her flat at 23 Cambridge Court, Sussex Gardens, Paddington.

But no one ever really knew where Hanratty was or what he was up to. He was essentially a loner and an enigma. He was beholden to no one. He had no employer, no wife, no partner he lived with. Whatever the nature of his relationship with Gladys Deacon may have been, it was essentially fleeting and intermittent. He was not a member of a criminal gang. He came and went as he pleased. He emerged out of nowhere, socialised, then disappeared again. He was a solitary criminal. No one really knew what he was up to, or where he was, or how he was spending his time.

It is consistent with everything we know about Hanratty that he should have been alone at night in a field at the back of an estate of houses, near a village which had previously suffered from a spate of burglaries. The cornfield off Marsh Lane at Dorney Reach was easily accessed by public transport. Early on the morning of the abduction Hanratty admitted that he had gone to Paddington Station, from where it was thirty minutes by train to the area. If you left the cornfield and headed on up Marsh Lane and then crossed the A4 you came to a station on the main line to Paddington. So far all this was consistent with Hanratty's past behaviour and modus operandi as a petty criminal. What was new was the gun.

When first interrogated about the crime, Hanratty, according to Lord Russell of Liverpool, made a "very significant statement". He told Superintendent Acott "quite voluntarily," at a time when "no mention whatsoever had been made of the murder weapon" that he had asked a friend to get him a "shooter" so that he could do some "stick-ups" but that his friend "wouldn't play" and so he never managed to get hold of one.

His Lordship believed it "extremely unlikely, to put it midly" that a man under suspicion of shooting someone dead would volunteer the fact that he had once tried to procure a gun for the purpose of armed robbery. "That he did say this, and said it quite voluntarily is, surely, one of the many pointers to Hanratty's innocence". In reality he was quite wrong in his assumption. Hanratty did not volunteer the information. It was extracted from him by police questioning.

When Hanratty came out of Strangeways prison on 24 March 1961 he went straight to London to see a criminal associate named Donald Slack (also known to use the name Fisher). He saw Slack a second time, after the A6 murder. On 2 October, according to Paul Foot, "he went to Ealing to sell a diamond ring he had stolen. He visited Donald Fisher." The shadow of a libel lawyer hangs over those sentences. Foot was circumspect in his phrasing but the insinuation is plain: Fisher dealt in stolen goods. He was a fence. Hanratty had known Slack/Fisher for around five years and had written to him from prison. When Hanratty came out of prison Slack/Fisher gave him a meal and £25. Hanratty asked him to look after a folder of personal material – apparently photographs and letters. This was material which he evidently did not wish his parents to see.

When Acott interrogated Hanratty after his arrest he told him that Fisher had revealed that on his first visit Hanratty had enquired about getting hold of a gun. It was "a very big shock" to Hanratty to learn that his associate had grassed on him. As Hanratty acknowledged, "it was the truth". He had indeed talked to Slack/Fisher about the possibility of obtaining a firearm. Hanratty desperately tried to play down the significance of this conversation. It was, he explained, just an idle boast. There was nothing to it. He hadn't really meant it. "He asked me what I had in mind [after being released from prison]. I said that screwing [i.e. breaking into houses and stealing property] was all played out. 'If you want to get rich these days,' I said, 'you've got to have a shooter and go after cash.'" But that wasn't what Slack/Fisher is supposed to have told Acott. He claimed that Hanratty had specifically enquired about obtaining a gun, not that he had been making a philosophical observation on how a criminal might best accumulate wealth.

Slack/Fisher later denied he had had any such conversation with Hanratty. "I have certainly never spoken to him about firearms or given him weapons of any kind." To campaigners this provides further evidence of Acott's underhand methods. He had tricked poor James Hanratty into incriminating himself! But of course a conversation about firearms clearly *did* take place between Hanratty and Slack/Fisher on the day of Hanratty's release from prison. Acott had no reason to invent one and Hanratty simply confirmed it. The probability is that Slack/Fisher did indeed grass on Hanratty. He did not wish this information to become public, or perhaps having informally tipped off Acott he chose to steer clear of any further involvement in such an incendiary, high-profile case. If Slack/Fisher did not volunteer the information then Acott must have had very good reasons for believing that he was just the man to have supplied Hanratty with the murder weapon, and he therefore tricked Hanratty into conceding that the two had discussed firearms. One of those who knew Hanratty best, Louise Anderson, evidently knew that he had got hold of a gun and that he kept it hidden at the France family home.

On Monday 21 August Hanratty went to the France's house in St John's Wood. There he collected a brown pigskin suitcase containing some clothes which Mrs France had washed, ironed and packed for him. He stayed several hours and had his tea there. This was obviously when he retrieved his gun and slipped it into the case.

Some time between 5pm and 7pm he left the France residence and said that he went to the left luggage office at Leicester Square underground station. He said he had a small case stored there, which he now collected. This is supposed to have contained stolen jewellery. He took it into a toilet cubicle and transferred the stolen goods to his suitcase. A likelier explanation is that this case contained the ammunition for the gun. Hanratty claimed that he left the pigskin case at the left luggage office and dumped the small case in a dustbin in an alleyway, and then walked to the Rehearsal Club. He stayed there half an hour, then went by taxi to the greyhound stadium in Hendon.

Before 10.30pm he was back at Leicester Square tube station, where he collected his case. He said he visited a Soho prostitute, claiming he was one of her regular clients, then went to the Rehearsal Club for a Babycham. (This, incidentally, contradicts the claim that Hanratty never drank.) He then took a taxi to the Broadway House Hotel in Dorset Square, which was full. They fixed him up with a room at the Hotel Vienna on Sutherland Avenue. He arrived some time between 11pm and midnight. He was given Room 24 – the basement room.

Paul Foot was very sarcastic about the idea that Hanratty "kept empty cartridge cases on his person" and that "two of these had dropped on to the chair" in his hotel room. But obviously that is not what happened. The likeliest explanation is that at some point between his arrival and departure Hanratty reloaded his gun in the privacy of his hotel room. At least two bullets had been fired from the gun – presumably a test shoot, to check that it worked. It is unlikely but just possible that he may even have fired the gun in the hotel room. In the morning, with the noise of traffic, it would not necessarily have been noticed. Cities are full of random background noise. The television personality Jill Dando was gunned down beside her front door on a quiet London residential street at around 11.30am on a weekday morning in April 1999 – neither neighbours who were at home or anyone else in the street at the time heard the gunshot or noticed that a murder was occurring in broad daylight. Noise would not have been the issue at the Hotel Vienna but rather the damage caused by the bullets. Had the gun been fired at a cushion there would have been powder-burns on the material, entry and exit holes in the cushion, and, most likely, bullet holes in the furniture and walls.

That Hanratty mislaid the cartridge cases is not remotely surprising. He was a sloppy criminal who just one week after being released from a stiff three-year sentence broke into a house and left his fingerprints behind on a window frame. His carelessness was reckless and foolish. Unlike an automatic pistol, a revolver does not eject spent cartridges as they are fired. They are ejected only when the weapon is opened for reloading. Hanratty presumably reloaded the gun in the hotel room and then put the two empty cartridges down on the chair and forgot about them. His attention span was short and he was careless by nature.

The cartridge cases were found in a dark, windowless alcove of the basement room which Hanratty had occupied. The cases were barely noticeable against the dark material of the upholstered chair upon which they were lying. Robert Crocker, the hotel chain director, did not notice them when he reached down to tweak the loose piece of material beneath the chair, sending one of the cartridge cases tumbling to the floor. Nor did Juliana Galves, manageress of the Hotel Vienna, spot its companion. She ran her hand over the chair and found it. It was such a gloomy location that she felt it, she didn't see it.

What made Hanratty so careless we shall never know. A knock on the door from a hotel chambermaid come to clean the room, when he was in the middle of reloading the gun? Did he reload the weapon in the morning, in a hurry? Or was it that he simply didn't care and left the empty cartridge cases for the hotel staff to dispose of? This is quite possible. He had signed the hotel register with a false name and address, so he thought he was untraceable. Secondly, he had so far not used the gun for a criminal purpose. He was not yet the A6 killer.

Why did Hanratty obtain a gun? Probably because, as he explained, to Donald Slack, he was considering moving on from burglary to armed robbery, where the proceeds were far more substantial. Moreover, London in the 1960s "was the heyday of the armed robber". There may also have been an element of bravado involved. Hanratty moved in criminal circles in which some individuals ostentatiously carried weapons. He had a vain and boastful personality. He was 24 and had spent almost five years in prison. He was no longer an apprentice crook. He was, in his own eyes, a true professional, a man who could show old dogs new tricks (*look Dixie – you can get rid of stuff under the back seat of a bus, bet you never knew that!*).

Hence Hanratty's sudden enthusiasm for changing his appearance. Some time in July 1961 – perhaps a month before the A6 murder – Hanratty had his hair dyed by Carole France. He was someone who stood out from the crowd. He did not just have deep-set staring blue eyes, he also had distinctive light auburn hair and was popularly known to his associates as "Ginger" Hanratty. When Carole France dyed his hair black Hanratty was thrilled by the transformation.

Bob Woffinden argued that the only reason Hanratty altered his appearance was because he must have felt that "if the police heard of any burglary being committed by a light-haired man, they'd automatically associate it with him." This is not at all persuasive. Eye-witness testimony never put Hanratty in jail for burglary. Indeed, it seems only once was he ever disturbed while engaged in housebreaking. Hanratty committed scores of burglaries and his physical appearance was irrelevant. It was fingerprint evidence which put him away, not descriptions of a light-haired man. Hanratty was just one burglar among many. In any case, he had spent the previous three years in prison. He was hardly Mr Big.

On 5 August Carole France re-dyed his hair black. It was probably during this month that Hanratty managed to buy a firearm. With his gun and his changed appearance he was now ready to commit an armed robbery – perhaps with a handkerchief wrapped around the lower half of his face, cowboy-style. This, of course, was exactly what the gunman in the cornfield did – he concealed his face in this way with a handkerchief.

Carrying out an armed robbery without a getaway car or an accomplice requires a certain amount of planning and a foolproof escape route. Running away on foot and hoping to escape by public transport is infinitely riskier than fleeing in a motor vehicle. In the past Hanratty had travelled to his chosen burglary neighbourhoods by bus and then walked. Having done a spot of housebreaking he returned with his loot the same way. It was a relatively leisurely form of criminality, with no hue and cry and no pursuit.

To get away quickly after an armed robbery a train is better than a bus. For a London criminal like Hanratty it made sense to choose a bank or a post office or even a shop which was outside the capital but not too far away. Ideally it should be in a busy urban area which would allow the robber to slip casually among the shoppers and make his way to a nearby railway station and coolly catch the next train back to London. Somewhere, let's say, like Maidenhead.

Did Hanratty ever plan to go to Liverpool? Perhaps – but not immediately and not on the morning of Tuesday 22 August 1961. Liverpool was mentioned to those who knew him to throw them off the scent. Hanratty was a compulsive liar, even to his friends. As the first stage of his furtive plan to carry out an armed robbery he went to a London hotel. Any hotel would do, and he ended up at the Hotel Vienna, convenient for Paddington Station. At the hotel he would load his gun and check that it was ready for the next day. In the interim he had time to kill. He dawdled at the Rehearsal Club, went to a greyhound track, and, so he claimed, visited a prostitute. But this last detail may simply have been fabricated, with the intention of establishing that he was not desperate for sex.

Hanratty told a tale involving a brown pigskin suitcase. Whatever truth there may have been in that (and Hanratty's narratives always mingled fact and fiction) it is interesting to note that when Florence Snell saw him leave the Hotel Vienna she said he was carrying "a green holdall". She was scarcely the most credible of witnesses and she may have been mistaken; on the other hand she had no reason to invent this part of her testimony and it was not in itself particularly incriminating. But if Hanratty was heading off to Maidnhead to carry out an armed robbery the holdall seems more likely than the pigskin suitcase. Whatever the truth of this matter, what is not in dispute is that James Hanratty left the hotel that morning between 8.30am and 9am and walked to Paddington Station. We can be quite sure he was carrying a loaded .38 Enfield revolver in whatever case or bag he had with him that day.

Whom he obtained that weapon from we shall never know. But there were a lot of firearms around in criminal circles at that time. The .38 Enfield revolver was commonly used as a weapon by the British Army and after the war many soldiers returned home with illicit firearms. My late father brought back a handgun from his military service and stashed this illegal weapon at home. My mother was unhappy having a firearm in the house and made him dispose of it. He took it away and threw it in a river. But thousands of other households contained weapons illicitly obtained during wartime, some of which duly found their way to the criminal fraternity. Harry Roberts, who in 1966 shot dead two police officers, had his own private armoury consisting of a Colt .38 Special, a 9mm Luger PO8 and a .38 Enfield. The least glamorous of those three handguns was the last one, which was James Hanratty's weapon. Roberts used his Luger.

8 The Abduction

> What I am trying to say is that it all came unexpected.
>
> John Fowles, *The Collector* (1963)

On the evening of this particular Tuesday in August Michael Gregsten and Valerie Storie spent between an hour to an hour and a half at the Old Station Inn at Taplow, on the A4 between Maidenhead and Slough. They had one drink each (money was tight and they were plainly lingering over their drinks). They spent their time looking at maps for a motor rally they were planning for their work social club.

Valerie estimated that they left the Inn at around 8.45pm, which meant they would have arrived in the cornfield at around 9pm. She believed the gunman tapped on the window at about 9.20-9.25pm. These timings were contradicted by the Inn's landlady, Mary Lanz. She estimated that the couple left at around 9.20pm, which meant the gunman didn't appear on the scene until around 10pm.

Lighting-up time was 8.35pm. Whatever time the couple drove into the cornfield it was definitely getting dark when they arrived; night had fallen when the gunman put in an appearance. Valerie Storie may well have been wrong about her times, since a local man, David Henderson, said he remembered seeing the Morris Minor parked with its interior light on near the field entrance at around 9.45pm.

What were Michael Gregsten and Valerie Storie *doing* in the cornfield? To Peter Alphon the answer was plain. They went there for sex. Among his lurid "confessions" was the claim that, in the role of gunman, he had ordered them to make love and watched as they copulated. This was a voyeuristic fantasy which said much more about Peter Alphon than it did about what occurred in the cornfield on that particular night.

Speculation about Valerie Storie's sex life seemed distasteful when she was still alive. She had to live for decades under the shadow of the violence which had killed her lover, left her a paraplegic in her early twenties, and cast her, according to the high-profile A6 campaign, as a vengeful and deluded woman whose false eye-witness testimony had sent an innocent man to the gallows. We now know that in fact she was entirely frank with the police about the nature of her relationship with Michael Gregsten. She acknowledged that sometimes they went to this field for sex. But that was not the only reason. On summer evenings they sometimes parked near the entrance and then walked down a path to the River Thames and watched boats going through the locks. They had last been to the cornfield two nights earlier, when they had had sex in the car. They had been there about twice over a three-month period. It was not a place where they went according to a fixed schedule; no one could have have known they would be in the field that night. On this particular evening, Storie told police, they had not gone there for sex, simply to talk. Rather than pay for more drinks at the Old Station Inn they went elsewhere to continue their conversation. Apart from the motor rally there was also the subject of their new life together. Michael had decided he was going to make a decisive break and leave his wife and children for Valerie.

There was a sudden sharp tap on the driver's side window. From where she was sitting, in the passenger seat next to the driver, Valerie could not see the gunman's head. She was able to perceive that the man was immaculately dressed, in a dark suit with a white shirt and a dark tie. Michael Gregsten wound down the window. "This is a hold-up," the man said. "I am a desperate man. I have been on the run for four months. If you do as I tell you, you will be alright." He demanded the ignition key.

The mystery gunman was, of course, James Hanratty – a man who did indeed dress immaculately (unlike, say, scruffy Peter Alphon, who also never wore a tie). It was a hold-up, which was something Hanratty had contemplated from the moment of coming out of jail. But in what sense was Hanratty "a desperate man"? He had not been on the run for four months but that was the exact length of time which had elapsed since his botched burglary in April – a crime which would bring the police to his parents' house. Another conviction for burglary would probably have resulted in a five-year sentence, which almost made it worthwhile to try something bigger, like armed robbery.

But if Hanratty had been planning a stick-up in Maidenhead evidently it hadn't worked out. The probability is that his nerve failed. Holding up a bank or a building society required reckless courage. If that is what happened this might explain why he resorted to using his weapon at the end of a long day. A couple in a car in a field, at night, were a very much easier target. There was no one around to interfere.

The scene played out in the cornfield was a random event. The crime was in no sense premeditated. Hanratty had no idea that he would find Michael Gregsten and Valerie Storie sitting in a Morris Minor just inside the entrance to the cornfield. What was he doing there? Twenty-one years ago, in *Shadows of Deadman's Hill*, I speculated that Hanratty had been walking along Marsh Lane when he saw the Morris Minor. After the book was published I received a letter from a local resident, shedding light on why and how Hanratty appeared at this location. I believe my correspondent is correct and has solved the enigma:

> For the last 20 years or so, one of my weekend pastimes has been to meet up with a few friends to go jogging at lunchtime in Maidenhead. We park our cars in River Road, just before Maidenhead Bridge and run a few miles along the river bank to about as far as Bray. This is a very scenic route and we pass some grand and secluded houses along the way. About half way along the route is a public footpath which leads to Dorney Reach. The footpath skirts what was the cornfield. (The entrance to

what is now the Thames Water site is in roughly the same position as the old entrance to the cornfield.) It means that Hanratty would have stumbled upon the Morris Minor from behind and without having had to pass by any properties in the area from where he could have been observed.

Therefore, I think the speculation in some quarters that Hanratty was 'wandering through a cornfield' is wrong. It would explain why Gregsten and Storie did not see the gunman approaching the car. Had Hanratty been walking down Marsh Lane from the A4 it would have taken him some 20-25 minutes to reach the cornfield. He would have passed many houses, during a period when it would still have been relatively light and he could have been noticed.

Also, had Hanratty walked from Maidenhead town centre along the A4 and turned right into Marsh Lane, he would not have needed to ask Storie and Gregsten, when they drove off along Marsh Lane, where a left turn would take them.

My belief is that Hanratty had already made a reconnaissance of the secluded riverside properties near Dorney Reach, with a view to doing a bit of business. These houses, then as now, are homes to celebrities. Maybe Hanratty, in his frustration at finding too many people at home, even in the holiday season, thought he would try his luck in the next village, i.e. Dorney Reach.

Interestingly, this neatly fits the testimony of Roy Langdale, who claimed that Hanratty talked to him about the crime. He said that Hanratty told him he was walking across a field when he came across the Morris Minor.

The crime, therefore, was the consequence of two unrelated, arbitrary events – Hanratty walking along the path beside the cornfield late at night, carrying a revolver, and Michael

Gregsten and Valerie Storie sitting in the Morris Minor near the entrance to the field. It seems improbable that James Hanratty had either murder or rape in mind when he knocked on the car window. Perhaps, at most, he contemplated turfing out the occupants and stealing the car. In the first instance he probably decided to rob them. A glance at their watches, however, told him that his prisoners were not wealthy.

The gunman acted on impulse and that impulsive gesture was to lead to extreme violence and tragedy. Everything that followed flowed from Hanratty's own damaged life and his impoverished, sociopathic personality.

Was Hanratty really a risk-taker who acted on impulse? Yes, he very definitely was. His burglaries were sometimes spur-of-the-moment affairs. Less than a month earlier, on 25 July, he was on a bus to Crosby in Merseyside. He got off the bus at a likely location and broke into a house chosen at random. Almost always the houses were empty and Hanratty was lucky. But on Saturday 2 September 1961 something quite revealing happened. He broke into a large house in Enfield that morning. He ransacked a room and began packing two cases with silver. Before he had finished he saw a woman walking up the path to the front door. Hanratty ran and hid in a downstairs toilet. He heard the woman unlock the front door and waited for her to shut it behind her. This didn't happen. Perplexed and anxious, he came out to see what was going on. He discovered that the woman had only stepped back outside to collect some bottles of milk left by the milkman. Hanratty ran and slammed the front door shut, hoping to escape from the rear of the house.

Next thing he was aware of was the woman staring in at him through a window. Hanratty returned to the front door and opened it. The woman said, "Who are you?" Hanratty ignored her question. "Come in," he replied. The woman was frightened and suspicious of this unexpected stranger in her house. She ran back down the path to get help. Hanratty ran to a back room, kicked open the French windows, sped down the garden, and made his getaway to an adjacent street. A bus came along almost at once and he boarded it. He made his escape and was not seized and arrested.

What, one wonders, would have happened if the woman had accepted Hanratty's invitation and stepped into the house? He would then have been face to face with a woman whose home he was in the process of burgling. What would he have done next? Would he have locked her in a room and then made his escape? Would he have threatened her? Would he have simply pushed her aside and then run off down the path?

This situation was one which had many possible outcomes. Would Hanratty have treated her with consideration or with violence? If she had screamed, what would he have done? Some fifteen years earlier, in October 1946, a lorry driver named Harold Hagger gave an early morning ride to a woman thumbing a lift. He assumed that Dagmar Petrzywalski would be willing to have sex with him, in return for payment. Or perhaps he simply planned to rape her, believing that any woman hitchhiking in the dark must be of loose morals. He pulled into a quiet rural lane and turned off the engine. When she resisted his advances he restrained her by the throat. She died almost at once. Hagger hadn't intended to kill her. He hadn't even been planning to find a woman for sex. The situation had simply got out of hand and he dealt with it impulsively, throttling her. Impulsive actions can have unforeseen consequences. Dagmar Petrzywalski, who had had many rides from friendly lorry drivers before, simply had the misfortune to be in that place when a man like Harold Hagger arrived on the scene.

It was the same with Hanratty. On 2 September 1961 he impulsively put himself in a situation which had many potential outcomes. It might well have ended in rape and murder. Because the woman ran off, it didn't. But Hanratty was quite prepared to put himself into a situation with himself as the jailer and someone else as the prisoner, without thinking through the implications and possible consequences. Even Hanratty's defenders acknowledge that this was a core aspect of his personality – as Woffinden at one point remarked, "He was, as ever, thinking very short term."

This is surely how the A6 case began. Hanratty was walking along the footpath from the river, heading for the cornfield entrance. He was, as became evident later, feeling frustrated and very sorry for himself. Plainly he had not had a good day. Whatever his plans for armed robbery or burglary had been they had not materialised. Suddenly, there ahead of him in the darkness, was a parked car, with a couple inside, a man and a younger woman. His immediate impulse was to rob them – perhaps even to steal their car. On impulse he pulled the handkerchief across his face, cowboy style. He slipped on a pair of gloves and walked up to the driver's side of the car. He rapped on the window, taking the couple by surprise.

Michael Gregsten wound down the window. He assumed it was the farmer who owned the field, come to complain that they were trespassing.

"This is a hold-up."

Gregsten could not see the man's face, because he was standing so close to the car. The man was smartly dressed – dark jacket, white shirt, tie. He was pointing a gun. It was an Enfield .38, although Gregsten wouldn't have known that. The type of firearm used raises a question almost never asked. How did Hanratty transport it around that day? The implication is that by the time of the encounter in the cornfield Hanratty was openly carrying it around. This seems unlikely. In the words of someone knowledgeable about firearms, "an Enfield .38 is a rather bulky weapon and awkward to conceal". Perhaps Hanratty was carrying a small case or holdall and Valerie Storie simply never saw it. If he was, he presumably laid it on the floor of the Morris when he got in and sat behind the driver.

Hanratty's initial motive was robbery. But he had now set in motion a chain of events the consequences of which he could not foresee. Because of what he had just done he would, in the end, be dead within eight months. The suffering he caused to others who were left to live with the consequences of his criminality would endure a lifetime.

The gunman demanded the ignition keys. Valerie told Michael not to hand them over. She seems to have been a young woman of remarkable fortitude. But he had a gun pointed at him. He handed over the ignition keys.

Variations on this moment were to be repeated at intervals throughout the events which followed. Michael was anxious, afraid, obedient, passive; Valerie, although also very scared, resisted – at first in small, surreptitious ways, later more openly.

The gunman told Gregsten to open the rear offside passenger door. He climbed inside and sat behind him, pointing the gun. He ordered his captives to lock their doors and not look round.

Hanratty, who was surely speaking the truth at this moment, said: "This is a real gun and I haven't had it very long. It's like a cowboy's gun. I feel like a cowboy." He sounded high, as if he was drunk or on drugs, but that would have been out of character. It was more the giddiness of power; of the control over these two people which the gun gave him. It was as magical as a wand. Hanratty added that it was .38 gun. This meant nothing at all to his middle-class prisoners.

Hanratty was in boastful mode, showing off. He was also experiencing something new. He was superior to these two nicely spoken people. He was powerful. A part of his personality was opening up. He felt almost light-headed. Something inside him was suddeny released. He felt buoyant, boastful, chatty. The adrenalin flowed. It kept him alert and awake through the long night which was to follow.

He tapped his pockets and there was a rattling noise. "These are all bullets," he told them. He was proud of his new toy. Before this moment it had been a secret, something furtive, something loaded in the gloom of a basement hotel room. He had only ever told one person about the gun and that was Louise. He could trust her. She was also a little frightened of him. He was confident she would never grass.

It was exciting, using his gun for the first time. He had an audience. He could put on a performance. He was a gunman, an outlaw, a cowboy; a desperate man.

But there was also something about the gunman which suggested what he was doing in that neighbourhood so late at night. "I thought he was a burglar," Valerie Storie said afterwards, "and he was waiting for someone." She was half right. He *was* a burglar – but Hanratty only ever worked alone. He was a chancer, looking for opportunities. The easy pickings he thought he would accumulate earlier in the day had not materialised, so now he was off seeking pastures new. And then he stumbled upon this car. After a frustrating day he could at least rob the couple inside, so that the day wasn't wasted.

But once he was sat in the back of the car what did Hanratty *want*? There was something about him which seemed to suggest he was a burglar but what was he waiting for? An accomplice, perhaps? After Janet Gregsten visited Valerie in hospital she told journalists, "The whole thing seems without rhyme or reason. It can only be the work of a maniac. Mike and Val got the impression that he might have been committing a burglary somewhere and wanted a getaway car."

All this was in a sense true. Hanratty was probably still bent on burglary when he stumbled upon the Morris Minor. The problem with Janet Gregsten's comments is that they conflate what happened later – murder, rape, a man who acted like a maniac – with the banal origins of the crime. It *was*, very much, without rhyme or reason. The problem was that the gunman himself did not know what he really wanted. It is highly unlikely that murder and rape were on his mind at first. The original impulsive plan was surely to rob them and, perhaps, to steal the car. But for the present Hanratty was enjoying his role as performer and man of power.

The gunman told them he hadn't eaten for two days, an odd remark for a smartly dressed man to make. He didn't look poor. After about five minutes he returned the key to Gregsten and told him to drive further into the field. He wanted to prolong the pleasures of command and control. Gregsten was ordered to turn the car round and park it beside what Valerie Storie believed was a haystack covered by tarpaulin (it was actually a combine harvester). The car bonnet was now facing the entrance to the field, ready to make an exit. This, too, was exactly in accordance with Hanratty's personality. He was a professional housebreaker who always checked his possible escape routes first.

All this was a new experience for Hanratty and he was plainly enjoying himself. He was living for the moment, not worrying what the consequences of his unlawful detention of two people might be. His nineteenth, twentieth and twenty-first birthdays had each been spent inside a prison cell. He had just done three years' corrective training. He had been pushed around, shouted at, locked up. He had undergone the harsh institutional rigour of life in some of the toughest, bleakest prisons in Britain. On the surface, outside prison, he usually seemed polite, deferential, no trouble. But not always. Deep inside he was damaged, corroded, hollowed-out by punishment. His late adolescence and early manhood had been blighted, were gone, were irretrievable. He was emotionally maimed. Whole areas of feeling just were not there. He was a cold, narcissistic sociopath, incapable of empathy.

Hanratty had a comprehensive experience of the humiliating realities of a brutal and desolating prison world that a couple like Michael Gregsten and Valerie Storie had no inklings of. But now, in an instant, all that had changed. His gun meant that he could boss them around.

Hanratty looked at his watch. It was getting late. There was still time to catch the last train back to Paddington. But it was new, this power, and he savoured it. He made it last. He looked at his watch again. It was a nervous habit he had acquired when he was tense, under stress. A housebreaker has to work fast, very fast. Every minute counts. Again he looked at his watch. What time was that last train? He was never very good at remembering things like timetables. But did it matter? If he was too late for the train he would take the Morris Minor.

He was in no hurry. He had no commitments. No wife or girlfriend waiting for him to come home, wondering where he was.

And he still didn't know what he wanted. He was enjoying himself. It was like the wild west. He was the outlaw. But no one would ever find out who he was. He had a handkerchief over his face and his hair was dyed. No one could possibly know that the gunman was none other than Ginger Hanratty.

"There's plenty of time," he said. And it was true, it was, really. James Hanratty had all the time in the world.

The gunman was chatty, conversational, almost good-humoured. "You'll be alright if you do as I tell you." Was he waiting for someone? Why didn't he *do* something? Gregsten and Storie asked Hanratty what he wanted. He replied: "It is alright. There is no hurry."

So they talked. They asked him where he had been. Hanratty always regarded himself as a smart operator. He was fly, was Jimmy. He fooled hotels, he never wrote his real name and address. Not at the cleaners, either. He was very, very clever. He would fool these people, easy. He told them he had been in the Oxford area. Because, of course, he hadn't. Why Oxford? Because they were posh, like the people who went to Oxford? Not really posh, of course. Posh people wouldn't be driving a Morris Minor. But posh to Jimmy. Well-spoken. Middle-class. Well, lower-middle-class, really. But this kind of class distinction was probably lost on Hanratty.

He told them he had been living rough for two days. He said the day before he had woken up wet through. He had been soaked by rain. Another obvious lie. He was smartly dressed. He wasn't a tramp. He wasn't bedraggled, dirty, scruffy. He was someone who cared about his appearance. He was James Hanratty – a man who was always fussing about his appearance, always popping into the gent's cloakroom at railway stations and sprucing himself up in front of a mirror.

The gunman asked Valerie and Michael where they lived. He asked if they were married. They said no. Not that he was particularly interested in these people. He was far too egocentric to care about anyone, really. Except, perhaps, his mum and his aunty.

He demanded their watches and they handed them over. James Hanratty was something of an expert where watches were concerned. They were good things to steal. You could slip them in your pocket and sell them quite easily. You asked people in the street. *Want to buy a watch, mate?* There were lots said yes. A valuable watch at a discount price. Fell off the back of a lorry. No questions asked. A bargain's a bargain.

Hanratty looked at Gregsten and Storie's watches in disgust. Cheap rubbish. A disappointment. What he didn't understand was that Michael Gregsten was always broke – a wife and two kids to support, plus a woman on the side – and Valerie Storie was a low-paid civi servant. They didn't have the kind of money that bought flashy, expensive watches. In any case they were not the kind of people who cared about such things. Later on that night Hanratty returned the watches. They were no good to him. It was one more disappointment in a day of disappointments.

Money was different. Any money was worth having, no matter how little the amount. The month before he had even stolen sixpences from a house near Liverpool. Hanratty instructed Gregsten to hand over his wallet. He looked inside. It contained three miserable quid! Pathetic – but better than nothing.

Now it was Valerie's turn. He told her to hand over her purse. For the second time that night she transgressed. She didn't play by the rules. She was a sparky, difficult, independent woman;

a feminist long before the term was invented. She wasn't ashamed of having an affair with a married man and she didn't care what people thought. Her work colleagues knew. They did not approve but it was none of their business. Her parents knew. She didn't care. Valerie Storie was not the kind of person to be ordered around by a thug with a gun. He wanted her purse, fine, he could have it. But first she took the banknotes out and slipped them inside her bra. The thug was so stupid he didn't notice.

Hanratty repeated that he was hungry. They told him to take the car and go. Go while it is still dark. Hanratty replied that there was no hurry. He was happy to wait until daybreak.

This was an ominous development. Perhaps this was when the thought of raping Valerie Storie first entered his mind. She was in his power, under his control. With his gun he could get them to do *anything*.

As if to justify what would later occur he returned to the theme of poor Jim Hanratty, victim of the world's cruelty. He said that he had never had a chance in life. "He said he'd been locked up in a cellar for days and been beaten and had bread and water." He said that he had been in institutions since the age of eight. He said he had been in remand homes and Borstal. He said he had done "C.T." He said he had "done the lot". He said he knew that next time he was in prison he would get "P.D." He said he had lived with the rich. He said he knew The Bear Hotel, Maidenhead. It had been renovated. It was a jumble of information which said a lot about a little while apparently revealing nothing of value.

Michael Hanratty later said that there were two reasons he knew his brother was innocent. One of them was that his brother would never have used the word "institutions". It was a shrewd and plausible point. Valerie Storie was specifically asked at the trial if the gunman had used this word. After a pause she said that he had.

There are three points to make about this moment. Everything that the gunman was supposed to have said was based on Valerie Storie's memories of a long, harrowing night which ended in an explosion of violence – the murder of her lover while he sat beside her, and then her rape. This long night of dialogue was mediated by her, over several narratives. Firstly, she had to try and remember a conversation which went on sporadically for over five hours. Secondly, the gunman spoke with a working-class London accent, using the diction and speech patterns of an uneducated person. In seeking to convey what he had said Storie undoubtedly at times superimposed her own educated middle-class rhetoric. On the face of it Hanratty would never have volunteered the word "institutions". He would have said clink, stir, choky, camp, or something along those lines. But people with learning difficulties and a very limited vocabulary do occasionally incorporate sophisticated language into their conversation. It is learned, just as slang is, from other people's conversation. Even children as young as two or three are capable of listening to adults and mimicking their words, long before they entirely understand what they mean. It is also the case that if Storie had introduced the word into their conversation Hanratty would have been able to pronounce it and echo her. One of the striking features of his language at the trial was the way in which he sometimes mimicked what others had said. At one point he replied to Graham Swanwick, counsel for the prosecution: "I must put it to you that you are quite wrong." So although Hanratty would never have introduced the word into the dialogue he conducted with his prisoners, he might well have used it.

Thirdly, Valerie Storie may simply have been wrong in this instance. She had a very strong personality. She does not give the impression of someone who would ever lightly own up to being wrong. As an intelligent woman she also realised the significance of the question. It was the classic thrust of a trial barrister – try and trip up the witness on one small point and then, having obtained an acknowledgement of error, inflate its significance to suggest that *everything* this witness has to say is unreliable.

Courtrooms are like theatres in their architecture and

what takes place there. Every trial involves a drama featuring a number of performances. A trial can become an entertainment, with the public gallery packed out. The barristers on both sides go through the motions, playing roles they have played many times before. To them it's a game. Some they win, some they lose. The game ends and they move on to the next one. Valerie Storie declined to play along. She refused to budge from any of her positions. Her response was combative. She may have been wrong in some aspects of her testimony but she was never going to admit it. If you gave an inch, they would take a mile.

Valerie Storie's memory of her masked assailant was that he "seemed to contradict himself most of the time". This is redolent of Hanratty in the dock at his trial in Bedford. It provided a rich stew of linguistic confusion. Hanratty's trial testimony surrealistically jumbled tenses and released a blizzard of malapropisms and other grammatical misdemeanours which sometimes had the court in stitches.

The gunman said he had been locked in a cellar. He had been fed on bread and water. He had been in institutions since the age of eight. What lay behind this rambling and apparently fictitious account of his childhood? It suggests that Hanratty was feeling very sorry for himself (hungry, desperate, a life of suffering). *He* was the victim – not the frightened couple he had held up at gunpoint and was holding captive. He was plainly, at some level, trying to justify his actions. He couldn't help it. His life had been hell. His past had made him what he was at this moment – a desperate gunman.

There were grains of truth in all this. Hanratty was a disturbed and damaged individual but on the face of it he came from a decent, caring, working-class family. His parents were devout Catholics. His family background was stable. His father lived with his mother. The Hanrattys were the incarnation of the stable, hard-working nuclear family. This, at any rate, is what books about the A6 case tell us, and there is no reason to disbelieve them. But something clearly did go seriously wrong in James Hanratty's early life. The problem is that, as with so much to do with Hanratty, we have only the sketchiest details of his childhood.

Where was Hanratty at the age of eight, when, according to his erratic conversation in the Morris Minor, he was first placed in an institution? Interestingly, he was not at home with his parents. During the war his father served in the navy and it seems was often away from home. Young Jimmy, the firstborn of four brothers, had his mother to himself from the age of three. Michael was born in February 1939 and was a baby when war broke out. The other two brothers, Peter and Richard, were born after the war was over.

In July 1944 young Jimmy, aged seven, was wrenched from his mother and life at home in Wembley, and put on a train at King's Cross with his younger brother Michael. They were evacuated from London to escape the threat of the V-1 flying bombs which were then pounding the capital. They had to stand all the way in a crowded train heading north. They were deposited in Barrow-in-Furness in Cumberland. There, members of the public picked out the chidren they wanted. The Hanratty boys stayed with a local couple, Mr and Mrs Everside, for a year. Hanratty's mother stayed at home, alone, at 29 Hillfield Avenue, Wembley.

It is a strange episode and we know virtually nothing at all about it. Who were Mr and Mrs Everside, who scooped up the Hanratty brothers and took them home? Where did they live? Were they a loving, caring couple? Did they have children of their own? Was there a dark side to their desire to house two small boys with them? Such an episode would never happen nowadays. We know all too well that some adults are not carers but abusers and exploiters. Even if the Eversides were a harmless couple with no ulterior motives, did they still believe in chastising the erring child? Discipline and physical punishment were part of British society for decades after the war. Teachers were permitted to slap children, smack their knuckles with wooden rulers, or beat their buttocks with canes. The physical assault of children, resulting in bruising and bleeding, was deemed socially acceptable. If this was occurring in schools, what was happening in the privacy of the home?

It is a striking coincidence that Hanratty claimed his suffering began at the age of eight. His eighth birthday was spent with the Eversides, in Barrow-in-Furness. Was his description of being locked up in a cellar the memory of an actual event? Was his bread-and-water punishment story real? It is entirely possible that these events occurred and were literally true, or that they were exaggerated accounts of real experiences. It is equally possible, of course, that they were purely imaginary and metaphors for the pain of separation from his mother. It seems unlikely after all this time that we will ever know the truth about this period of James Hanratty's early life. But it must have left him conflicted. He surely loved his mother and missed her. But perhaps he also hated her for allowing him to be removed from his home and cast into the company of strangers. Hanratty's conversation in the Morris Minor suggests that it was in his eighth year that his alienation from his family and from society first began. Something traumatic occurred when he was eight years old and it damaged him forever.

There are classic examples of great artists whose work was shaped by a disturbing childhood experience. In February 1824, two days after his twelfth birthday, Charles Dickens was sent to work at a tumbledown blacking factory beside the Thames. It stank of dirt and decay. It was overrun with rats. Dickens worked a hard, bleak ten-hour day, packing pots of boot blacking. A few days later his father was arrested for debt and incarcerated in the Marshalsea prison. For a child these experiences were shattering. They haunted the novels he wrote as an adult.

At the age of five Alfred Hitchcock was locked in a cell at Leyton police station for a few minutes. It was whimsical gesture by a policeman who had been asked by Hitchcock's father, who ran a greengrocer's nearby in the same street, to punish his son, who had been naughty. Hitchcock was traumatised by the experience. For the rest of his life was terrified of police officers. He put the experience to brilliant artistic use in many of his greatest movies.

In Hanratty's case his emotional wounding may of course simply – complexly – been the deep emotional disturbance of a child whose father vanished from his life and who was then torn from his mother and his home in bewildering circumstances and dumped with strangers for a year. The brothers do not seem to have returned from the north when the war ended but some time later. The reason for this is unclear. When the boys did get back to London they found that their mother had moved to Elthorne Court, Church Lane, Kingsbury. Their father later returned home and in 1947 they moved to a semi-detached council house, 12 Sycamore Grove, Kingsbury. At the age of eleven Hanratty was sent to St James' Catholic School, Orange Hill Road, Burnt Oak. There it became obvious that James was maladjusted. A school doctor identified him as backward and recommended that he be sent to a special school. His parents refused to accept this advice and Hanratty remained at the school until July 1951, when he was 14.

There were two white cottages at the edge of the cornfield, quite close to where they were parked. A light went on outside one of them and someone came out, evidently putting a bicycle away in a garden shed. Hanratty was suddenly worried that the car might be spotted with the three of them inside and that someone might decide to come over and see what was going on. By now it was 10.30pm – perhaps later. Gregsten, Storie and Hanratty had now been together for thirty minutes or more.

The figure with the bicycle went back into the cottage and everything was quiet again. They talked some more. Then the gunman decided it was time to move on. He said he was hungry. He said they should go and get some food, then come back to the field. They told him that further along Marsh Lane was the Bath Road, which went to Maidenhead one way, Slough the other. The gunman said he didn't want to go to Slough.

Hanratty told Michael Gregsten he would have to be shut up in the boot. (Perhaps the thought of rape now entered his mind. With Gregsten out of the way it would just be him and Valerie.) Gregsten and Hanratty got out of the car. Perhaps Hanratty's possible sexual intention had communicated itself to Valerie, or perhaps she was simply fearful of being alone with this man and his gun. She transgressed a third time. The moment the men were outside the car she leaned over and managd to break the restraining strap on the back seat. This meant that Michael would be able to escape from the boot simply by pushing the seat back. Then she transgressed a fourth time. She dared to disagree with the gunman's plan. She told him that if he shut Gregsten in the boot he would kill him. There was, she claimed, a crack in the exhaust. Fumes leaked from it into the boot. Gregsten would be asphyxiated.

The gunman believed her. He handed the ignition key back to Michael Gregsten and told him to start the car.

> Carrying a gun has the bully boy flavour of the ersatz
> male, the fellow with such a hollow sense of inadequacy
> he has to bolster his sexual ego with a more specific
> symbol of gonodal prowess.
>
> John D. MacDonald, *Darker than Amber* (1966)

They rolled forwards out of the field.

At the entrance they turned left, up Marsh Lane.

They drove on into the night.

Soon they came to the A4. At the junction Gregsten asked the gunman which direction he should take – left or right. He gave him the names of the towns which the road linked. "I've had enough of Maidenhead," Hanratty said. So they turned right.

In Slough they stopped briefly at a machine that sold cartons of milk. But it only took sixpences and none of them had that particular coin. So on they went. Storie noticed the time on the Post Office clock in the high street. Exactly 11.45pm.

They continued east, along the A4. At some point Hanratty passed over their two watches. They were worthless. They could have them back. Storie puts hers on and, because Gregsten was driving, put his watch on her wrist as well.

Hanratty asked how much petrol was in the car. They lied; told him only a gallon. In another 20 miles it would run out. They stopped at a Regent garage near London Airport. Hanratty told Gregsten to ask for two gallons and said he would shoot if he asked for help from the pump attendant. He gave Gregsten a one pound note.

When the attendant handed back the change – a ten shilling note and a threepenny piece – Hanratty gave Valerie

Storie the threepenny bit. "You can have that as a wedding present," he jeered. There was hostility present, now.

He gave Gregsten new instructions. Turn off now. Left. Towards Hayes.

There was a long night ahead.

Those who campaigned for Hanratty's innocence paid little attention to the route taken that night. Since they believed he was in Rhyl at the time it mattered little. The gunman's route was confusing. It seemed random and mystifying. For some it could be explained by the fact that Peter Alphon was disturbed and a little crazy. It made sense if the gunman was Alphon.

"When they reached the junction with the A4," Lord Russell wrote, Gregsten "was told to turn right in the direction of Maidenhead." It's a revealing slip.

Paul Foot wrote that the gunman forced Gregsten to drive "through Slough, Hayes and Greenford, where Gregsten was told to turn right towards London through Harrow and Stanmore. Near London airport, the car turned into a Regent garage." Also wrong. They headed for Hayes *after* they had been to the garage.

The gunman knew west London. He wasn't lost. The route was perfectly coherent. They did not go wrong or make mistakes. Hanratty knew where they were and where he wanted to go.

Gregsten and Storie talked in a low voice. Most of the time the gunman didn't seem to mind but from time to time he objected. "Be quiet will you," he chided them. "I am finking." It was a phrase he kept on repeating. And Valerie Storie always remembered how he pronounced "th" as "f". *Fings. Finking.*

The precise route taken is not certain because it was night and Valerie Storie was unfamiliar with some of the neighbourhoods they passed through. But they seemed to stick to main roads and the route was coherent in terms of their final destination.

Beyond Hayes they joined the Greenford Road (A4127). This was Hanratty's territory. He had mentioned a café in Northolt but when they reached the intersection with Western Avenue (A40) he told Gregsten to keep going straight ahead. They continued along Greenford Road and through Harrow.

Somewhere in Harrow they stopped at a cigarette machine and Gregsten was allowed to get out and buy a packet of cigarettes. Storie lit one for her lover and one for the gunman. Earlier, in the cornfield, Hanratty had said he didn't smoke. But now he took a cigarette. Storie saw for the first time that he was wearing black gloves.

They drove on, through a part of London which Hanratty knew very well. Wembley, where he had once worked for the local authority, was a mile or so to the east. They came to Watford Road (A404). They continued on, meeting Kenton Road. To the east lay Kingsbury and the Hanratty family home. They continued north, along the A409.

Hanratty was the classic back-seat driver. He fussed continually over Gregsten's driving. "He was a very nervous passenger," Storie remembered. "He kept saying, 'What gear are you in? Why did you change gear there? Mind that car! Be careful of those traffic lights!'" Presumably Michael Gregsten was both nervously erratic in his driving (as might anyone be with a loaded gun pointed at the back of their head) while simultaneously hoping to attract attention.

At last they began to leave the outer suburbs behind. Now they were in Hertfordshire. On they went, through Watford and the villages of Aldenham and Park Street.

On the A5 Gregsten managed to attract the attention of another driver by surreptitiously flicking the Morris's manually controlled reversing light. A car came alongside and someone inside it gestured towards the rear of the Morris. Hanratty ordered Gregsten to stop and the two men got out to check the rear lights. Hanratty, who was never very bright, had forgotten that the ignition keys were still in the car. Storie contemplated slipping into the driver's seat and simply driving off into the night, leaving the two men stranded at the roadside. It was an existential dilemma – one of those "What if …" moments. In the end she could not bring herself to abandon her lover with the mysterious gunman. She and Gregsten were still hoping for a peaceful outcome to their ordeal. The gunman was welcome to take the car. Besides, he had power over them in the cornfield and he had done nothing to hurt them. He might be odd and probably unstable but he had shown no sign of wanting to harm them. The two men returned to the car. They drove on. Gregsten continued to try to attract the attention of other motorists, without success.

They reached a fork in the road. To the left, the A5 continued. Straight ahead was the A6, to Luton and Bedford.

Straight ahead.

Beyond Luton the gunman said he was tired and needed "a kip". Twice, he told Gregsten to pull off the A6 and go down a side road and park. But the first road had a PRIVATE – NO PARKING sign, and the second road had houses on it. Hanratty was looking for somewhere lonely where they would not be disturbed. Luton was by now some eight miles behind them. They were halfway to Bedford. Valerie Storie remembered they passed through Barton-le-Clay and Silsoe. They continued on, through Clophill. Another fifteen minutes and they would be in Bedford.

They continued on and there, as the road curved slightly and round to the left, Hanratty spotted an RAC box by a lay-by. He told Gregsten to pull in. Instead, Gregsten ignored the command and drove past. Hanratty became angry. He threatened Gregsten again and told him to do a U-turn and go back.

Gregsten obeyed. He turned into the side entrance, and then again, along a concrete strip which ran parallel to the trunk road. There was a low grassy bank, perhaps five metres wide, which separated this concrete strip from the A6. It was a cul-de-sac, with nothing but vegetation at the far end. Gregsten was ordered to drive to the far end, then turn round, so that the bonnet of the Morris was facing back towards the lay-by exit. This manoeuvre was a repeat of the one in the cornfield. A housebreaker always makes sure of his escape route.

It was journey's end for two of the occupants of that humdrum little car.

One aspect of Hanratty's identity not mentioned by Jean Justice and Paul Foot, and unwittingly revealed by Bob Woffinden, is his connection with Bedford. Justice either didn't know or didn't care. Lord Russell of Liverpool did not seem to know. Paul Foot makes no mention if it. Yet Bedford was, as Woffinden nonchalantly acknowledged, "an area he knew reasonably well". Hanratty's mother had a sister, Anne, who lived in Bedford. Hanratty was close to "Auntie Annie", "Uncle Fred" and their daughter Eileen. As a child Hanratty spent some summer holidays with the Cunninghams, along with his brother Michael. Rather strangely – it is not clear why – Annie Cunningham (1895-1977) was later buried with her nephew James.

Bedford provided a refuge for Hanratty during a disturbed adolescence and difficulties at home. In July 1952 he had been found by the police lying unconscious in the road, having come off his bicycle for reasons unknown. He remained unconscious for ten hours. After a few days in hospital he was sent home. He promptly ran away. Four weeks later the police contacted his family. Their son James was in the Royal Sussex Hospital in Brighton. He had been found once again lying unconscious in a street, having collapsed from self-neglect (presumably lack of food and drink). All this was indicative of a deeply disturbed adolescent who, for whatever reasons, plainly did not regard his family home as a place of comfort and security.

He was transferred to a mental hospital – St Francis' Hospital, Haywards Heath. The doctors suspected a brain haemorrhage and performed an exploratory craniotomy. But there was nothing physically wrong with him. The consultant psychiatrist, in the language of the time, diagnosed James

Hanratty as a "Mental Defective".

The operation had involved him having all his hair shaved off. He was returned home looking like a freak. But instead of staying with his family he was packed off to Bedford for two weeks, to stay with the Cunninghams. The report of Dr Toakley, the neurological registrar at St Francis' Hospital, stated "We have written to his own doctor, and in an attempt to solve family difficulties, have persuaded his parents to let him stay with his aunt."

Something was very wrong at home and Auntie Annie in Bedford was evidently the solution to those immediate difficulties. The report also noted that when Hanratty ran away from home the clothes he wore "were his way of striving for independence". Perhaps he favoured the nascent Teddy Boy look, with tapered trousers and a long narrow tie. The older James Hanratty, of course, became obsessed with looking smart, trim, successful, affluent.

We know virtually nothing of what his parents James and Mary Hanratty were really like in their younger days, or what the young James's relationship with his three brothers was like. We know nothing of life at 12 Sycamore Grove. But when Hanratty talked to the psychiatrists at Haywards Heath there was a suggestion "that his home life was very unhappy and unstable, that he was frightened of his mother and had no filial feelings towards his father, although none of this has been substantiated."

We know enough of Hanratty's background to understand that when he took his prisoners on the road to Bedford his choice of destination was neither haphazard nor innocent. It was the world turned upside down again and another tribute to the power that a handgun gave him. He had been sent to Bedford on more than one occasion. Now he was making others go there. Except, of course, that he hadn't really thought about what he would do with them once he got there.

10   Deadman's Hill

> Dick became convinced that Perry was that rarity, "a natural killer" – absolutely sane, but conscienceless, and capable of dealing, with or without motive, the coldest-blooded deathblows.
>
> Truman Capote, *In Cold Blood* (1966)

It had been a long night and Hanratty was tired. He was never very good at planning things in advance. He was always impulsive and indecisive. It ws still the middle of the night. He could put a decision off until later. First he needed to tie these people up. He needed a good kip. He needed time to think.

The gunman told his captives he had to tie them up. They begged him not to shoot them. Just take the car and go, they urged. But he didn't want to do that. Not yet. He had power; he didn't want to give it up.

"If I was going to shoot you I would have done it before now," Hanratty said, with impeccable logic. It must have given them hope. All this long, baffling night Michael and Valerie had resisted the gunman in small ways but had never attempted anything drastic, like deliberately crashing the car, or attempting to disarm him. They had done what any couple in their position would have done, which was to hope that in the end the gunman would at worst steal their car and leave them standing at the roadside in the dark.

There was a rug in the Morris and the gunman said: "What about cutting that rug up?" They pointed out that there was nothing to cut it with. Hanratty made Gregsten get out of the car. They went to the boot to look for something suitable. A seach of the tool kit produced a piece of rope. Hanratty made Gregsten take off his tie and get back into the car. He told Storie to turn round and face him and put her hands together in front of her. She appeared to submit but in fact resisted. "As he put the tie against my wrists I held them apart very slightly." This left the tie loose. Next he tied the rope to her wrists, securing one end to the door handle. It was done very clumsily and ineffectively. Hanratty wasn't any good doing things like this. He had learning difficulties and poor co-ordination.

Now he needed to tie Gregsten up. There was a duffel bag containing laundry at Storie's feet. What happened next is far from clear. According to Valerie Storie the gunman said to Gregsten, "Give me that bag up." Michael Gregsten picked it up with both hands, turned to his left, and just as he was lifting it over the back of the seat Hanratty fired two shots into his head in quick succession, at point blank range. In the confined space of the Morris Minor the noise was tremendous. Michael Gregsten collapsed forward over the steering wheel. There was so much blood pouring out that Storie could hear it in the darkness. She screamed.

Hanratty shouted angrily at her to stop. Valerie Storie, as ever uncowed by her captor, retorted: "You shot him, you bastard! Why did you do that?"

The gunman replied: "He frightened me. He moved too quickly. I got frightened."

Gregsten's body moved – the final muscular spasms of a dying man – and flopped back against the seat. His head fell back.

When the Home Office pathologist Keith Simpson examined Michael Gregsten's body at Bedford mortuary the next day he estimated that he had been shot between 3am and 4am. Valerie Storie believed it was earlier than this and that the killing had occurred at around 2.15am.

Michael Gregsten, Simpson later wrote, had been "shot 'through and through' from left ear to right cheek. The skin was tattooed round the entry wounds, and the range could not have been more than inch or two; the shots had evidently been fired in rapid succession, before the head had moved." Simpson concluded that Valerie Storie's account of the shooting of Gregsten and, afterwards, herself, and of the sexual assault on her, was borne out completely by the medical evidence.

Paul Foot described Hanratty as "essentially gentle and harmless" and says that Acott could not find a single episode of violence in his past. He was echoed by Bob Woffinden, who became distinctly lachrymose as, with violins playing faintly in the background, he described Hanratty's arrest for rape and murder: "it was all over for the gentle fugitive". At the trial Woffinden (who was not there) describes Hanratty as appearing "pleasant" and says "Many were struck by his deference, his general mildness of manner and what appeared to be his essential openness." This is to ignore all those who found the man in the dock cocky and arrogant. Moreover none of the crime journalists who attended the trial seem to have regarded Hanratty as anything other than guilty. In the end, however mild-mannered the defendant may have appeared to some observers, the jury were unanimous in agreeing that he was the murderer (and, it followed, the rapist).

In any case, apart from displaying a curiously sentimental reluctance to acknowledge the human capacity for explosive acts of violence, Foot and Woffinden's claims are not biographically accurate. Hanratty, far from possessing an "essential openness", was a serial liar and a man of the shadows, who used a pseudonym even for the most banal transaction, like sending flowers to his mother. He could also, on occasion, act in an impulsive, unpredictable and violent manner. On the evening of 26 July, less than a month before the A6 murder, Hanratty was involved in a brawl in Liverpool. He described how he had been approached by two men, one wearing a "knuckleduster", who demanded the cash he had on him. Woffinden excuses what happened next on the grounds of self-defence. Hanratty "knew a fight was about to start. He punched the one who had spoken to him." Hanratty's account of the brawl may well be accurate. However, the essential point is that he struck the first blow. *He* committed the assault. Until

Hanratty punched the man nothing had occurred apart from allegedly threatening words.

What occured inside the Morris Minor was essentially a replay of what had happened in Liverpool. As Michael Gregsten turned with the duffel bag, Hanratty sensed – rightly or wrongly – that Gregsten was going to throw the bag in his face. Hanratty reacted impulsively. He lashed out to defend himself. But this time he didn't throw a punch. This time he pulled the trigger of his .38 Enfield revolver. Twice. He may have done it on impulse, without thinking. It was, nevertheless, a deliberate and calculated act. To pull the trigger on a.38 Enfield requires effort. It is not a gun with a delicate, hypersensitive firing mechanism that can go off almost by accident. When Hanratty pulled back the trigger he knew what he was doing. At that range the consequences were not in doubt. Whatever may have been going through Hanratty's mind at that moment, he was shooting to kill.

There was another act of extreme violence in James Hanratty's past. He was eighteen years old when it happened, in August 1955. The year before he had been made to have psychiatric treatment at the Portman Clinic. They had tried to make sense of him at the Institute for the Study and Treatment of Delinquency. But they had failed. And so it was that in August 1955, in the boys' wing at Wormwood Scrubs, he had slashed his wrists. But, inept as always, he had botched it. They saved his life. Afterwards the prison medical officer diagnosed him as "a potential psychopath with hysterical tendencies".

There is no reason to think that the killing of Michael Gregsten was in any way premeditated. Hanratty had ample opportunity to execute him from the moment he first rapped on the car window in the cornfield. In the end it was the tragic, unintended consequence of a bizarre set of circumstances – Hanratty obtaining a gun, coming across the two lovers in their car, deciding on impulse to rob them, enjoying his new-found power, and stretching the situation out. Hanratty was unintelligent, uneducated, a criminal simpleton, at the very least a sociopath. He was impulsive and indecisive, unable to think through the consequences of his actions. Within a week of leaving prison after a tough three-year sentence he was stupid enough to leave his fingerprints behind at the scene of a burglary. That meant he would get a five-year stretch when the police caught up with him. A gun in the hands of a man like Hanratty opened up a vista of lethal possibilities.

With the sound of the gunshots still ringing in their eardrums and the blood pouring loudly from the fatally wounded victim, Hanratty and Storie were both in a state of shock. Afterwards, she recalled, they argued. Time blurred. Was it for five minutes – or fifteen?

> I said to the man, "For God's sake, let me get Mike to a doctor quick. I will do anything you want if you will let me take the car and get Mike to a doctor." He said, "Be quiet, I'm finking." I said, "Let me move Mike. I will take the car. I will take you anywhere you want to go but let me try and find help for Mike." He said, "No, he's dead," so I said, "Let me take Mike somewhere. I must try and get help." Then he said, "Yes, alright, he is not dead." I said, "If I see a car coming I will stop them and ask them to give you a lift. I will not say anything about what has happened as long as we can get help." Again he said, "Be quiet will you, I'm finking."

Perhaps twenty minutes elapsed. One moment the gunman would say "No, Mike is not dead" and the next, "Yes, he is." By calling his victim "Mike" Hanratty was, characteristically (and just as he did at his trial) absorbing and imitating the phraseology of someone else. Storie remembered how the gunman "kept contradicting himself" – again, just as Hanratty did under cross-examination. She added, "I thought he was slightly round the twist."

Finally Hanratty seemed to understand that there was no

possibility of Michael Gregsten being still alive. He had killed a man. He was now a murderer. He had crossed a threshold. If he were caught and successfully prosecuted he would be hanged.

From the duffel bag he removed a pair of pyjama trousers and used it to cover the dead man's bloody head. His thoughts now turned (or perhaps returned) to rape. He no longer had anything more to lose. A conviction for rape was nothing compared to a murder charge.

From the moment Hanratty first entered the Morris Minor with his gun Valerie Storie was at risk of sexual assault. He may have contemplated it from the beginning, when he wanted to lock Michael Gregsten in the boot. Now that obstacle was finally removed. Moreover, in her terror, Valerie Storie had said, "*I will do anything you want* if you will let me take the car ..." To Hanratty that might have seemed like an invitation to have sex with her.

Valerie was the kind of young woman who was outside Hanratty's subterranean world. She had class. In normal circumstances he would never have been able to persuade her into bed. She was an educated middle-class civil servant; he was a semi-literate oaf whose major activity was burglary. Perhaps that made her all the more desirable.

He asked Valerie her name. She told him. He asked her to get into the back of the car with him. She refused. The gunman ordered her to kiss him. She refused. He threatened to shoot her. She turned to face him. He had removed the handkerchief that masked him.

A car passed and she caught a brief glimpse of his face in the momentary illumination flooding in from its headlights. "The light was only on his face for a few seconds as the vehicle went past and then we were in complete darkness again." This was to become a key moment in the case. What did the gunman look like? What did Hanratty look like? Was it possible that Valerie Storie had misidentified her attacker?

*

The first person to speak to Storie after her long ordeal was over was John Kerr, an eighteen-year-old Oxford university student. According to Kerr, Storie told him that the man had "big staring eyes, fairish brown hair" and was "slighty taller" than Storie herself, who was five feet three and a half inches tall.

The next person to listen to Storie's account of what had happened was Detective Constable Gwen Woodwin. The first description of the suspect was then issued by police: "man aged about 25 years, smooth face, big eyes, smartly dressed in a dark grey or black suit. When speaking says 'fings' instead of 'things'."

This description, given to a sympathetic woman constable, was an essentially accurate description of James Hanratty, whose twenty-fifth birthday was just a couple of months away. And of course Hanratty's single most distinctive feature was indeed his big, staring eyes. It is a feature which is evident in some photographs of his face (and which is not noticeable at all in any of the pictures of Peter Alphon). It was something which became very evident during Hanratty's trial: "In moments of agitation, or when he was striving to get a point across, his large blue eyes did seem to be almost protruding from his head."

Then Detective Superintendent Acott barged in, a perfect specimen of Metropolitan Police *machismo* (a tradition which seems to have worsened in the twenty-first century, reaching depths which would probably have shocked even an old-school sexist cop like the DS). Acott didn't believe a word of Valerie Storie's account: "from the start it was treated as highly suspect". After Acott's questioning a revised description was issued: "Man aged about 30, height 5' 6", proportionate build, dark brown hair, clean-shaven, brown eyes, fairly pale face, has a distinct East End of London accent. Wearing dark lounge suit and believed tie and shirt."

This was still a recognisable picture of Hanratty with one very obvious exception: he did not have brown eyes. In fact Valerie Storie never at any time described the gunman as having brown eyes. Nor, as the first description wrongly stated, had she ever said that the man had told her his name was Brown. The word "brown" had mistakenly crept into police statements from the very beginning, probably as the result of someone misreading their own or someone else's hasty, barely decipherable handwriting. What a campaigner like Paul Foot failed to appreciate was that a central plank of his argument – that Valerie Storie was an unreliable witness, and that the gunman had had brown eyes – was simply false. Probably the error resulted from the misreading of a word beginning with "b" – "big eyes" or "blue eyes" or "big blue eyes".

On 26 August Valerie Storie assisted a photofit expert as he endeavoured to produce an image of the wanted man. On 28 August, after further police questioning, a revised description of the wanted man was issued: "aged between 25 and 30, about 5' 6", proportionately built, slender, brown hair, clean-shaven, a very smooth pale face, with icy-blue large saucer-like eyes". In a later version this last part became "very large, pale blue, staring eyes and brown hair combed back with no parting". These were all reasonably accurate descriptions of James Hanratty.

The Hanratty campaign built itself on a number of rotten foundations. One was that Valerie Storie was an inconsistent witness, who changed her testimony. For example, it was argued, she told the first person to speak to her that her assailant had "fairish brown hair". But how perceptive was John Kerr? He turned up for work as a road traffic enumerator by the roadside RAC box located just before the entrance to the lay-by for vehicles heading north to Bedford. The bodies of Gregsten and Storie lay near the far end of the lay-by. They were fully visible to him but he did not notice them. If he saw them at all it was as discarded rubbish. His attention, not unnaturally, was focused on his job – watching out for passing motor vehicles and recording their passage.

Valerie Storie was groaning and calling for help but Kerr did not hear her. He was there for 35 minutes before someone noticed her. It was a passing pedestrian, an elderly man, who first came across the couple. He walked over to Kerr and told him that there was a distressed woman lying there.

Kerr went over to see for himself. It was a shocking and traumatic scene for a teenager to witness. Firstly there was the bloodied corpse of a man. Beside him on the ground was a woman who had been shot several times. Her skirt was up above her waist, exposing her legs and knickers.

When Kerr spoke to her he did not hear her clearly. He was in a state of shock and Valerie Storie was struggling to speak through the pain of her injuries. It is hardly surprising that communication between them was garbled. Valerie told him her name. He wrote it down as "Mary". Kerr believed that she told him that her attacker had "fairish brown hair". She may have said "fairly brown hair" or she may have said something completely different. Thirty years later Kerr recalled that he had asked if she meant hair the same colour as his, and she had agreed. His hair was light brown and, he insisted, had not changed at all in colour over three decades. But this kind of anecdotal evidence is of limited value, subject as it is to the vagaries of time and the fallibility of human memory. Memory, notoriously, is not so much comparable to a photograph as to a painting which is altered with each new remembering.

Besides, a crucial question is what exactly was the colour of James Hanratty's hair in the early hours of Wednesday 23 August 1961? The answer is that we don't know. Woffinden describes him as normally having "fair auburn hair". Auburn, of course, signifies a reddish brown. But to his friends Hanratty was known as "Ginger". Some time in mid-July or later his hair had been dyed black by Carole France and on 5 August she touched it up with more dye. When Hanratty turned up three days after killing Michael Gregsten, Carole France commented that the dye was beginning to fade from his hair. She therefore re-dyed it black. We consequently don't know what Hanratty's hair really looked like in the week of the murder.

Apart from Valerie Storie's description of her attacker, the only testimony we have on this subject is that of Eileen Cunningham. She claimed that she saw Hanratty five days before the crime and that his hair was "absolutely jet black". She helpfully added, "You would not have been able to tell he was really ginger." But her statement is highly suspect because she was Hanratty's cousin and she was keen to help prove that he was not the gunman. Her statement was not made to the police but to the defence.

There is one interesting piece of testimony which indicates what Hanratty's hair probably looked like at the time he shot Michael Gregsten. On 2 September 1961 Carole France re-dyed Hanratty's hair black. On 11 September Hanratty met an acquaintance named Laurence Lanigan who noticed the unusual colour of Hanratt's hair. "You could see it was dyed because it seemed to have two shades." In other words, after just nine days the black dye used by Carole France had dramatically faded. At the time of the A6 murder some two weeks had elapsed since Hanratty had had his hair re-dyed by Carole France. This suggests it probably did look some shade of brown. If someone whose hair is naturally ginger has it dyed black and then after two weeks the colour is fading then, in the passing light of a car at night, it may well have appeared "fairly brown".

Paul Foot used two photographs of Peter Alphon alongside the photofit image of the suspect based on Valerie Storie's description. He thought there were striking similarities. But the pictures are undated and unsourced and were probably taken in the period when Alphon first became involved with Jean Justice. Alphon was consciously trying to style himself as the A6 killer. Louis Blom-Cooper, a firm believer in Hanratty's guilt, used a photograph of Peter Alphon looking nothing at all like either of the two photofits, with a completely different hairstyle to that of the wanted man. At Hanratty's trial the clerk of the court held up a copy of the photofit based on Storie's description and there were smiles and whispers. The face shown greatly resembled that of the clerk of the court himself. Charlotte France believed that one of the photofit faces *did* look like Hanratty. In the revised edition of his book on the case Bob Woffinden grudgingly conceded that "one of the original identikit pictures had vaguely resembled Hanratty".

At the end of the twentieth century just six pictures of the adult James Hanratty were in the public domain. The striking thing about them is how different he looks in them. Adolescent in some, older beyond his years in others. He looks normal; he looks weird and threatening. His hair is smart; his hair needs a comb. He looks boyish and innocent; he looks like a man, with a man's secrets. His face seems puffy; his face appears lean and smooth. He stares back at the observer, faraway in time, his living human reality lost forever.

In one of the photographs he does indeed bear a resemblance to the photofit based on Valerie Storie's description. His hair is slicked back and his eyes are big, prominent, inescapable. This is the image which none of the books asserting his innocence uses, other than the Penguin edition of Foot's book, which puts it on the cover but in a deliberately distorted and incomplete form which drains the image of its power and significance.

In the darkness of the lay-by at Deadman's Hill James Hanratty told Valerie Storie a second time to kiss him, or he would shoot her. Reluctantly, she acquiesced. Then he sat back in the car with the gun still in his right hand. Perhaps he was thinking.

At Wormwood Scrubs the teenage Hanratty had been diagnosed as a potential psychopath. When Hanratty was in Durham Prison the prison doctor identified him as an actual psychopath. But what does it mean to say that James Hanratty was a psychopath? The actor Brian Cox, reflecting on playing characters who are very bad, commented "you cannot act evil; the element of evil is dormant. Evil manifests in action. Power and control are the active ingredients that bring evil awake." Power and control – exactly what possession of a handgun gave to James Hanratty. Cox described the conclusion of the consulting prison psychologist Gustave Gilbert at the Nuremburg trials. Evil involved an absence of empathy: "the individual's psyche suffers from what can only be described as a form of spiritual stroke resulting in an emotional blackout".

Absence of empathy was at the core of James Hanratty's personality, as was illustrated time and time again. When he was given privileges and placed in a position of trust at Maidstone Prison he promptly abused this favourable treatment. The episode "underlined Hanratty's social isolation from the prisoner group". Hanratty's father gave up his job with the council and sacrificed his pension rights in order to finance a window-cleaning business and keep his eldest son away from crime. The moment his parents went away on holiday Hanratty abandoned the window-cleaning equipment in a garden and disappeared to his old criminal haunts.

Hanratty had no understanding of the feelings of others; no notion of gratitude or obligation. When Terry Evans bumped into Hanratty in Rhyl in July 1961 he found him work at the local fairground and took this stranger home with him, generously putting him up for the night. Hanratty repaid him by stealing a pair of shoes from him and abandoning the fairground job. He was lazy and unwilling to try his hand at salaried employment. Breaking into houses and nicking stuff was a much easier way of acquiring money.

Hanratty was ruthlessly egocentric and utterly incapable of empathising with any other person. Inside, he was emotionally blank. A researcher at Maidstone Prison who observed his behaviour said that what was striking about Hanratty was his "gross social and emotional immaturity".

The last letter which Derek Bentley wrote before his execution in 1953 was about the family cats and dogs and the marriage of his sister Iris. It bubbles with life, with everything in the future that would be lost to him. Compare that with the very last recorded words of James Hanratty, shortly before dawn prior to his hanging. Hanratty was concerned not with people or feelings but with an inanimate object – his car. "But please Mick," he wrote to his brother, "remember it is a very fast car, and whatever you do take care when you drive it. With a car of this standard it is very powerful."

Here, at the end, the old themes resurface: power, control, and worrying about his brother's driving, just as he fussed about Michael Gregsten's. As a sociopath, Hanratty was unable to discern any irony in someone like himself, who had never passed a driving test, and whose own driving (from what little we know about it) seems to have been execrable, passing on sage advice to others.

Next Valerie Storie leaned over the seat and with her left hand tried to grab the gun. Once again Valerie was displaying her feisty side – her refusal to submit to everything this armed thug demanded. But Hanratty was bigger and stronger than her. "That was a silly thing to do," he complained. "I thought you were sensible. I cannot trust you now."

He told her to get into the back seat with him.

She refused.

He repeated his demand.

Again she refused.

Exasperated, he said: "I will count five and if you have not got in I will shoot."

She had no choice. But even now she resisted. "I got out of the car slowly, trying to play for time, hoping that someone would come by. He was still sitting in the car and he opened his rear door and with the gun on me, pointing towards me all the time, he said 'Come on, get in.' I said no. So he got out and, with the gun almost touching me, said 'Get in.' I got in the back of the car. He followed me and shut the door."

She was in the off-side passenger seat, immediately behind Michael Gregsten's corpse.

Hanratty tried to kiss her again. He groped her. Resourceful as ever, she managed to slip the seven one-pound notes from her bra into her raincoat pocket.

> "He tried to touch me and he tried to kiss me. Then he said, 'Take off your knickers.' I said no. Again he threatened to shoot me if I did not agree. So I was forced to take them off. He then put the gun on the back window shelf of the car."

Hanratty, who was wearing black gloves, tried to take them off. He found this difficult. He wasn't used to wearing gloves. He was clumsy. He held out his hands and said to Storie: "Pull."

She could feel that the gloves were of "a very thin nylon-type texture". Having got the one glove off he put it in his pocket. He undid the zip of the fly of his trousers and pushed her back into a half-sitting, half-lying position, with the bag of washing wedged under her back.

His erect penis protruded.

"Put me in," he said.

She obeyed.

Valerie told the police that the rape took only "a very, very short time, a minute or so." She thought Hanratty seemed strangely detached. This perhaps confirms the idea that this rape was about power, possession and punishment rather than sexual pleasure. "He didn't seem particularly excited," she remembered. "He seemed sort of anxious to get it over with. He didn't seem sexually excited."

As a rape victim Valerie Storie had to endure not only the rape but also the ordeal of having the fact that she had been raped given the widest publicity in the national press. She was named. Her photograph was published. The world knew what had happened to her. After this she had the further ordeal of having to appear at Hanratty's trial and face her attacker. She also had to endure the incomprehension of male interpreters and commentators. Those attitudes were perpetuated in later years by those who campaigned for Hanratty, who insisted that her evidence was unreliable, and that she had sent an innocent man to the gallows. The title of Paul Foot's book, *Who Killed Hanratty?*, insinuated that Valerie Storie was among the guilty, along with those who investigated the crime and later managed the judicial process. Foot evaded the actual details of the rape and with him, as with Justice, Woffinden and others, the wheel, as so often in masculine constructions and interpretations of rape, turned full circle: the victim was in some way guilty and at fault for everything that occurred.

Detective Chief Superintendent Acott, personifying attitudes which were institutional in the Metropolitan Police and which persisted for decades afterwards, remarked that Valerie Storie's account of her ordeal was initially regarded with extreme scepticism and suspicion. "It sounded so fantastic that from the start it was treated as highly suspect – like the majority of accounts given by women who have made allegations of rape."

Paul Foot and Bob Woffinden's hero Jean Justice suggested that Valerie Storie wasn't really raped at all. "It is significant here," he commented, "that one of the nurses from the Bedford General Hospital said in evidence at Ampthill that the state and position of Valerie Storie's knickers indicated that the girl had not been raped in the classical sense of the word." Here, grotesquely, Justice insinuated that the sex was consensual. This was a coarse and incomprehending misreading of Storie's wish to put her knickers back on after her assault, which Hanratty allowed her to do. Ironically this ensured that Hanratty's DNA became imprinted on the fabric, allowing his guilt to be established scientifically some four decades later. But of course the deluded Jean Justice was also convinced that Peter Alphon was telling the truth when he fabricated the voyeuristic fantasy that he was the one who had had sex with Storie and that she was "relaxed" as he penetrated her. Her co-operation, according to Alphon, made "a difficult task just about possible even under the cramped conditions that obtained".

Complacent and patronising male attitudes to rape also distorted the prosecution case. According to the argument presented at the Bedford trial Hanratty was a crazed sex maniac who had planned the assault on Valerie Storie from the very beginning. This made no sense at all. Neither did the arguments of the campaigners, who introduced complacent and highly prejudiced assumptions about rape to bolster their case for gentle Jim Hanratty's innocence. Foot and Woffinden both made the point that Hanratty had ready access to sex through his use of prostitutes (or so he claimed – this may have just been another of his innumerable lies and deceits). If James Hanratty wanted sexual gratification, the argument ran, he did not have to resort to rape. But that simply displayed a wilful incomprehension of what rape can involve.

Hanratty's rape of Valerie Storie was not simply about gratification. It was about punishent and humiliation. This woman had spent the entire night disagreeing and arguing with Hanratty. She was being punished because she was a woman who was not compliant. She was a woman who stood up for herself – the kind of woman James Hanratty had no experience of. She was difficult, independent, with opinions of her own. Gregsten had played the game; Gregsten had done what he had been told. Valerie had not. She was also a woman way outside his league.

In a way, she fascinated him. He kept asking her what her name was. Valerie told him, but he couldn't seem to remember it. He kept forgetting and asking her again what it as. She would tell him and then he would forget again. She estimated that six times he asked her name. Six times he forgot it.

The gunman's mental processes were absolutely characteristic of James Hanratty. He had learning difficulties. He found it difficult to process information. He always preferred to let someone else dial a telephone number for him if at all possible. He could never remember names. Not Terry Evans's. Not even

Louise Anderson's. He stayed in Louise's flat, he took her out for meals, he even proposed marriage to her. But he just couldn't remember her surname.

But not even Louise was like this woman. Valerie Storie was different. She spoke BBC English in a BBC voice. She surely had enjoyed the kind of privileges which had always been denied to James Hanratty. She had a car and a boyfriend. Hanratty didn't have a car and he didn't have a partner. This woman had everything. She not only had to be punished and humiliated for being difficult and hostile. In raping her Hanratty was having his revenge on a society which had made him what he was – uneducated, a loner, a prisoner. The best years of his young life had been spent in prison cells. Now he had the chance to even up the score.

Two years after the A6 murder a novel would be published about the abyss of language, culture and understanding which can exist between an uneducated working-class male and a cultured middle-class female. John Fowles's *The Collector* is a novel about an abduction and it may even owe something to the A6 case (it seems to have been written around the time of the crime and subsequent trial). The voice of Fowles's inadequate, inarticulate working-class kidnapper bears some striking resemblances to the voice of James Hanratty in his prison letters.

Fowles returned to the theme of the war between the classes in his short story "Poor Koko". This is the tale of a working-class housebreaker and his unexpected meeting with a cultured middle-class author. The burglar is not simply interested in theft. Confronted by the representative of a class he loathes he punishes the author by tying him up and then burning the manuscript of an unfinished book which the author has spent four years writing. "Poor Koko" is the fable of "tongueless man" and his destructive capacity; of the revenge of the underclass.

Valerie Storie thought that it was about 2.30am when the gunman raped her. As a psychopath, Hanratty was not perturbed by the smell of fresh blood which pervaded the car or the presence of a corpse propped up in the driver's seat. After he had ejaculated Hanratty withdrew his penis, tucked it back into his underpants, zipped up his fly, and sat back.

What he said next is not mentioned by Blom-Cooper, Jean Justice, Paul Foot or Bob Woffinden. "You have not had much sex have you?" he said to the woman he had just raped. What he meant by this crass remark, presumably, is that Valerie Storie displayed no sexual enjoyment. It reflected Hanratty's impoverished personality in a number of ways. Firstly, he was, or so he said, a regular user of prostitutes. If this was true, perhaps they complimented him on his amazing lovemaking and simulated delight as he reached his climax. Secondly, he displayed the coldness and lack of emotion associated with psychopaths. Thirdly, he had what was for its time a not uncommon chauvinistic male attitude to rape – that a woman being raped might begin to enjoy the experience (a belief which finds dramatic expression in the director Sam Peckinpah's 1971 film *Straw Dogs*).

The final irony is that Hanratty's rather gloating remark was almost certainly inaccurate. Although he adopted the role of experienced man of the world, his own sexual experience was very limited, since he had spent much of his adolescence and early manhood in prison cells. Most of the sexual activity of his short life would have been masturbation. Valerie Storie had probably had far more sex than Hanratty in the past two years, or even in the five-month period since his release from Strangeways Prison on 24 March 1961. The only information about Hanratty's sex life came from Hanratty himself – a man who was a habitual liar. It was also in his interest to portray himself as something of a Don Juan at a time when it was commonly believed that rapists were motivated by sexual frustration.

Hanratty looked at his watch. He was anxious about the time. He looked again, and then again. It was something he did when he was under enormous stress. Valerie said, "Well, look, I must call you something." The rape had been a hideous parody of sexual intimacy but when she said, "What shall I call you?" Hanratty, embarrassed, blurted out the truth. "He sort of said, 'Jim.' That's the only name, obviously not his proper name I shouldn't think."

To campaigners for Hanratty's innocence this moment was clear proof that he was framed, as no one would be so stupid as to give their real name in such circumstances. Even Valerie Storie didn't believe that her attacker was really telling the truth when he said his name was Jim. But this is to misunderstand Hanratty's personality. He had learning difficulties. He wasn't very bright. Valerie Storie's question took him by surprise. He blurted out the truth.

In context, it's entirely credible that Hanratty did indeed say his own name. Campaigners, however, wrenched this admission from its context and utterly misrepresented it. Bob Woffinden described how the gunman in the car "offered a few scraps of information about himself, suggesting that he spent a considerable time in custody ... and inviting Valerie Storie to call him 'Jim'. The car stopped at least twice: once at a garage, and once at a milk machine." This is a deeply dishonest and manipulative account of Valerie Storie's testimony. By rearranging the chronology of the gunman's conversation Woffinden made it seem as if he had announced that his name was Jim long before they reached the lay-by at Deadman's Hill. Put like that the name-uttering is ripped from its context and the case for a frame-up becomes more plausible.

A similarly grossly misleading version of what occurred was put forward in Woffinden's Channel 4 documentary *Hanratty: The Mystery of Deadman's Hill*. The authoritative voiceover by an unseen, unidentified narrator, asserts that the A6 killer had said "Call me Jim". This false statement then cuts to a shot of a man saying "That was a set-up. Hanratty was framed, definitely framed." The man voicing this opinion can hardly be regarded as an impartial commentator since he is none other than the accused man's father, James Hanratty senior. But this collage is essentially meretricious since the gunman never at any time said "Call me Jim". He did not "invite" Valerie Storie to call him that.

The name Jim was torn from his lips by a sudden, unexpected question from the woman he had just raped. He was caught off guard. In response to her sudden question, she remembered, "He sort of said, 'Jim.'" In other words, suddenly taken by surprise, he blurted it out. He muttered it, half in embarrassment, half in a kind of grotesque parody of post-coital pillow talk. Probably in some part of his mind he already knew that he would have to kill this woman. She was the only living witness to his killing of the car's driver. Hanratty had nothing to lose by telling her the truth.

Besides, this wasn't the first time James Hanratty had been stupid enough to admit his real identity and incriminate himself. When he went into a jeweller's in Liverpool just a month before the A6 murder he successfully sold some stolen silverware for twenty-five shillings. The jeweller suddenly and unexpectedly produced a purchase ledger and asked him to sign it. "This took me by surprise," Hanratty admitted, "so I used my own name and address." Despite regularly using a bogus name, "Jim Ryan", and bogus addresses, Hanratty lacked the imagination to come up with a fake identity. What happened after the rape was no different to what happened at the jeweller's. When Valerie Storie took him by surprise and turned the tables on him by demanding to know his name he couldn't stop himself mumbling "Jim".

After telling her his real name Hanratty may, of course, have decided that there could be no other choice than to shoot her. In demanding to know his name, and by getting him to blurt it out, Storie may well have inadvertently signed her own death sentence – or what would have been a death sentence had Hanratty not once again proved himself to be a blundering, dull-witted incompetent.

Storie urged him to take the car and go. She warned him it was almost daybreak. Once again he said, "Be quiet, will you. I am finking."

He decided to take the car. But first it was necessary to remove Michael Gregsten's body. He said: "You will have to get him out. I must not get blood on me." She managed to manoeuvre the top half of her lover's cold body out of the car but then his feet caught in the pedals. He was too heavy to lift. She told Hanratty he would have to help.

He managed to get the legs free and out of the Morris. Storie dragged the corpse along the side of the car, then round the back. She laid it at the edge of the concrete strip, beside the ribbon of vegetation which separated the lay-by from the A6. She then asked Hanratty if she could get her things from the car, which he agreed to. She put her basket and the duffel bag with the laundry on the ground beside Gregsten. She urged the gunman to take the car and go. He asked her to start the car for him and show him the position of the gears. This she did. He wanted to know how the lights worked and she showed him. Leaving the car with its engine running, Valerie returned to the body of her lover. Hanratty followed her. He seemed undecided about what to do. He told her he was worried she would go for help. She promised not to and urged him to depart. The car stalled. She re-started it and showed him again how the gears worked. (Already Hanratty, whose learning difficulties were severe, had forgotten.) The gunman sat there in the driver's seat with the engine running. Valerie returned to the corpse and sat down on the ground. The gunman got out of the car and walked up to her. He said, "I think I had better hit you on the head or something to knock you out, or else you will go for help." Storie promised not to and once again urged him to go. She stood up. She put her hand in her raincoat pocket and took out one of the pound notes she had hidden there. She held it out. "Here you are. You can have that if you will go quickly."

Hanratty took the pound note. He walked two or three metres, then turned and opened fire. There were four bullets left in the chamber. The first tore into her. The second sliced into her spine. She lost all feeling in her legs and collapsed. Hanratty fired twice more. He reloaded and fired again. One hit her. Altogether five bullets had penetrated her body. The second one paralysed her. Because of the injury it caused she would never walk again.

Valerie Storie lay perfectly still. She closed her eyes and pretended to be dead. Hanratty prodded her body. He stood over her, then, evidently believing her to be dead, he returned to the car. He got in and slammed the door. He put the headlights on and drove off, back the way they had come.

It was some time between three and four in the morning, Wedesday 22 August 1961. The abduction that was to resonate in criminal history for decades afterwards was finally over. The mystery man with the gun was gone. One of his captives was dead. But the other, though shot five times, was still alive.

> "I was playing for time. Just for time. I played the wrong way, of course."
>
> Raymond Chandler, *The Big Sleep* (1939)

At 6.30pm on the day the mystery gunman fled Deadman's Hill, the stolen Morris Minor was found abandoned. It had been parked on a residential street in north-east London, on Avondale Crescent in Ilford, very close to Redbridge underground station on the Central Line.

It remains unclear what time Hanratty drove away from the scene of the crime. Valerie Storie believed it was around 3am, some 45 minutes after Michael Gregsten had been murdered. Keith Simpson, the pathologist, estimated that Gregsten had died some time between 3am and 4am. A traffic census taker, John Smith, reported that a car which he believed to be a Morris Minor drove past at speed a little before 4am. He was based just south of the village of Silsoe, some ten minutes drive from Deadman's Hill. But there were many other "sightings" of the getaway car that morning, once the crime had received national publicity. It is difficult to say with any confidence if any of them were accurate. Some were plainly of other cars, and the power of suggestibility necessarily qualifies these sightings.

Two which were regarded by the police as accurate involved a badly driven Morris Minor seen in daylight in the early morning in the area where the car was later found abandoned. John Skillett and Edward Blackhall were travelling west along the A12 into London when a grey Morris Minor being driven at speed almost collided with them. A little later they caught up with the car at Gant's Hill roundabout. Blackhall wound down the window and Skillett, the driver, shouted abuse at the driver, who just laughed contemptuously. Shortly afterwards they saw the driver turn right, heading towards Redbridge underground station.

Shortly after 7am James Trower was standing on Redbridge Lane when he heard a driver crunching his gears. He glanced across and saw a Morris Minor turn left into Avondale Crescent. As the car passed the driver momentarily looked across at him.

When Peter Alphon was subsequently held on suspicion of being the A6 killer and put on an identity parade James Trower was unable to identify anyone. Edward Blackhall picked out someone else. (John Skillett was away on holiday and not present.) When James Hanratty was put on an identity parade Edward Blackhall once again picked out someone else. Trower and Skillett both picked out Hanratty.

Michael Hanratty said that one of the reasons he knew his brother was innocent was because he always blushed if confronted with something he was guilty of, and his brother didn't blush when Valerie Storie identified him at the trial as her attacker. In the light of this argument it is interesting that when Trower and Skillett both picked out Hanratty he "did go very red".

Defenders of James Hanratty have never been short of ingenious excuses for the mass of circumstantial evidence indicating his guilt. Perhaps the prize should go to Lord Russell of Liverpool, who argued that even though two eye-witnesses had identified Hanratty as the driver of the Morris Minor in Ilford this did not mean that he was the killer. On the contrary, his Lordship argued, the killer had abandoned the car elsewhere and then Hanratty had come across it and stolen it: "the man then driving the car might merely have been 'driving it away without the consent of the owner', having found it, apparently abandoned, somewhere else." The notion that James Hanratty was wandering around before dawn on Wednesday 23 August 1961, somewhere between Bedfordshire and London, when he came upon a damaged Morris Minor with blood inside, which had been

240

abandoned by the A6 murderer, and which he then decided to steal, suggests that Lord Russell might well have enjoyed a successful career as a writer of TV crime scripts which depend on an amazing twist for their plot climax. The theory was so outlandish that not even Paul Foot or Bob Woffinden chose to incorporate it in their own convoluted conspiracy narratives.

Was the Morris Minor which Skillett, Blackhall and Trower saw the one used in the crime? In 1971 Paul Foot was in no doubt: "This was plainly the murder car, and the man driving the car was plainly the murderer." However, Charles Drayton, a milkman, said he had been in a near collision with the Morris in Bedford at 5.30am. He claimed to have made a mental note of the car's registration number: "I remembered this so well because I have always regarded 8 as my lucky number and 47 was my round number in Norwich and also the number of my house there. The letters BNH stick because they remind me of a racehorse named Bahrain owned by the late Aga Khan which I used to back each time it ran. I am quite certain about this vehicle and the index number." While Drayton's conviction that he had seen the killer's car is not in doubt its reliability is altogether more dubious. That anyone remembers a not especially memorable registration plate with this degree of accuracy for the tortuous reasoning given is highly questionable. Bob Woffinden, however, regarded it as a credible sighting.

Drayton was far from being alone in believing he had seen the killer's car. A couple reported an early morning encounter on the A6 at Deadman's Hill with a man and a stationary Morris Minor with its headlights blazing. When they stopped to offer help he swore at them and hid his face. But eleven other witnesses were convinced they had seen the Morris in Derbyshire. When this hitherto unknown fact was revealed by the Criminal Cases Review Commision in 1999, Paul Foot was ecstatic. In his eyes these revelations were another pointer to Hanratty's innocence. Contradicting what he had confidently written 28 years earlier, Foot wrote: "Two witnesses who identified Hanratty as a man they had seen driving the murder car in London on the morning after the murder were discredited by the rather shocking fact that the murder car was nowhere near London at the time." But this "shocking fact" was not a fact at all. It was a supposition, and the other sightings of Gregsten's Morris were self-cancelling, in view of the contradictory times and geographical locations involved. Besides, none of those supposed eye-witnesses saw the driver. Rather like the Rhyl alibi, the power of suggestibility was plainly involved.

Bob Woffinden argued that the Morris probably wasn't dumped on Avondale Crescent until shortly before it was found at 6.45pm. This seems most unlikely. By the afternoon of 23 August every police officer in England was looking for the car. It also has to be remembered that there were far, far fewer cars on the roads in 1961 than is the case today. Hanratty's choice of disposal site was, whether intentional or not (and probably not), a good one. A sleepy residential street with little through traffic ensured that the car would not attract immediate attention.

More evidence emerged later which suggested that every one of those momentary sightings in Derbyshire and elsewhere were mistaken. This is perhaps unsurprising, since Morris Minors were then one of the commonest cars to be seen on English roads. What was never disclosed to the defence at Hanratty's trial – and which should have been – was that the police had discovered that Michael Gregsten kept a record of the mileage each time the car was filled with petrol. On 22 August 1961, the odometer was recorded as 51,875 miles. When the vehicle was recovered in Avondale Crescent, the odometer reading was 52,107 miles. Thus, 232 miles had been travelled in this period.

It was calculated that Gregsten had driven some 57.4 miles during that Tuesday, which included among other things a trip with his two boys to a park in Watford, a visit to a launderette to collect washing, and a journey to Cippenham, where he had a haircut. The precise route taken from the cornfield to the A6 and Deadman's Hill is not known but was probably in the 58-65 miles range. This suggested that the car was driven a minimum of 109.6 miles before it was discovered abandoned on Avondale Crescent. The most direct route between Deadman's Hill and this location in Ilford was, at the time, 48.6 miles. Hanratty's route was plainly an erratic one. It was also, obviously, unplanned. Hanratty drove off in a blind panic. He knew he had to dump the car but he could only do so at a location where he could quickly put some distance between himself and the incriminating vehicle. That meant using a bus, train or underground train. But it was night-time. There was nowhere obvious to go.

Hanratty's meandering route to Ilford plainly involved him in collisions with stationary objects, judging by the damage visible on the car when it was later located. Depending on what time he drove away from the lay-by, his speed was on average somewhere between 27mph and 36mph. In those days car ownership levels were still very low. Hanratty had the roads largely to himself until daybreak, when it became easier for him to work out where he was and where he needed to go. He probably decided to dump the car on Avondale Crescent the moment he spotted the distinctive underground station sign at Redbridge station. The London underground was perfect for a quick getaway. It also gave him the chance, finally, to get some kip.

The route he took to Ilford is anyone's guess. He may have driven south until he reached London and the North Circular Road, headed east, turned off, ended up in Brentwood, and turned back. Alternatively he may have returned to St Albans, turned off east to Harlow, then travelled south-east to Brentwood to pick up the A12 into London. There are many possible permutations of the killer's route to Ilford. The execrable driving is consistent with Hanratty's panic, fatigue, learning difficulties and poor motoring skills, and the circuitous route which he seems to have taken indicates his ignorance of north east London. The location of the dumped car is also psychologically revealing. All Hanratty's past family associations were with North West London; in order to deflect suspicion away from himself he therefore chose to dump the car in an unfamiliar area, at the opposite side of London to the one he knew best.

The killer's getaway raised two questions. Did the killer's driving ability and knowledge (or rather lack of it) match Hanratty's? Secondly, why was there no forensic evidence to connect him to a blood-splattered car in which a rape had been committed? Defenders of James Hanratty argue that he was an experienced car thief and a good driver, unlike the A6 killer, who seemed perplexed by the controls of a Morris Minor and who damaged the car in the course of his getaway. When the car was found the front number plate was bent back and almost unreadable and there was a dent in the middle of the rear fender.

How good a driver was Hanratty? According to Louis Blom-Cooper, other prisoners at Maidstone Prison regarded Hanratty as a blusterer and a bit of a joke. He had boasted that when he was released he was going to get himself "a big Yankee motor": "This occasioned some raucous laughter, since he had earlier admitted that he could not drive."

Hanratty's version was different. According to him he was released from prison in February 1957 and later met a man ("Bill, from Bloxwich, Walsall") who taught him how to drive. Scrutiny of Hanratty's record of imprisonment reveals that if he had driven *every day* during his days of freedom between February 1957 and August 1961 his driving experience would have been at most fifteen months. In fact it was plainly very much less than that. When Hanratty was released from prison in March 1961 he spent much of the period before the A6 murder with no access to cars. His driving experience definitely amounted to less than a year; quite possibly less than six months. It was sporadic, not continuous. Hanratty, of course, had never taken a driving test. There is absolutely no reason to believe that Hanratty was a good driver. His personality – a sociopath, a risk-taker, impulsive, uneducated, with learning difficulties – suggests he was probably a very bad one. It is hard to imagine a careful, cautious, courteous and considerate driver. On the contrary, he was almost certainly the classic reckless driver – impatient, in a hurry, selfish, inconsiderate, egocentric.

It remains unclear if Hanratty's car thefts were solitary acts or committed with others. Nor is it clear why he was caught for those offences. His very limited experience of cars seems to have been with bigger, more expensive models. He had probably never been inside a humble Morris Minor before abducting Gregsten and Storie. The fact that he kept asking Gregsten what gear he was in seems perfectly consistent with Hanratty's learning difficulties and his inexperience. He found it difficult to process information or remember it. That the abandoned car was found damaged is also consistent with what we know about his limited driving skills. One of the few people Hanratty ever gave a ride to was Carole France, who described how he "drove zig-zagging, he was driving from side to side up the road".

The acid test of Hanratty's driving abilities was what happened when he hired a car in Limerick on 5 September 1961. Within 48 hours he crashed it, colliding with an oncoming car and damaging its offside front wing and both offside doors. Hanratty sprang out and told the other driver that he accepted full responsibility. He then handed over his details, supplying the man with a false name and a false address. Later, when he abandoned the car at Dublin Airport, it had fresh damage to it, including a dented number plate – just like Michael Gregsten's Morris when it was found.

Later that month Hanratty used the proceeds from his burglaries to buy his first car, a Sunbeam Alpine. This, too, is psychologically revealing, as this particular two-seater sports car symbolised Hollywood glamour and a devil-may-care attitude. It is the car that Cary Grant drives in Alfred Hitchcock's *To Catch a Thief* (an irony which Hanratty is unlikely to have been aware of) and which Elizabeth Taylor drives in *BUtterfield 8*. In the year that Hanratty was hanged it was the car used by James Bond in the first of the 007 films, *Dr. No* and it was still the symbol of sexiness and transgression a decade later when used in *Get Carter*.

In short, Hanratty's brand choice was a classic instance of projection: a man with a shrivelled, barren personality trying to cast himself as the sexy romantic outlaw. The Sunbeam Alpine was the glamorous carapace concealing his inadequacies with women, with language, and with human emotion.

The ever-naïve Bob Woffinden put forward a different image of Hanratty, portraying him as a harmless, gullible, gentle innocent. When the Sunbeam Alpine was purchased, Woffinden remarks that "Hanratty had overlooked some glaring mechanical defects. The rear bumper was dented, and the nearside light had been knocked out." But it seems highly unlikely that any second-hand car dealer would sell a car in that condition. It would indicate that the previous owner was a bad driver. Any dealer would fix those cosmetic issues.

It seems patently obvious that Hanratty, a serial liar, did the damage himself after buying the car and then airily claimed to people who saw it that the vehicle had been in that condition when he bought it. The dent to the back bumper matched the damage done to the Morris Minor; plainly Hanratty had a habit of reversing into stationary objects. Soon after obtaining the Sunbeam, Hanratty had to return it to the garage for repair. One of the gears had gone. Once again Woffinden makes excuses. He would have us believe that the gears were faulty when Hanratty bought the car. This is possible, of course. But an even likelier possibility is that Hanratty wrecked the gearbox himself as a result of his execrable driving.

Where did Hanratty go on Wednesday 23 August 1961 after dumping the car in Ilford? He said he had gone for a shave that morning, which may well have been true – but it was somewhere in London, not Rhyl. What else? Breakfast, coffee, sleep.

He was surely shattered, worn-out, running on empty. Nervous energy and adrenalin had kept him going through the long night. Now he needed a rest. A bath and a bed.

Maybe he went to a hotel. Somewhere cheap, where

nobody paid much attention to who came and who went. Not that he had anything to worry about. He had worn gloves. The people in the car, he believed, were both dead. There was nothing to link him to the crime. It had been random, after all. And nobody knew about his trip from Paddington to Maidenhead. This was the amazing thing. He had done something much bigger than he had ever done before and he had got away with it. He was a free man. Nobody knew his dark secrets – only Jimmy Hanratty.

A bath, rest, a long sleep.

He didn't see the news until later. When he did, he couldn't believe it. That bloody woman was still alive! He had pumped seven bullets into her (or so he thought – two had missed) and she wasn't dead. She was indestructible. He should have put shot her in the head, like the other one. Too late now.

Still, at least he was in luck about some things. The *Evening News* said he was thirty! With brown eyes and a dark brown suit. So it was alright. She hadn't really seen him at all. No one would ever guess that Jim Hanratty was the A6 killer. Now all he had to do was get rid of the gun and the spare ammo. He could do that in the morning. He knew just the place to hide it where no one would find it for weeks and weeks. Months. Maybe years.

He only stayed the one night at the hotel. A false name and address, obviously. He didn't want people remembering his face.

There was something else. He didn't just need to get rid of the gun. There was all that unused ammo, too. *Five cartons and a number of loose cartridges* ... Stashed in a left-luggage office somewhere (Paddington Station, perhaps. Or Piccadilly Circus tube). "Cartons" is a vague term. Twenty cartridges to a box is standard. But there are smaller packages, like the single-load "six-pack". Next morning Hanratty went for a short ride on a 36A. Upstairs, the back row ... It took about twenty seconds to lift up the seat and slip the stuff into the cavity. They wouldn't find it until they replaced the seat. That might be years away ...

So – no worries.

There was nothing to tie Jimmy Hanratty to the crime. But all the same, just to be on the safe side, it was best to put together a bit of an alibi. So he went to Liverpool. In the papers they had more news about the crime. There was a lot of nonsense about the killer being a hitchhiker! The more he read, the more he knew they had got it all wrong. And that made him feel very safe indeed.

In Liverpool he put his case in the left luggage and then he went for a meal. After that a trip to the flicks. *The Guns of Navarone*. It was wonderful. He wandered around a bit. He bought an evening paper and saw they were still banging on about a bloke with brown eyes. He was safe. It was time to go back to his old haunts. He sent a telegram to "Dixie": HAVING A NICE TIME. BE HOME EARLY FRIDAY MORNING FOR BUSINESS. YOURS SINCERELY. JIM. He had to give his name and address, so he said it was Mr P. Ryan, Imperial Hotel, Russell Square, London.

He caught the midnight train back to London. It was a stopping train and took all night. It got in at 5.20am. There was absolutely no point in him sending the telegram other than to establish that he had been in Liverpool. It was a sort of alibi.

Upon arrival Hanratty killed time, then turned up on the France family's doorstep at some point after 8.30am. They welcomed him in and asked what he had been up to. He said he had been in Liverpool with his aunt. (Nothing about two nights in Rhyl.) He said he had taken his aunt to the greyhound stadium there. But "Dixie" seemed a bit suspicious. He seemed to know that Hanratty had been at the Rehearsal Club on Monday night. His guest admitted that he had. He said he had gone to a hotel afterwards and then on to Liverpool the next morning. He still had his receipt from the Hotel Vienna and because "Dixie" seemed suspicious he showed it to him. Quite why "Dixie" France was so suspicious of Hanratty as the possible A6 killer, and at such an early stage, has never really become clear. But plainly he had good reasons for his suspicions, and he also appears to have felt a weight of personal responsibility when it became evident that his associate was indeed the guilty man. This, too, has never been satisfactorily explained. Did he supply Hanratty with the Enfield .38? Probably not. Did he somehow know that Hanratty had obtained a gun? Perhaps he had heard a whisper at the Rehearsal Club. His acute sense of guilt after the crime has never been satisfactorily explained.

Carole France was at work that day but the next day, Saturday, she helped him out again. The dye was fading in his hair. "Uncle Jim" asked her to re-do it, so she did. Now it was nice and black again – not like it had been when he had abducted the couple in the cornfield.

But that same day he had a horrible shock. It was all over the papers. Some cleaner had found the gun he had hidden under the seat. He couldn't believe it! So soon! That had never been part of the plan.

Someone smarter than Hanratty would have disposed of the gun more sensibly. The obvious place was the Thames. Chuck it off a bridge at night. Or even throw it from the Embankment. There were plenty of dark lonely places by the river. The same with the ammo.

And now "Dixie" was giving him those funny looks again. Hanratty decided to leave the France home.

He went off to stay with Louise.

That week there was more in the papers. This time they published two identikit pictures of the killer. One of them didn't look much like him. The other one was a closer fit.

This was the week when, very slowly, the net began to tighten around James Hanratty, both for his burglaries and for the A6 murder.

On 27 August Hanratty's parents were visited by police, who had identified him from fingerprints as having engaged in housebreaking since his release. They wished to interview him. His parents had no idea where he was. But the household had a telephone, at a time when telephone ownership was very far from universal. On 1 September Hanratty ordered a dozen roses to be sent to his mother, with the cryptic message *Don't worry – everything's all right.* Perhaps someone in the family had tipped him off about the police visit and the reason for it. If so, he knew the bad news. But there was worse to come. The papers had a new description of the killer. He was a man with staring blue eyes.

Suddenly Hanratty was behaving recklessly again. On Saturday he went to a house near the lake in Edgeware and broke in at the back. Then a woman walked up the drive. He said, "Come in." But she ran away, and so did he.

That weekend he went back to the France family home. He wanted Charlotte to wash some clothes for him. While he was there they showed the identikit pictures on the television news. Charlotte pointed to one of them and said, "Oh, doesn't that look like you?"

"Dixie" was giving him those funny looks again. That made him fink. He told them he needed to go to Ireland. Over there you could get a twelve-months driving licence on application, with no test. All you had to do was fill in a form. Then you could come back to England and use it without having to take a stupid driving test.

But of course that wasn't the real reason. The chances of being stopped by the police on an English road and asked for your licence were remote. It had never happened to him, not even driving a stolen motor.

The real reason was to get far, far away from England. It had made him a bit frightened, Charlotte thinking the identikit picture looked like him. But he had to give them a reason for going abroad and this was the best excuse he could think of.

He went out the next day and bought a new suit and two shirts and new shoes. On Monday he booked a flight to Dublin, using the name Ryan. He phoned Charlotte from London Airport. His flight had been delayed. He thought there was a man watching him. Paranoia. The knowledge of his guilt was getting to him.

He spent a night in Dublin and next morning obtained his driving licence. He could have returned to England on the next flight but of course that wasn't his real purpose in going there. The real reason was that he was nervous the police might be on to him, somehow. He felt the need to lie low and put some distance between himelf and the sites of his criminal activities.

From Dublin he went west. It was a psychologically revealing choice. He wanted to get as far away from things as he possibly could. He hired a car from Ryan's, saying his name was Ryan. They didn't bat an eyelid. He spent the night in Limerick and the next morning he drove to Tralee to watch the races and have a bet or two. Afterwards he drove to Cork. There he shared a hotel room with a commercial traveller named Gerrard Leonard. They decided to go to a dance-hall. Leonard wanted a drink. Hanratty, supposedly, did not smoke or drink, but just as he had accepted a cigarette from Michael Gregsten, now he had a lager and lime.

In the morning Hanratty asked Leonard if he would mind writing some postcards for him. But Hanratty could never remember names. Just as the A6 killer couldn't remember Valerie's name, no matter how many times she told him, now he couldn't remember Louise Anderson's. He asked Leonard to address a card to "Louise Andrew".

Later, after leaving Cork, Hanratty collided with an oncoming car. After that incident had been dealt with, he drove on. He went to Tipperary, Killarney, and Limerick, arriving back in Dublin on Friday evening. He stayed there two nights and caught the Sunday night plane back to London, arriving in the early hours. He had been out of the country exactly one week – long enough for the trail to have gone very cold and for any suspicions aroused by the identikit pictures to have ebbed.

He could not have been more wrong. On the very morning that he arrived back in London the two cartridge cases were discovered at the Hotel Vienna. At long last the police would come into possession of a tangible piece of evidence connecting James Hanratty to the A6 murder. From this point on many of the pieces would begin slowly to fall into place, indicating who the masked gunman was. But before that happened Hanratty would have the unexpected pleasure of seeing the police put two and two together to make five and arrest a wholly innocent man.

Back in London, Hanratty sold some stolen goods to Louise Anderson.

Another of the enduring mysteries of the A6 case is what exactly the relationship was between the 24-year-old Hanratty and the 48-year-old widow, Anderson. They each denied it was sexual (and if it was that would have been especially shocking for the era in which they lived). But if it was simply a friendship between crooks it was an oddly romantic one. Hanratty took her out for meals and drives in the countryside. He sent her carnations with the message LOVE FROM JIM. He stayed at her flat and he proposed marriage. This all sounds like a lot more than just friendship.

The police plainly leaned on Anderson, so that she escaped prosecution for her criminal activities as a dealer in stolen goods in return for her co-operation with the prosecution. But something had also changed in her attitude to Hanratty. She was passionately convinced of his guilt and could barely restrain herself in supplying statements to incriminate him. Her animus towards him seemed to go far beyond the co-operation exacted from her by police pressure. Her conviction of his guilt seems to have been entirely genuine rather than opportunistic. Her attitude was unchanged when Paul Foot visited her nine years later, in August 1970. As far as she was concerned Hanratty's guilt was a solid fact.

On Saturday 16 September Hanratty seized the opportunity to take Carole France out without her father (or presumably her mother) knowing. He took her to the funfair at Battersea, then over Chelsea Bridge to a pub. Paul Foot quoted from Hanratty's account of what happened: "we went across to a pub near the embankment and had a kiss and a cuddle on the embankment … Her father would go potty if he knew." Just as Woffinden's use of ellipses was not always innocent, the same applied to Foot. What Hanratty actually said was that after the kiss and the cuddle he led her to a deserted street behind Victoria coach station: "I was intimate with her. I had no Durex. Her father would go potty if he knew."

What are we to make of this admission of Hanratty's? Was he lying and trying to deflect belief in the charge that he was a rapist on the grounds that he was successful with women and had ready access to sex when he wanted it? Foot, somewhat obscurely, asserted that "In other parts of his statement, Hanratty embellished his story of his relationship with Carole France." Woffinden believed that a sexual encounter did take place, which he breezily described as an "escapade". But if this episode really did occur than it surely reveals Hanratty in the role of sexual predator (and perhaps even rapist).

To Carole France, 16 years old, Hanratty had always been "Uncle Jim" – a kind friend of her mother and father, and generous with gifts of cash. But at the first opportunity, Hanratty seized his chance. He took her to a funfair, fed her alcohol, then led her to a backstreet. Was Carole a virgin? Quite possibly she was. Was it what would in later years be known as a date-rape? He had sex with her – probably standing up in a doorway. Swift penetration. The pleasure entirely Hanratty's. He didn't care if he got her pregnant. He didn't care that, according to him, he regularly used a prostitute, with its attendant risks of catching and transmitting a sexual infection.

Of course, only Carole France knew the truth of what happened. But the probability is that if they did have a sexual encounter it was an entirely predatory one on Hanratty's part. It may even have been rape. Hanratty was a morally blank individual, ruthlessly egocentric and narcissistic. He betrayed the trust of others repeatedly. He had no real friends. When it was over he packed Carole off home in a taxi. She seems to have kept what had happened to herself, as rape victims so often do. But at the trial it was noticeable that she was far more hostile to Hanratty than her mother or her father were. On 21 May 1962 Carole France took an overdose. It seems most unlikely that the cause of her failed suicide attempt was grief at the recent execution of James Hanratty.

On 20 September 1961 Hanratty bought a second-hand Sunbeam Alpine car, using the proceeds of his many burglaries. "There's every indication," benignly remarked his defender Bob Woffinden, "that in this brief period he was at his happiest and most confident". To Woffinden this is the sunshine before the storm – the last joyous days of a gentle rogue before he was cruelly taken in for questioning and charged with a crime of which he was entirely innocent. But a far more plausible explanation of Hanratty's apparent good mood is that it was cockiness. He had committed the biggest crime in the country and got clean away with it. He had also gone on breaking into houses without getting caught and made so much dosh he could now afford to buy himself a motor. He was rolling in cash, with a flash car. He was also getting sex. He had had Carole France. The good times had arrived. He was the man he had always boasted of being. A major league criminal. A success.

On Friday 22 September there was the best news of all. A6 MURDER: THE POLICE SEEK A MAN'S HELP. It was all over the *Evening News*. It was the lead story on the wireless news and on the telly that night. When he saw the headline his heart had knotted, very painfully. But then he read on and relaxed. The coppers thought some bloke called Peter Alphon was the A6 murderer! Whoever he was. It was unbelievable.

There was something else. Tomorrow it would be exactly one month since he had shot that bloke and raped his woman. And he had got away with it! He knew what he would do next.

It was obvious, wasn't it?

It was Saturday 23 September – precisely one month after the A6 murder. It was the day that all the newspapers had headlines about a man in custody for the crime. It seemed obvious that the police had finally got their man. And what did James Hanratty do on this most significant of days? He drove his new car to Gladys Deacon's house in Stanmore. She was a girl he had started seeing. It was a surprise visit: she wasn't expecting him. And then what? In Woffinden's words, "He took Gladys for a drive. They headed north to Bedford, an area he knew reasonably well."

Woffinden seemed blithely unaware of the implications of this trip. It indicated that on this very significant date, at a time when a man was in custody on suspicion of being the killer, James Hanratty drove up the A6 to Bedford. He retraced the major part of the route taken by the masked gunman one month earlier.

The significance of this trip to Bedford is starkly obvious. A man frequently described as "cocky" was revisiting the scene of the crime, secure in the knowledge that the police had someone else in custody for it. Hanratty was gloating. He couldn't believe his luck. He had got clean away with it. All the more reason to go back in daylight and take a look at where he had shot dead that geezer and raped his woman. Did Hanratty pull over at Deadman's Hill and park in the lay-by? We'll never know. No one ever asked Gladys.

In Bedford they had tea at a restaurant, then Hanratty went off on his own, leaving Gladys in the Sunbeam. He said he had gone off to sell some jewellery but he couldn't find the fence so he returned to the car. That was his story anyway. It might have been true or he might have been up to something. It's another of those dark corners in Hanratty's furtive, singular life and we'll never know what the truth is.

They went back to London. Another triumphant passage past the scene of the crime. He took Gladys to Battersea funfair. It was his idea of giving a girl a good time. Then he drove her back to Stanmore. He said he had sex with Gladys in the car. It might have been true, and if it was it was another way of signalling that he was, after a fashion, reliving the crime – having sex with a woman at night in the back of a car. But since Hanratty was a serial liar this may not have been true. Perhaps he invented the story to show he wasn't the kind of man who had to force himself on a woman. Where Jim was concerned, there were plenty of girls willing. He said he spent the next day, Sunday, with Gladys, in London.

But then things took a sudden turn for the worse. On the Monday the papers trumpeted what had happened. This man Peter Alphon had been put on an identity parade. Valerie Storie had failed to identify him as her attacker. The case against Alphon collapsed. The police were forced to recognise that they had got the wrong man. Now they needed to take another look at the facts surrounding the discovery of the two cartridge cases at the Hotel Vienna.

It hardly seems a coincidence that this was the day "Dixie" France couldn't hold back his suspicions any longer. "Dixie", it seems, went to Scotland Yard. He grassed on his associate. Hanratty himself seems to have panicked at the news that the case against Alphon had been dropped. He went off to a hotel in Finsbury Park to await developments.

Then: nothing. The police said they currently were not looking for anyone else in connection with the crime. It looked like they didn't have a clue. Hanratty was, it seemed, safe after all. He went off to stay with Louise. She later told police that she had become afraid of Hanratty and his attentions. To deflect them she introduced him to Mary Meaden, a girl who sometimes worked in her shop. Hanratty asked her out and on Thursday they went to see the Harry Secombe show. Hanratty didn't try anything on with Mary. She wasn't that sort. He knew right away that she was the kind of person he wanted to settle down with. The next day, Friday, he took her to the pictures. Afterwards he proposed. She said it was far too soon to decide on something like that. Hanratty said he didn't mind waiting.

When did James Hanratty first learn that the police wanted to interview him in connection with the A6 muder?

His defenders believed that the first he knew of it was on 5 October. His behaviour, however, suggests that he suspected the police were on his trail perhaps a week before this date. Chief Superintendent Acott visited the Hanratty family home on 26 September. He claimed to be there regarding car offences committed by their eldest son. He did not mention the A6 murder and his parents do not appear to have grasped who this senior detective and his associate were. On 28 September, Acott stopped Hanratty's father on his way home and talked to him again. Was James Hanratty tipped off by a family member about these two visits? Even if Mr and Mrs Hanratty did not understand who Acott was, their elusive son Jim would have known at once that the Detective Superintendent was not visiting the family home about something as relatively minor as burglary or motoring offences.

Apparently Hanratty's father first learned the truth from a journalist, who called at the family home on the evening of 29 September and broke the shocking news that his son was wanted for questioning in connection with the A6 murder.

The next day, Saturday, the newspapers reported that the police had a new suspect. He wasn't named but he was described as aged around 25, wearing a dark suit, with black or brown hair brushed back. He had prominent blue eyes. The effect on Hanratty was dramatic. He missed his date with Mary Meaden and instead broke into two houses in Stanmore. He was looking for a jacket to replace the one he was wearing – the one he had worn on the night he shot Michael Gregsten. Hanratty, cocky as always, had continued wearing the suit he had worn that night. But even though he was not very bright, he was bright enough to understand that some of Gregsten's blood might be soaked into the jacket. Now he was suddenly in the frame it was time to act.

He found what he was looking for. He took the jacket

from a wardrobe and scarpered. He stole nothing else. James Hanratty, jewel thief and stealer of petty cash, burgled two houses for a single item of clothing. It was another indication of his guilt and his panic – as was his action in ripping his existing jacket and dumping it.

The next day, Sunday 1 October, he briefly saw Mary. He talked to her about his hair. He was very worried about how he looked. He didn't tell her why, of course. But if the police were looking for someone with black or brown hair he needed to go back to being ginger. He couldn't be certain it was him they were looking for, since they hadn't named their new suspect. But he couldn't afford to take chances.

That same day, at 6.10pm, a man rang Stoke Mandeville Hospital, where Valerie Storie was a patient. "I am the man who shot Valerie Storie," he said. "I will be there at 11.30 to finish her off." He said he was calling from Windsor, which turned out to be true. The man also rang Windsor police. The next day the man rang the hospital again, with another threat, and again the day afterwards. Campaigners attributed these calls to Peter Alphon but if it is entirely possible that they were coming from someone involved in the case it is equally possible that the culprit was Hanratty, expressing his fury at the way the tide of events seemed to be turning against him. He must have bitterly regretted that he had bungled killing Valerie.

It would have been unusual for Hanratty to remember Valerie's full name – but now he had the newspapers to remind him. It was also characteristic of Hanratty to boast where he was phoning from. When he phoned Acott, five days after the first telephone threat to Storie, he remarked, "You'll never guess where I'm speaking from: Liverpool." As indeed he was.

On Monday 2 October Hanratty went to Ealing to see Donald Fisher – the man he had gone to visit on his release from prison and with whom he had had the conversation about getting hold of a gun. They went to the Wembley greyhound stadium. Fisher remembered that "Hanratty was worried about something, because when we got to Wembley he didn't want to go in the main entrance in case he met his father." The next day Hanratty went to a barber's in Kilburn to try and get the dye taken out of his hair. Every aspect of his daily life indicated his guilt and his knowledge that he was the un-named man the police were looking for.

On Thursday 5 October he knew for a fact that the game was up. The newspapers mentioned a man called Ryan who had left a rented car at Dublin Airport. Hanratty phoned "Dixie" France, unaware that "Dixie" had grassed on him. "Dixie" advised him to give himself up. Hanratty said he wouldn't be paying him a visit and rang off.

The next day Hanratty phoned Scotland Yard and talked to Superintendent Acott. "I know I've left my fingerprints at different places and done different things … but I want to tell you, Mr Acott, that I didn't do that A6 murder."

What is odd about Hanratty's first reponse to the knowledge that the police were after him for the A6 murder is his evident lack of bewilderment. An innocent man, who had been in Rhyl at the time of the crime, would surely ask: Why me? What on earth makes you think I had anything to do with that terrible crime? I wasn't even in the area when it happened! But Hanratty didn't react like that all. His response, curiously, was to start talking about fingerprints. Because of course he knew very well he had wiped the Morris clean of his prints. He knew there was nothing tangible to connect him to the car where the crimes of murder and rape had taken place.

In his first telephone conversation with Acott, Hanratty displayed the characteristic indecision of the gunman in the Morris. "I think I'll ring a paper and ask them what to do," he said. "I'll think about it. I'll phone you between ten and midnight and tell you what I've decided. I must go now. My head's bad and I've got to think." Except of course he didn't say "think" but "fink".

He did indeed have a think. In his first two calls to the police Hanratty said nothing at all about having an alibi. His third call was from Liverpool. He said he had gone there to visit some criminal acquaintances. "I asked them to say I couldn't have committed your murder but they wouldn't listen." Despite being offered a hefty bribe they declined to get involved. Since he was the murderer, Hanratty had to try to fabricate an alibi. He settled on Liverpool but claimed his acquaintances did not want to back him up. It all reeked of implausibility. Hanratty initially told Acott he had spent "five days with these three friends". Acott asked if there was a single other person, apart from these three un-named friends, who had seen him in Liverpool at this time. Hanratty said there wasn't. Later, Hanratty trimmed the time to three days. Later it became two nights in Liverpool. But each new revision collapsed under scrutiny and in the end Hanratty was forced to come up with something new: two nights in Rhyl. This alibi was as vague and insubstantial as the Liverpool one.

Hanratty had plenty of time to work out an alibi. He fled to Liverpool, arriving on Saturday 7 October. On Monday 9 October at 4.45pm he was in the Scotland Road (at around the time he would later claim to have been there on a Tuesday in August). Believing he had almost been caught by the police he went to a hairdresser's to have his hair bleached. Despite later claiming to have been in Rhyl when Michael Gregsten was shot dead, Hanratty made no attempt to go to Rhyl and seek confirmation of that supposed alibi. From Liverpool he went to Blackpool. On 11 October at 11.10pm he was spotted eating alone in a Blackpool café by two detective constables. When he stepped outside he was arrested.

What followed reinforced all the other indications of Hanratty's guilt. At Bedford county police headquarters James Trower and John Skillett each picked out Hanratty from the ID parade as the man they had seen at the wheel of a badly driven Morris Minor in Ilford early on the morning of the murder. It was noticed that when Hanratty was identified by these two eye-witnesses he went bright red, just as his brother Michael said that he did when he was accused of something of which he was in fact guilty.

The next day Hanratty faced the prospect of an even more troubling ID parade. He would have to stand in front of the woman he had raped just over seven weeks earlier. Of course, if he was innocent he had nothing to fear. In the event Hanratty displayed the extreme stress and tension which he had exhibited during the crime itself, including a repeatedly expressed desire to know what the exact time was. A fellow participant in the parade, Antony Luxemburg, described Hanratty's behaviour when he was brought into the room and told that he could stand wherever he wanted to in the line-up: "he had this extraordinary tension, the most intense human being I've ever seen in my life, it was absolutely electrifying".

Peter Alphon had been placed on a parade with nine other men and was not recognised by Valerie Storie. The odds were better for James Hanratty: he was obliged to attend a line-up with twelve other men. Valerie Storie asked each person to say, "Be quiet will you, I am thinking." In Woffinden's words: "She was listening for a cockney accent, someone who said 'finking'" However, according to the speech and phonetics expert who examined Hanratty in prison, although the suspect might well say "finking" in the natural course of a conversation, from sheer habit, he was perfectly capable of prouncing the diphthong "th": "If in any circumstances it were vitally important to him to use 'th' instead of 'f', he could certainly produce the sounds." Valerie Storie's request was not therefore as damaging to Hanratty as his defenders assumed it to be.

After being identified by Valerie Storie as the man who had raped her, Hanratty was taken to Ampthill and charged with the murder of Michael Gregsten. Asked if he had anything to say he made no protestations of innocence, simply replying, "No." Other signs of Hanratty's guilt followed thick and fast in the aftermath of his arrest and interrogation. He admitted he had talked about obtaining a gun but desperately tried to downplay its significance. Even more damningly, when Acott told him about what had been found in the Hotel Vienna bedroom, Hanratty acknowledged that in response "I asked Superintendent Acott what size the bullets was. I was so excited and depressed with his new evidence that he had sprung on me, I was flabbergasted, and I knew at this stage that matters looked very, very serious against me." There is no reason to doubt this. Hanratty must indeed have been astonished to learn that two cartridge cases he had carelessly left behind had lain there undiscovered for three weeks. But if he was as innocent about guns as he liked to pretend, why was Hanratty's immediate response to ask what size the cartridges were? Similarly, he admitted boasting to Charles France that the best place to get rid of unwanted stuff was under the upstairs back seat of a London double-decker bus. And Hanratty continued to cling to his bogus Liverpool alibi until the moment it collapsed and he hurriedly fabricated a new one, inventing two fictitious nights in Rhyl.

The first time Hanratty met his defence barrister Michael Sherrard he told him he was apprehensive about his photograph appearing in the press. But if he had really been in Rhyl during the Tuesday and Wednesday when the A6 crime had taken place, surely it was to his advantage, since witnesses to his presence there might recognise him and come forward? On the other hand if Hanratty had spent the night of 23 August staying under an assumed name at a small London hotel or boarding house he would have been very anxious indeed not to be recognised.

Paul Foot argued that "There was not a trace of a confession to anyone". But of course Hanratty's fellow-prisoner Roy Langdale alleged that Hanratty had admitted his guilt to him and supplied details of the crime which were then not in the public domain. He was was not alone in claiming that Hanratty had privately admitted his guilt. In 2001 Peter Dunn, who had reported on the Bedford trial for the *Observer*, revealed that in 1992 he had interviewed John Needham, an RAF corporal involved in Hanratty's second identity parade. "Mr Needham told me that during a casual chat, Hanratty, who seemed to the corporal to be 'openly cocky about it', said to him: 'They know I did it, I know I did it, but I don't think they can prove it. It's not up to me to help them.'"

Someone who knew Hanratty very well and who was in no doubt that he was the A6 killer was Louise Anderson. She claimed that Hanratty had confessed to her that he had killed a man. He didn't say who it was but she was in no doubt that he meant Michael Gregsten. Someone else who knew Hanratty, Charlotte France, claimed that he had said falteringly to her, "Now I've done something that scares. Something I've never done before and I don't understand."

A fifth narrative about a confession by Hanratty emerged in 2002. "Cassandra", a journalist on Paul Foot's old newspaper *The Daily Mirror*, had a strange tale to tell. When Hanratty was hanged one of those present was a Catholic priest, Canon Anthony Hulme. Years later he was given a lift down the A6 to a church function in Luton by a churchgoer, Robert Leggat. "This is an eventful place," Hulme remarked. Questioned by Leggat about the case, "he said that [Hanratty] had confessed the crime to him but was now forgiven. It was a very sombre thing, not a throwaway comment or anything like that." "Cassandra" accounted for Hanratty's confession by asserting that "James Hanratty was the kind of lapsed Catholic lad who, whatever he had done, would know he'd go to Hell if he didn't square things with his maker at the last minute."

Five apparent confessions. Every one might be false or, equally, every one might be true. We'll never know. But we do know that Hanratty was guilty. We also have two very revealing utterances which came from the mouth of James Hanratty himself. One came at the very end of his trial in Bedford. After the guilty verdict, which clearly stunned Hanratty, the judge asked him if he had anything to say.

"I am not innocent," Hanratty said. He then quickly corrected himself. "I am innocent, my Lord, and I will appeal."

That is the orthodox transcript of this moment of the trial. Jean Justice, who was present, remembered it rather differently:

> When [the foreman of the jury] pronounced the word "Guilty," there was a shocked gasp from the gallery. Hanratty collapsed against the front of the dock, his face crumpled in disbelief. "I'm not – innocent," he stammered brokenly. "I mean I'm not – I mean, I will appeal, my Lord."

Obviously at a conscious level Hanratty was struggling to say "I am not guilty" or "I am innocent". His slip was regarded generously by commentators as the momentary confusion of a man at a moment of extreme stress. But Freud argued that "the most insignificant and obvious errors in speaking have their meaning" and he devoted an entire chapter to slips of the tongue in his classic study *The Psychopathology of Everyday Life*. This book continues to supply insights into the workings of the human mind and remains a valuable study of human behaviour and language use. Freud argued that slips of the tongue signify something intentionally withheld, something repressed, something pushed out of consciousness which bobs up unexpectedly in speech. A verbal slip expresses "a thought-content which is at pains to remain concealed but which cannot nevertheless avoid unintentionally betraying its existence in a whole variety of ways".

A remarkable modern instance, underlining Freud's perspicacity, came in May 2022 when former American president George W. Bush gave a speech about foreign policy. Intending to criticise President Vladimir Putin for Russia's invasion of Ukraine, Bush instead denounced "the decision of one man to launch a wholly unjustified and brutal invasion of Iraq". Bush inadvertently acknowledged his own criminality. James Hanratty was no different. Hanratty *knew* he was guilty. At the climactic moment of his trial he could not help himself from blurting out the truth:

"I am not innocent."

It was not the only occasion when Hanratty's subconscious took control of his speech utterance. When he was arrested in Blackpool, Hanratty told the two police officers they had the wrong man, saying "I'm Peter Bates". This was not a pseudonym he had used before. Why "Peter Bates"? Both names had intriguing associations. "Peter", of course, was the name of the first suspect in the case – Peter Alphon. And "Bates" just happened to be the name of the murderer in Alfred Hitchcock's sensational film *Psycho*, released in Britain on 15 September 1960.

Hanratty could not have been to see it then because he was in prison. He did not come out until 24 March 1961. It is possible that he saw this movie at a cinema during the period between that date and his arrest outside the Stevonia Café in Blackpool on October 11 1961. It should be remembered that the culture of cinema-going was entirely different at the start of the 1960s than it is today. Television had yet to eat into the massive cinema audience. Televisions had small screens and everything was in black and white. Films were rarely shown on TV and the Christmas Day film on television was a major national cultural event. There were only two TV channels and many homes still did not own a television. Most people went to the cinema on a regular basis. Some movie theatres showed four or five different films in a week. Programmes involved two films – the "A" film, featuring top movie stars, and a supporting feature, the "B" film, usually a low-budget black-and-white drama cranked out at speed and starring minor actors or unknowns. As the history of Hammer films shows, these "B" features were sometimes of impressive quality. The opportunities for movie-going were therefore extensive. Moreover, there was no break in programming as there is today. In those days films were projected continuously, and if you chose to enter a film half way through or stay and watch the entire show again, you were free to do so. Ironically *Psycho* was an exception: partly for publicity purposes Hitchcock insisted that no one be permitted to enter the cinema once the film had started.

New films lingered on for weeks or even months, unlike today. It is entirely possible that Hanratty saw *Psycho* between his release from prison and his arrest. Much of his life in that period is a mystery and a blank. We do know that he often went off to see fims on the spur of the moment.

Of course "Peter Bates" *might* have been an entirely random choice of pseudonym. But from a Freudian perspective it makes perfect sense. "Bates" connects with some key moments of *Psycho* and Hanratty's own behaviour. *Psycho* includes moments which parallel Hanratty and the A6 murder, such as a false name in a hotel register, an uneasy conversation between a fluent, confident, independent woman and a hesitant, disturbed, inadequate psychopath, a sudden wholly unexpected explosion of violence, a blood-splashed crime scene, and the need to drag a dead body away. But very much more specific than these broad parallels is the central theme of a psychopath's relationship with his mother. Norman Bates loves his mother; he also hates his mother. He is a loving son but also a matricide. In killing his mother he becomes his mother.

James Hanratty's strange relationship with his mother has never been mentioned, let alone discussed, in books about the A6 murder. But it surely lies at the root of his troubled psyche. In the Morris Minor he spoke of his punishment and imprisonment beginning at the age of eight – the very age when, as we know, his mother wrenched him from her protection and love and handed him over to strangers in the north of England.

When the police closed in on him for the A6 murder, Hanratty's concern with not upsetting his mother became an obsession. At one point, bizarrely, he even telephoned Scotland Yard to complain about press coverage of the hunt for him. He blamed it on Detective Superintendent Acott, and said "Tell him it is worrying my mother."

While on the run he sent his mother some artificial flowers, with a note saying, "I am sorry to have caused you this trouble." When he was finally arrested Hanratty asked the police to keep his real name a secret. He justified this absurd and unrealistic request by saying, "I want you to keep calling me Jimmy Ryan because I don't want to embarrass my parents." Hanratty's relationship with his mother and father was surely a tortured and complex one. They both vanished from his life when he was a child, leaving him with a trauma which may well have been accentuated by abuse as well as emotional deprivation. He rejected them when he was a young teenager. He ran away from them. He rebelled against everything his devout, respectable church-attending parents stood for. He became a career criminal and a jailbird. Yet, as he plunged ever deeper into a life of crime, he maintained the façade of a loving son. He remembered their birthdays. He was always sending his mother flowers. He stayed in touch. When he was charged with murder they stood by him. Paul Foot states that before the A6 case neither parent had ever been inside a courtroom, without apparently realising that if true it means that they coldly shunned attending his earlier court appearances when he was a teenager.

Chief Superintendent Acott, who had the measure of his prisoner, seems to have believed that it might be better for Hanratty if he pleaded guilty with diminished responsibility. Hanratty fiercely rejected that option. His insistence on his innocence continued the family tradition of *keeping up appearances*. His mother and father had stoutly rejected the idea that there was anything wrong with their son as a schoolboy. They refused the social stigma of having him sent to a special school. In denying him the attention and care he needed they did him no favours. Now, James Hanratty, having committed one of the most horrifying crimes of the decade, simply went into denial. At times the denial of his true self appeared almost comical. Hanratty solemny told the Bedford court, "I try to live a good and respectable life except for my housebreakings." But of course he had also privately admitted regular visits to a Soho prostitute, apart from his burglaries and car thefts.

In the face of all the evidence Hanratty was trying to affiliate himself with the values of his churchgoing parents. But he was also sly and evasive. "The man who committed this crime is a maniac and a savage. *I know what you have proved here.* I am not a man the court can approve of, but I am not a maniac of any kind. I can prove it with my past girlfriends" (my italics). On another occasion he told the court, "I'm a crook but I ain't a maniac."

But of course this assumes that a "maniac" is someone identifiable as such by looking at them and considering their behaviour in public. But even the Yorkshire Ripper had a wife and came from a respectable family. At the apex of his criminality, Joseph James DeAngelo, the "Golden State Killer" and serial rapist, lived with his wife and children. Jean-Claude Romand was a top medical professional who worked at the World Health Organisation in Geneva and lived a respectable and affluent life with his wife and two young childen – that, at least, was the image he presented to the world. In reality he had no medical qualifications and no job and sponged off his wealthy parents, while persuading others to let him invest their savings, which he used to fund his lifestyle. When after eighteen years of living a fantasy existence his lies began to unravel, he murdered his wife, his two small children, and his parents. Beneath the charming personality lay a sociopath who was incapable of feeling, and a compulsive liar and fantasist. Ironically, he may even have read Jean Justice's *Le Crime de la Route A6.* Among Romand's innumerable lies and fantasies was the story of how (just a few years after Justice's book appeared) he was abducted at gunpoint and taken in his car on a mysterious journey. Some thirty miles outside Lyon he was beaten up at a lonely spot. Then he was allowed to return in his car. When he told his friends they asked what the men had wanted. "That's just it, I haven't a clue. I don't understand any of it."

The notion that Hanratty could not have been the A6 killer because he was not "a maniac" is not remotely plausible as an argument since perfectly ordinary-seeming people can indeed have a dark side, or explode into violent anger. Episodes of "road rage" often involve individuals who are respectable members of society with no criminal record. Another contemporary example, often in the news, is neighbours who fall out over car parking, resulting in fatal assaults. In addition, underlying Hanratty's self-justifying argument is the myth that a rapist must be someone without a sexual partner.

The most revealing part of Hanratty's testimony at this point is his remark, "I know what you have proved here." He had a cocky certainty that there was no forensic evidence to link him to the crime, and that therefore he would be acquitted. He seems to have managed to convince himself how the case would appear to an outsider and that a verdict of Not Guilty was inevitable. "It was quite obvious to me inside that I never committed this crime," he remarked, rather oddly. It sounds as if in seeking to rationalise his crime out of existence he may have even begun to convince himself of what he regarded as the plausibility of the defence case.

It would not have been the first time he had blanked out an uncomfortable reality. In his troubled adolescence, when Hanratty was in the Royal Sussex Hospital, his father had paid him a visit. He found his son "semi-comatose" and unable to recognise him. But it was noticed that this appeared to be an act, since Hanratty "had spoken quite intelligently" to a fellow patient. Besides, Hanratty's respectable family background is not a sound basis on which to absolve him of criminal tendencies. As the novelist Graham Greene once provocatively remarked, "A Catholic is more capable of evil than anyone". Ironically, James Hanratty bears more than a passing resemblance to the young, repressed, tormented criminal protagonist of Greene's classic novel Brighton Rock.

Hanratty never at any point seems to have referred to Valerie Storie or her sufferings as a rape victim and a paraplegic. She, too, was blanked out. Hanratty not only shut out the crime and its horrors, he also went into total denial about the consequences of his arrest and impending trial. "Please do not worry too much," he reassured his mother, insisting that he would soon "straighten out" the little matter of his arrest as a murderer and rapist. This insouciant attitude continued to the opening days of the trial. It was noted that Hanratty adopted the role of "interested onlooker, someone who joined in moments of light relief, rather than the man in the dock". At times Hanratty's detachment produced pure comedy. Jean Justice remembered the "gales of laughter" in court when Hanratty remarked, "I've sat here day after day, week after week, and never missed one moment of this trial." Justice was also glumly aware that at times Hanratty did not present himself very convincingly in the witness box. He remembered Detective Superintendent Acott's "satisfied grin" when Hanratty produced "his unconvincing Rhyl alibi". He regarded Hanratty's assertion "I could have lived with a girl in London for a week any time I wanted to" as a transparently "empty boast".

Hanratty comprehensively blanked out reality in all its incarnations, from the crime itself, its surviving victim, and his own culpability, as well as the inevitable judicial consequences. In the month following his arrest Hanratty "discussed his inevitable release". On 18 January 1962, just before the start of his trial, Hanratty chirpily assured his younger brother Peter that he would be home again soon. Hanratty always thought he was smarter than he was. He believed he had outwitted the police. He boasted that their interrogation techniques hadn't worked with him: "It's surprising what the law can do to a innocent man," he wrote. "They can turn him inside out in no time but me being so used to the game they did not find it so easy." But in fact Hanratty had presented no difficulties to an experienced murder detective like Acott, who easily extracted the damning gun conversation from his prisoner.

Mrs Mary Hanratty was a devout Catholic. By committing murder and rape her son James had very publicly shamed her. He had, metaphorically, killed her. In this he was like

Norman Bates. As the psychiatrist explains at the end of *Psycho*, "Matricide is probably the most unbearable crime of all – most unbearable to the son who commits it. So he had to erase the crime, at least in his own mind." Or as Hanratty wrote to his mother: "You and I know that it is not in me to commit such an awful offence." He simply blanked out what he had done at dead of night in that lay-by in Bedfordshire. He told his defence lawyer, "I am not that kind of person. I don't even like talking about it. It upsets me. If I had done it, I would rather have taken my own life than do this to my mother." His final excuse was that "Though I am a bit of a crook, I wouldn't hurt a mouse." In this he was echoing Norman Bates, incarcerated, guilty, delusional, in a world of his own, believing that anyone who understood "what kind of a person I am" would know that he "wouldn't even harm a fly".

12   Tunnel Vision

> It has been a long dark tunnel, but we can see light at the
> end of it.
>
> Bob Woffinden (1999)

Thirty years after the execution of James Hanratty, Channel 4
broadcast Bob Woffinden's documentary *Hanratty – The Mystery
of Deadman's Hill*, in its "True Stories" series. It was shown twice
more in the following three years. It represented the most
powerful expression of the miscarriage of justice campaign and
provided a wholly uncritical rendering of the strong opinions of
those three central figures, Jean Justice, Paul Foot and Bob
Woffinden. Jean Justice's passionate, febrile account of his deeply
personal engagement with Peter Alphon, set forth in an obscure
paperback published in Paris by a controversial French publisher
of pornography, was now repeated in a highly polished TV
documentary which purported to be setting out an objective,
factual account of a crime and its aftermath. A conspiracy theory
contained in an obscure, little-read book was now reaching an
audience of millions.

   Television is one of the most powerful of all modern
means of communication, and was especially so before the advent
of social media and satellite TV, when there were far fewer
channels available to watch. But as a source of information, the
television documentary is often a dubious and highly subjective
medium. It simplifies the complex. It favours the image over
language and logic. A collage of images can carry a manipulative
charge. Image follows image, with no time for reflection. The
subjective nature of the medium is given a veener of objectivity
through the use of presenters or voiceovers. Conventionally these
have been male, often middle-aged, sometimes famous, either as

professional presenters or successful actors. Presenters proffer the illusion of the detached, impartial seeker after truth. Voiceovers in particular carry a particular authority as the calm, unseen voice of reason, objectivity and truth. A voiceover pulls everything together and presents what appears to be solid, objective conclusions. Like a conventional Victorian novel, Woffinden's *Hanratty – The Mystery of Deadman's Hill* has a single, omniscient, authoritative point of view. Its thesis is that Hanratty was innocent of the crime for which a jury found him guilty. No alternative perspective is permitted.

Woffinden's documentary begins with an extract from one of James Hanratty's prisoner letters: "Mum, what have I done to deserve this? No one can imagine what it is like to experience something like this ...". These words are read out against a dramatised re-enactment of his execution in Bedford Prison in April 1962. The voice of the unseen narrator then intervenes: "Thirty years ago this week, James Hanratty was hanged for the A6 murder. His innocence has been proclaimed ever since. Now there is disturbing new evidence that he was wrongly executed." A photograph of Hanratty is shown, while soft, melancholy piano music plays in the background. Another extract from a prison letter is read out: "Mum, somebody somewhere knows the truth and will come forward. No matter what happens we know that the country has made a terrible mistake."

It is a deeply emotive beginning and an inaccurate one. No one was proclaiming Hanratty's innocence in 1962 apart from his defence team and a handful of individuals. Few of those who attended the trial doubted Hanratty's guilt. The following year the thriller writer Eric Ambler published *The Ability to Kill*, a collection of essays about true life murders. One of the cases he dealt with was a very recent one: the A6 murder. Ambler was unimpressed by Hanratty: "he was, without a doubt, a deeply stupid man". Like others, he thought that Roy Langdale's tale of Hanratty's confession was probably true: "A man of Hanratty's mentality would be quite capable of telling a fellow prisoner that he was the 'A6 killer' simply in order to make himself seem important." Having described the crime and the ensuing trial, Ambler's conclusion was unequivocal: "There was, and is, no reasonable doubt that he was guilty." But Ambler's blunt account of the crime subsequently faded from view and was forgotten. No book about the crime mentions it. Attitudes like Ambler's were replaced by the influential and high-profile campaign to exonerate the man found guilty of the crime. In terms of publicity, *Hanratty – The Mystery of Deadman's Hill* was probably its crowning achievement.

Having given a misleading account of the aftermath of the trial, the documentary goes on blatantly to re-write the narrative of the A6 murder according to Woffinden's hugely one-sided agenda. The scene in the cornfield is re-enacted not as it happened, in darkness, but in broad daylight. Nothing is said about the proximity of houses to the Morris Minor. Nothing is said about Hanratty's record of burglaries carried out at night. Events are telescoped to suit Woffinden's polemical agenda. The gunman gets into the car and off they go. The hesitancy of the mysterious gunman and the time spent in the cornfield, along with all the revealing conversations, is airbrushed out. The journey from Buckinghamshire to Bedfordshire, which took perhaps three hours or more, and which was filled with revealing dialogue between Michael Gregsten, Valerie Storie and the gunman, is re-enacted in less than 40 seconds. The gunman's revelations about himself, which in many respects matched Hanratty and provided damning circumstantial evidence that he was indeed the couple's masked abductor, is simply excluded. Nothing whatever is said about the significance of the route in relation to Hanratty's life, his knowledge of north-west London, or his association with Bedford. The scene at Deadman's Hill is similarly misrepresented. The car is driven into the lay-by, the gunman shoots Gregsten and then rapes Storie and drives off – all in the space, it appears, of a few minutes. The tortuous conversations between Valerie Storie and the gunman are omitted.

By telescoping the chronology of the crime and leaving out almost all of the gunman's behaviour and conversation, this dramatic re-enactment of the crime drains it of significance. It is, in short, a travesty of what actually occurred. It blanks out a mass of evidence indicating that the masked gunman was indeed James Hanratty. This documentary's diversion of attention away from Hanratty and his criminal past is one of its most striking features. When it does briefly advert to Hanratty's criminal career the programme insinuates that Charles France was responsible.

Janet Gregsten's visit to Valerie Storie in hospital is summarised thus: "afterwards Mrs Gregsten said the killer must have been a maniac". In fact what she actually said was "The whole thing seems without rhyme or reason. It can only be the work of a maniac. Mike and Val got the impression that he might have been committing a burglary somewhere and wanted a getaway car." A balanced TV programme would have given the whole quotation and the information that Hanratty was indeed a burglar who operated alone on foot at night. But of course *Hanratty – The Mystery of Deadman's Hill* was no more interested in contemplating the possibility that James Hanratty might indeed have been the gunman than was Jean Justice.

Its maker, Bob Woffinden, had a dogmatic and one-dimensional perspective from the very start. In his first piece of writing on the subject of the A6 murder he wrote, "The question of Alphon's guilt is debatable; the question of Hanratty's innocence is not." Hanratty's supposed innocence was an article of faith. It was not open to critical scrutiny. It was an attitude which resurfaced when subsequent DNA testing indicated a link to Hanratty. Paul Foot breezily shrugged aside the science: "Bob Woffinden and I ... were asked about these tests and could only say that the case for Hanratty's innocence is stronger than it ever was, and that if the DNA suggests otherwise there must be something wrong with the DNA."

Hanratty – The Mystery of Deadman's Hill goes on to portray the discovery of the cartridge cases at the Hotel Vienna as suspicious. In its re-enactment of the scene the two cases are shown, illuminated and unmissable, one of them gleaming goldenly against the smooth background of a flat bedside chair. This, too, is a travesty. The chair was not beside the bed but at the foot of it, in a gloomy alcove of a dimly lit basement room. The cases were not visible even to the two people who entered the room on 11 September 1961 for the sole purpose of checking its condition. Robert Crocker discovered them only when he re-arranged the chair's torn covering and one of the cases rolled off. Standards at the Hotel Vienna were low and the room was not "cleaned regularly", as the documentary blithely asserts. It had been empty and unused for several weeks. The cartridges were not placed there to be spotted and to incriminate Hanratty, as Woffinden's programme falsely insinuates.

The documentary then introduces the figure of Peter Louis Alphon. "Alphon, an unemployed drifter, was already under police scrutiny. In several respects he matched Valerie Storie's description of the killer." The first statement is quite untrue. Alphon had been questioned about his odd behaviour at the Alexandra Court Hotel and then let go. That was that. He was in no sense under surveillance. In any case, the notion that the A6 killer would afterwards have manifested strange behaviour was a dubious one, based more on prejudice and the myth of an oddball "maniac" than an understanding of murderers and their lives. The eternally elusive Jack the Ripper was almost certainly a local man who appeared entirely normal, and who very probably had a wife or a partner and quite possibly a family. Besides, Alphon's odd, anti-social behaviour was entirely characteristic. It owed nothing to him having just shot a man dead or committed a rape.

Furthermore, to assert that Alphon matched Storie's description of the killer is a bit rich in a programme which cynically excludes the extensive dialogue in the car between the gunman and his victims, which offered striking parallels with the past life and existing mannerisms of James Hanratty. Hanratty's brother Michael assures viewers that his brother James was "a very good driver", with not a word said about his failure ever to take a driving test, his lack of driving experience, or the fact that when Hanratty hired a car he managed to crash it within 48 hours. John Skillett, viewers are informed, "identified Hanratty as the driver" of the badly driven Morris Minor, "but his passenger Edward Blackhall, better positioned, insisted it was not Hanratty". But viewers are not informed that on the ID parades Blackhall *twice* picked out innocent men as the driver, indicating his utter unreliability as an eye-witness.

The Liverpool alibi is quickly and misleadingly bundled out of the way: "he couldn't say where or with who he stayed". But the truth is that Hanratty described staying at a flat which turned out to be as imaginary as its occupants. He was a liar and when his lies were exposed he was forced to fabricate a new alibi. The programme then portrays the Rhyl alibi as authentic and verifiable. Brenda Harris, daughter of the woman who ran "Ingledene" describes what happened when her mother was shown a photograph of Hanratty: "My mother was confident, you know, that she knew him. She said, 'Oh, he stayed at my guesthouse.' She recognised him straight away." But this is a complete fiction and a classic example of how some stories get better in the re-telling, especially after thirty years. "No one else had breakfast that season in our own living room," Mrs Harris helpfully adds, again demonstrating how memories become more polished as the years roll by. In fact Hanratty claimed he had breakfast in "a general room", not someone's cosy parlour.

All the inconsistencies and question marks associated with the Rhyl alibi are simply airbrushed out. Viewers are not even told that Hanratty knew the town and had been there before. *Hanratty – The Mystery of Deadman's Hill* tells whopper after whopper. "Hanratty's description of Ingledene's interior matched up. The green bath is still in the attic today." But Hanratty's description of the room in which he stayed did *not* match that of the attic bathroom. Although he was studiously vague about many details Hanratty was definite that he had stayed in a room with curtains and a sink. The attic room had neither.

Having concluded that Hanratty had no motive for the crime, *Hanratty – The Mystery of Deadman's Hill* revives the idea first put forward by Jean Justice and later insinuated by Paul Foot, that the crime was planned in advance. To make this point the programme draws on the views of a man who, viewers are informed, attended the trial and "was increasingly disturbed at the quality of the evidence against Hanratty". This impartial observer is revealed to be Jean Justice. He appears not as the obsessive, unstable semi-deranged author of the febrile gay romance *Murder vs. Murder* and its equally defamatory sequel *Le Crime de la Route A6* but as a distinguished elderly commentator on the topic. His books, wisely, are not mentioned.

The programme rehashes the *Daily Sketch* story of "Mrs Gregsten's Amazing Intuiton". It dramatically asks: "How could she have picked [Hanratty] out of the millions on the London streets long before anyone suspected him? No one has ever explained this extraordinary intuition." But, very misleadingly, the programme makes no mention of the location of the sighting or the coincidence of the proximity of Charles France's home (where Hanratty was staying) to Wiliam Ewer's umbrella shop, where Janet Gregsten was helping out. Nor are Janet Gregsten's denials that the story was accurate mentioned. Charles France seems to have suspected Hanratty of the crime at a very early stage. This, too, goes unacknowledged.

The final part of *Hanratty – The Mystery of Deadman's Hill* is devoted to the argument that Peter Alphon was the true killer. It is proposed that the gun was dumped on the bus to incriminate Hanratty, that the cartridge cases were deliberately placed in the Hotel Vienna basement room to connect him to the crime, and that when the gunman said "Call me Jim" it was a deliberate attempt to frame him. These claims are made with scant regard for accuracy (the gunman in fact never used the words "Call me Jim").

A witness to Hanratty's hanging, David Lines, quietly

describes the execution and the emotional impact it made upon him. But the programme, partial as ever, fails to inform the viewer that Lines attended the trial and came away from it convinced of Hanratty's guilt. Next, the narrator solemnly informs the viewer that Scotland Yard holds sixteen boxes of material on the A6 case, which it refuses to allow the Hanratty family lawyers to access. The Yard, viewers are told, also possesses exhibits which could be DNA-tested but these are also withheld. Soft piano music plays. A photograph is displayed of Hanratty as a child. Another of his mawkish "Dear Mum" letters is reverently intoned as the camera pans across Carpenders Park cemetery to his grave. The last words of the documentary are Hanratty's, asserting his innocence. *Hanratty – The Mystery of Deadman's Hill* is a triumph of misrepresentation and, as an account of the A6 murder, a caricature.

It evoked a complaint to The Broadcasting Complaints Commission from Janet Gregsten. She felt she had been tricked into agreeing to participate in a documentary which she had been led to believe "would be about the need to reform the legal system". Her interviewer was Bob Woffinden, of whom she had apparently never heard. She found him "cynical and basically hostile" and his attitude to her had been "one of disbelief". After this experience she had obtained a book by Woffinden about the Hanratty case (this must have been *Miscarriages of Justice*, as his A6 book had yet to appear), which confirmed her doubts about his attitude to her. She had therefore pulled out of the programme. The programme makers had then broadcast it, including the claim that she had spotted Hanratty at Swiss Cottage long before he ever became a suspect, despite being well aware that she herself strongly denied that any such episode had ever occurred.

In a distinctly tepid, equivocal and fence-sitting judgement the Commission grandly released its response to Janet Gregsten's complaint, published on 24 September 1993. It found "a degree of unfairness in the way the programme described Mrs

Gregsten's supposed identification of Hanratty as the murderer of her husband without making it absolutely clear that the story was open to doubt."

Bob Woffinden had no sense of irony. A fervent believer in a conspiracy theory where the A6 murder was concerned, he later grumbled that John McVicar's book about the murder of Jill Dando put forward "one of the most preposterous [theories] advanced in modern criminal history". Woffinden accused McVicar of "gratuitous insults" in his description of Dando, which was a bit rich coming from a man who was an uncritical admirer of Jean Justice's first A6 murder book, which sneered that Valerie Storie was "by no means slim" and claimed, falsely, that she had been forced to have sex while the gunman watched.

Some twenty-three years after his tendentious Hanratty documentary, Bob Woffinden could be found bitterly complaining about a television programme which he regarded as dishonest and one-sided. It concerned the convicted murderer Russell Causley, who Woffinden strongly believed was innocent of the crime for which he was convicted. Presenter Mark Williams-Thomas, argued that Russell Causley was undoubtedly guilty of his wife's murder. Woffinden, again with no sense of irony, raged against what he sarcastically called this "self-styled 'Investigator'". In fact Williams-Thomas was a former Thames Valley Police officer, so, unlike Woffinden and most people who write about crime, he was not an amateur. This was a case in which the victim's body was never found. "Had MWT [sic] fully analysed the Crown's courtroom evidence, then viewers would have realised that the case against Causley at trial was essentially non-existent," Woffinden complained. But of course that was Woffinden's argument about Hanratty, and his own television documentary showed him to be an utterly unreliable guide to the weight of evidence in a criminal case.

The year after Woffinden's manipulative and one-sided documentary was first broadcast on Channel 4, another programme about the A6 murder was shown, this time on Channel 5, as part of a weekly "Great Crimes of the 20th Century" series. In contrast to the high production values of Woffinden's effort, this new programme was, although produced for BBC Worldwide Television, a low budget scissors-and-paste job. With a careless and slovenly script by Elkan Allan, it consisted of thirty minutes of old black-and-white newsreel and documentary footage, with a linking voiceover. Heavily influenced by Paul Foot's book, it was riddled with quite basic errors of fact. Although repeated in 2001, this documentary probably reached a much smaller audience than Woffinden's programme but made its own small contribution to the popular perception of James Hanratty's innocence. By now it was more or less baked into non-fiction crime books. James Morton's *Bent Coppers: A Survey of Police Corruption* (1993), referring to the poor public image of the British police, commented that it did not help that there had been "a series of clear miscarriages of justice over the century which have taken years to unravel". His list of examples included one "James Hanratty".

The 1999 paperback edition of Bob Woffinden's book on the case was the high-water mark of the Hanratty campaign. Its title – *Hanratty: The Final Verdict* – confidently expressed his conviction that soon even the legal establishment would exonerate the dead man of the crime and officially proclaim him innocent. Woffinden and Foot had pinned their hopes on improved DNA analysis of vital materials, namely Valerie Storie's knickers and the handkerchief used to wrap up the abandoned gun. They hoped that genetic fingerprinting would supply the scientific proof of Hanratty's innocence. But in 1997 the results were still inconclusive. However, this did not seem to matter, since the campaigners rested their confident assumptions on various arguments. Firstly, the identification evidence of the Redbridge witnesses, they believed, had been discredited because the car they had seen wasn't Gregsten's Morris. Secondly,

Hanratty's Rhyl alibi "withstood the closest examination". Moreover there had been "massive non-disclosure of vital evidential material" and the investigation of the crime had involved "numerous examples of serious misconduct by senior police officers".

Much of this was wishful thinking, combined with gross exaggeration or simple self-delusion. To Woffinden, however, it seemed the logical climax to forty years of harrowing injustice. "Even at the time of the execution on 4 April 1962, there was a widespread unease about the conviction," says the blurb on the cover of the Pan paperback edition of Woffinden's Hanratty book (almost certainly written by the author). But that is simply not true. There was at the time no general sense that an injustice had been been done. The so-called "A6 Committee" consisted of little more than Hanratty's immediate family and a handful of very vocal supporters – notably Jean Justice and Paul Foot. Both men brought their own agendas with them. Justice was a failed law student whose relish for an attack on the legal establishment was magnified by his identity as a flamboyant homosexual in an era when the police and judiciary hounded, humiliated and imprisoned gay men, and by his own passionate obsession with the perpetually teasing Peter Alphon. He seems to have been equally emotionally engaged with blue-eyed Hanratty, describing the death of this 25-year-old career criminal as nothing less than a "martyrdom".

Alphon purported to loathe homosexuals but his enigmatic relationship with Jean Justice suggests he may simply have been in denial and have discovered his true sexuality once Justice began lavishing attention on him. The language of *Murder vs. Murder* is highly charged, with Justice describing a "very close friendship" in which "we felt an extraordinary affinity for each other". He writes that Alphon was "powerfully attracted to me". This was plainly in part because Alphon, a lonely drifter, felt flattered by the attention Justice gave him. But there was need on both sides. Justice writes that he planned to "gradually lead him up to the highest pitch of ecstasy" and then trap him. But there seems to have been rather more than simply the A6 murder at stake. "I needed Peter. Every juke-box, thumping out its swinging beat and witless yrics, reminded me of him." Quite what the relationship was between the two men remains unclear; it certainly sounds as if it might at some point have become a physical one. Alphon had nothing whatever to do with the A6 murder but he used the possibility that he *might* have had to ensnare the ever-gullible, besotted Justice. It is hard not to sympathise with the senior police officer in Vienna who, when faced with Jean Justice, tapped his forehead and said to him, "You – sick."

Paul Foot brought his revolutionary politics to the affair. From his perspective James Hanratty was a young, uneducated working-class man from an Irish background, which instantly made him something of a romantic figure for an upper-class Left radical like Foot. The Irish had suffered for centuries at the hands of the English state. The police existed to repress the working-class. The judicial establishment was the incarnation and voice of a corrupt ruling class. The politics were briskly summarised by a comrade of Foot's:

> The police conform to the violence and bigotry of the rotten system they stand guard over. The state, of which the police force is a part, is the possession of a ruling class which willingly lets no part of it slip from its grasp.
>
> The police, the army, the prisons and the court system are part of the machinery of class rule. Over 80 per cent of high court judges are educated at public schools.

However, "the state is not monolithic ... the release of the Tottenham Three and the Birmingham Six, show how campaigning can force concessions."

Foot would not have dissented from this analysis, which

explains his understanding of the case. Poor Jimmy Hanratty had been framed by a corrupt police force and hanged for a crime he had not committed. Rather than admit error, successive governments and the judiciary protected the wrongdoers and perpetuated a stark injustice. When Hanratty's father forlornly paraded outside the House of Commons with a placard proclaiming his son's innocence it is not hard to guess who was responsible for the phrase "murdered by the state".

Foot, like Justice before him, became entangled in the endlessly elusive, endlessly shifting "confessions" of Peter Alphon, which were no sooner made than quickly retracted, and which were seamed, protectively, with quite deliberate errors. Foot's researches resulted in *Who Killed Hanratty?*, which in turn inspired others. Bob Woffinden's *Miscarriages of Justice* (1987) simply and naïvely accepted everything in Foot's book as indisputable fact.

Woffinden channelled the theories of Jean Justice and Paul Foot in his own lengthy work on the A6 murder. Its credibility seemed enhanced when the Criminal Cases Review Commission decided to refer the case to the Court of Appeal on the grounds of police misconduct, lack of disclosure and flawed identification evidence. That raised the question of the extent to which these were technicalities and how significant they were in relation to the question of Hanratty's guilt or innocence.

Non-disclosure included alleged sightings of the Morris Minor on the morning of 23 August 1961 and Valerie Storie's anxiety about the passage of time since the crime: "My memory of this man's face is fading ... I am so afraid that when confronted with the man I may not be able to pick him out." The defence would no doubt have made a great deal of these two aspects. However, the other sightings were almost certainly all erroneous. The fact that two of the Redbridge eye-witnesses successfully picked out Hanratty from a line-up was damning evidence against him. Similarly, the jury was informed that Valerie Storie had originally picked out the wrong man on the first identity parade, so they were aware that her eye-witness evidence was open to question. There was nothing here that seemed likely to have changed their minds and persuaded them to bring in a Not Guilty verdict.

Evidence of identification is certainly open to question, especially when the evidence against Hanratty involved only momentary glimpses of the killer. Eye-witness evidence identification, in theory, should always be regarded as inadequate in itself to ensure a conviction (a judicial convention sometimes conveniently disregarded, not least when Peter Hain was charged with bank robbery). This advice stems from the famous case of Adolf Beck, an entirely innocent man wrongly identified in 1895 and then again in 1904 as a thief and a fraudster by no less than sixteen eye-witnesses who all swore he was the man who had cheated them. This flagrant miscarriage of justice, which was aided and abetted by a hostile and arrogant judge and the malpractice of officials at the Home Office, became the textbook example of why eye-witness identification always needs to be treated with extreme caution.

That said, Hanratty's defence raised no concerns about the conduct of the ID parades. Even if the three eye-witnesses who picked out Hanratty were simply making lucky guesses, it was in the end subject to cross examination. The same cannot be said for the dubious eye-witness "evidence" which supposedly backed-up Hanratty's claim to have been in Liverpool and Rhyl at the time of the crime. Most of it was never subjected to critical scrutiny in a court of law and, unhappily, it emerged during the course of the trial, when memories were very obviously shaped and coloured by the high-profile media coverage.

Paul Foot's discovery of fresh eye-witnesses in later years was problematic because it emerged in the hothouse atmosphere of public campaigns and television journalism. Mr Justice Brabin once persuasively cautioned against this type of evidence, which he considered could be "buffeted" by the passage of time and external influences:

Stale evidence is often bad evidence. When recollection begins to fail imagination often takes its place and a witness is sometimes unable to distinguish the one from the other. A witness doing his best to tell the truth may, without realizing it, be giving evidence for it in his imagination, but giving it with the same confidence and demeanour that would mark his evidence if it were accurate. There comes a time when recollection almost entirely vanishes and the imagination of one witness is competing with that of another in recounting events which both have really forgotten. It can happen that what is spoken about as reality is in the main make-believe.

This is what the testimony from Rhyl amounted to: stale evidence, without merit. There was a basic contradiction in the campaigners' argument that the eye-witness evidence of Valerie Storie, John Skillett and James Trower was quite wrong whereas that of the later Rhyl witnesses was substantially accurate. If the eye-witness evidence of the first three was subject to the standard limitations of such testimony, why was the evidence from Rhyl magically exempt from those limitations? None of the supposed evidence from Rhyl involved the use of identification parades, and most of it was never tested in court. That which was tested in court was disbelieved by the jury.

The eye-witness evidence against Hanratty was only part of the case against the defendant. There was actually a broad spectrum of evidence. He exactly matched Valerie Storie's description of the gunman's smart appearance and cockney accent. His past matched the content of the gunman's revealing conversations. He was the only person at the Hotel Vienna who could be connected to the two discarded cartridge cases. His response to their discovery was not bewilderment but to shrewdly ask what size the bullets were (an odd question for someone who claimed to have no experience of firearms). The murder weapon

286

was discarded at precisely the place which he had once boasted made a good one to discard unwanted property.

Finally, there was Hanratty's failure to establish where he was on 22-24 August 1961. If he was really in Rhyl he had no reason to conceal this from his friends and family, yet he did not mention Rhyl until January 1962. He firstly provided a false alibi, then when that was discredited he invented a new one which was strategically vague and impossible to verify. Nor had he made any attempt to track down those who could have confirmed his supposed alibi, even though he had plenty of opportunity to do so.

The house of cards built by Justice, Foot and Woffinden came crashing down in April 2001 when it emerged that fresh, more sophisticated DNA testing had taken place on the semen on Valerie Storie's knickers and the mucus on the handkerchief used to wrap round the murder weapon. When compared with DNA extracted from Hanratty's teeth after his body was exhumed, there was a perfect match. Most damning of all, on the handkerchief there was DNA from only one individual: James Hanratty. This was scientific proof which underlined what had been obvious for forty years. James Hanratty was the murderer of Michael Gregsten and the man who raped Valerie Storie.

13   The Final Verdict

> The English criminal process is concerned not with the
> truth about the crime, but solely with the assessment of
> criminal responsibility.
>
> Louis Blom-Cooper, *The A6 Murder* (1963)

When *Shadows of Deadman's Hill: A New Analysis of the A6 Murder*, was first published in 2001, the Court of Appeal had yet to rule on the case. I anticipated that if the Court upheld the appeal on the basis of non-disclosure and police misconduct, this would not in itself mean that the conviction was necessarily a wrong one. It was a point made by Sir Louis Blom-Cooper in his book *The Birmingham Six and Other Cases*. He asserted that if a jury's verdict is overturned by the Court of Appeal this does not automatically signify that the defendant was innocent.

An identical conclusion was reached the following year by the Channel 4 documentary *Hanratty: The Whole Truth*, written and directed by Clive Maltby. First broadcast eight days before the Court of Appeal announced its judgement, this programme unequivocally asserted that James Hanratty was guilty of the A6 murder and the rape of Valerie Storie. With rather unnecessary hyperbole it promised "to lay to rest the most infamous murder case of the twentieth century". At the core of this 2002 programme was a lengthy interview with Valerie Storie, speaking publicly for the first time since her appearance on BBC's *Panorama*, broadcast on 7 November 1966. That experience had left her disillusioned and bitter, since the central thrust of the *Panorama* programme was that a terrible miscarriage of justice had occurred and that James Hanratty was innocent. Now she was for the first time participating in a documentary that asserted

Hanratty's guilt and which, quite literally, gave her the last word. She recounted her memories of the crime, intercut with a dramatic re-enactment of the abduction and what followed. Storie recalled her attendance at the identity parade, where she picked out Hanratty. "It was the eyes," she recalled, saying that when she looked at Hanratty, "He knew that I knew."

A range of other figures appeared, many for the first time. Michael Gregsten's oldest son, Simon, spoke of the terrible memory of being bluntly informed as a child that he would not be seeing his daddy again, because daddy was dead. He described the pain suffered by his mother, which lasted to the end her life, when campaigners insinuated that she had been involved in the crime. Janet Gregsten had been particularly upset by Bob Woffinden's *Hanratty – The Mystery of Deadman's Hill.* It seemed as if by broadcasting *Hanratty: The Whole Truth* Channel 4 was belatedly making amends for its meretricious 1992 documentary promoting Woffinden's dogmatic belief in Hanratty's innocence. Woffinden was not interviewed for the programme but in one of the old newsreel clips showing Hanratty campaigners at a press conference, Woffinden could be seen, a figure at the end with a pudding basin haircut.

One of Charles France's younger daughters, Roberta France, appeared for the first time. She rubbished the idea that her father was involved in the crime. His suicide, she said, came from his sense of remorse that he had allowed a murderer and a rapist into his home to mingle with his family. Her own enduring distress was obvious.

On 14 October 1961 Hanratty had been taken in a police van to Stoke Mandeville Hospital for the identity parade before Valerie Storie. On the way it had called at RAF Halton to collect men for the parade. John Needham, a former RAF police corporal, told the programme makers how he talked to Hanratty when he was brought to RAF Halton. In the course of a genial conversation he said Hanratty had casually remarked "They know I did it. I know I did it, but I don't think they can prove it." Once the police had selected enough RAF men who most resembled the suspect they went on to Stoke Mandeville. Hanratty travelled with the airmen, who were startled to find the infamous suspect among them.

Jonathan Whitaker, a Principal Forensic Scientist for DNA profile interpretation at the Forensic Science Service, explained that the likelihood of the DNA evidence connecting Hanratty to the crime being wrong was one in 500 million. He also dismissed the notion that contamination might be responsible for the analysis, stating that the samples involved primary contact, not secondary contact.

In the event the Court of Appeal upheld the original verdict. It marked the effective end of the long-running A6 campaign. Paul Foot had been astonished by the DNA evidence, which had provided the opposite conclusion to the one he had been confidently expecting. Now he rejected both the science and the judgement. He remarked:

> The DNA findings conflicted grotesquely with the alibis. If Hanratty was guilty, as the DNA suggested, he could not have been in Liverpool and Rhyl. If he was in Liverpool and Rhyl, there must be something wrong with the DNA. All of us who had followed the case over the years hoped that the appeal would solve this contradiction.

Foot's tunnel vision about the case continued to the end of his life. As far as he was concerned the alibi evidence was rock solid. Although I had torn it apart in some detail in *Shadows of Deadman's Hill*, as far as I am aware Foot never replied to my critique. When I publicly challenged him in *The Guardian* newspaper he stayed silent, which was oddly uncharacteristic of such a passionate polemicist and debater as Foot.

When Foot died in 2004 the political organisation to

which he had dedicated his life produced *Paul Foot 1937-2004: A Tribute*. It included an admiring piece by Julie Bundy about *Who Killed Hanratty?* claiming that it "rocked the established order" and "became a model for future investigations into miscarriages of justice". These conclusions were wishful thinking. The case against Hanratty was always far stronger than Foot, blinded by his romanticisation of a sociopath, ever acknowledged. In this instance he was no Chris Mullin, whose book, *Error of Judgment: The Truth About the Birmingham Pub Bombings* is an enduring classic. Bundy asserted that Foot established that Hanratty's alibi "was true". This preposterous claim was followed by Michael Hanratty's equally absurd allegation that "They were against my brother from the beginning. They had to fabricate things to get it to court."

Bob Woffinden's reactions to the DNA evidence and the conclusions of the Court of Appeal were identical to Foot's. He continued doggedly to insist on Hanratty's innocence, in the face of all the evidence. When Woffinden died even a sympathetic obituarist in *The Guardian* felt obliged to acknowledge that, though Woffinden was instrumental in getting the crime exhibits retested for DNA, "the results indicated that Hanratty was indeed guilty".

Others were less inflexible than Foot and Woffinden. Michael Sherrard QC, Hanratty's defence barrister, told members of the Law Society that although he still maintained that the evidence had been too weak to justify conviction, he accepted the DNA results: "The wrong man was not hanged. That was an immense relief to me."

The Court of Appeal's 2002 judgement ran to over 31,000 words. It made many points in rejecting every aspect of the case put forward by the campaigners. Firstly, it pointed out that at the original trial the judge's summing up could not be faulted, even though at the time Michael Sherrard had appealed against it on the grounds that it was unfair to the defendant: "The summing up was clear, it was impartial, it was not only fair but favourable to the prisoner and contained no misdirections of law and no misdirections in fact on any of the important issues in the case."

Woffinden had argued that the Morris Minor seen early in the morning in Redbridge was not Gregsten's, which he argued had only been parked there much later in the day. The Court rejected this hypothesis, saying that regarding the presence of the motor car in Avondale Crescent, "this evidence broadly fitted with that of Doris Athoe. She lived at 6 Avondale Crescent ... She said that she had seen it 'round about 7 o'clock in the morning' and that it remained there on the occasions ('at least twice') that she had passed up and down the Crescent. Her deposition was read and thus the time at which the car was left was not in issue."

The Court noted that Peter Alphon was not the A6 killer. "No witness connected with the murder picked out Mr Alphon." Moreover the DNA evidence exonerated him. The figure at the heart of Jean Justice, Paul Foot and Bob Woffinden's books was briskly dismissed as an irrelevance. Four decades of conspiracy theories collapsed in an instant.

The Court dismissed the argument that the DNA evidence was not admissible or relevant. It further considered the conflicting views of expert witnesses. The campaigners were keen to make the case for contamination but the Court noted that "the dangers of contamination were recognised even in 1961 and that the practice was to take elementary precautions such as making sure that clothing from victim and suspect were not examined on the same day".

Mr Greenhalgh, who saw the file and examined the fabric in 1995, told us that he considered the risk of contamination to the fabric to be very low. We quote from his evidence.

"As I examined the item, the piece of blue material from the knickers was in a sealed packet inside the two envelopes. I did not observe any damage to that packaging which I considered likely to be a risk of contamination. As far as I was concerned they were sealed, although the outer envelopes were not sealed there was no indication of any liquid damage on the brown paper envelopes, as might have been expected if a liquid sample had leaked onto them."

Collectively, where most of the forensic experts were concerned, "the general tenor of the evidence has been that they each considered the possibility [of contamination] to be remote". The Appeal Court's judgement also revealed that Valerie Storie had in fact seen her attacker's face on a number of occasions, not just once:

"When I got in the back of the car there may have been cars passing. I think there were some heavy lorries. I only had an opportunity to see a side view, possibly a three quarters view whilst I was in the back when any vehicle went past. I can't really say how many vehicles went past – not more than about 6 or 8 but I didn't really count them. Their headlights would illuminate the man's face for less than 10 seconds."

The judgement further provided context for Valerie Storie's notorious remark that her memory was fading:

[There was] an interruption of DS Acott explaining that he intended to show her photographs when she said "My memory of this man's face is fading" to which he responded "Yes but if you see the face, it will come back to you".

The Court also observed that, where the law was concerned, standards of disclosure were different in 1961 than they are nowadays. For example, where Acott's notebook was concerned,

"The notebook would fall to be disclosed under contemporary common law rules; it is less clear that it represented an inconsistent statement by 1962 standards." Although the campaigners put forward what was regarded as crucial new evidence, the Court concluded that "none of this evidence was without its difficulties for the defence and although this represents the high watermark of non-disclosure in this case we do not consider that, on its own, this feature reveals such fatal unfairness as itself to render the conviction unsafe".

Summing up, the Court observed that

> the critical question is the conviction of James Hanratty of murder unsafe ultimately relates to the single issue which dominated the trial and this appeal, the identity of the killer. In our judgment for reasons we have explained the DNA evidence establishes beyond doubt that James Hanratty was the murderer. The DNA evidence made what was a strong case even stronger. Equally the strength of the evidence overall pointing to the guilt of the appellant supports our conclusion as to the DNA.

Although there were shortcomings regarding disclosure these were not in themselves of any great significance:

> the procedural shortcomings fell far short of what is required to lead to the conclusion that the trial should be regarded as flawed and this conviction unsafe on procedural grounds. The trial still met the basic standards of fairness required. We are satisfied that James Hanratty suffered no real prejudice.

Finally, the Court expressed, in a suitably muted and euphemistic manner, the obvious exasperation of the judges that such a flimsy case should ever have been referred to it, tartly commenting that "there have to be exceptional circumstances to justify incurring the expenditure of resources on this scale, including those of this Court, on a case of this age". The Criminal Cases Review Commission's investigation of the A6 murder was apparently a multi-million pound affair and, in the end, a gross waste of public money.

The Court of Appeal's judgement was effectively the end of the Hanratty campaign, both in terms of legal options and in the sphere of public opinion. Six days after the Court's decision BBC TV broadcast *The A6 Murder* in its *Horizon* series. It allowed leading figures from the campaign to make the case for Hanratty's innocence. Paul Foot accused the police of "bending the evidence" to fit James Hanratty. Michael Hanratty concurred. "Acott and [Detective Sergeant] Oxford murdered my brother." (It has never been noted that Michael was happy to inherit the proceeds of Jimmy's criminal activities as a burglar in the shape of his Sunbeam Alpine car, originally purchased with stolen cash and jewellery. Beneficiaries of crime make questionable moralists.)

Whereas Channel 4 featured Simon, the eldest son of Michael Gregsten, *Horizon* interviewed his younger brother, Anthony McKinlay Gregsten. He spoke of his mother's ordeal at having to go and identify her husband's corpse in the lay-by. He also reminded viewers of how his father had largely been marginalised and forgotten in this long-running saga. The name which had endured was Hanratty's, who was often even hazily remembered by the general public as the victim not the murderer. He had a point. James Morton tartly makes the point that in a list of notorious murders the case of Maxwell Confait is one of the rare instances where the crime is remembered by the name of the victim, not the killer. Hundreds of thousands of words have been written about James Hanratty and his life and background. But the man Hanratty murdered, Michael Gregsten, remains a marginalised figure, little more than a phantom. Hanratty erased him from existence and the books about the case performed a second erasure. There are more photographs in circulation of the killer than his victim.

One surprise figure in the *Horizon* programme was John Kerr, who, as a teenager, was the first person to speak to Valerie Storie as she lay wounded in the lay-by. He had attended the trial and remembered that Hanratty did not make a good impression. Whereas Bob Woffinden's at times lachrymose book presented Hanratty as a gentle innocent, Kerr recalled that observing him in the witness box, "He came across as a cocky, arrogant person … he certainly looked a nasty piece of work." He also believed that "Hanratty's demeanour and appearance probably weighed a great deal with the jury in coming to their decision."

Another interesting revelation was that Michael Sherrard was firmly convinced that the length of time taken by the jury to reach their verdict was very good news indeed. Sherrard was confident that when they finally trooped back into court after almost ten hours of deliberation their verdict would be Not Guilty. Sherrard told the Hanratty family that he was enormously optimistic about a positive verdict. This was cheering news and made the Guilty verdict all the more of a shock.

At the heart of *The A6 Murder* was the DNA evidence. The science behind the DNA analysis was explained in considerable detail, with commentary from a range of forensic scientists. Samples of two exhibits were tested: Exhibit 26, the knickers, and Exhibit 35, the man's white handkerchief used to wrap the murder weapon when it was hidden under a bus seat. It proved beyond reasonable doubt that Hanratty was both the rapist and the gunman. Most damning of all, there was no other DNA to be found on the handkerchief at all. Hanratty's defenders insisted on the possibility of contamination but this was rejected by all the scientists except the one retained by the campaign. His arguments for contamination were rejected by the Court of Appeal.

The DNA saga glaringly exposed the hypocrisy of the Hanratty campaigners. As far back as 1994 they had urged the Home Office to use the new and developing science of "genetic fingerprinting" to test the surviving exhibits. As Bob Woffinden explained, "We had hoped that state-of-the-art forensic analysis might be able to provide a DNA profile of the gunman which could then be matched with a putative profile for James Hanratty (to be obtained from his mother's and brother's DNA)." When this was done the original tests were inconclusive.

Finally, later than the publication of the paperback edition of Woffinden's book, results were obtained. The gunman's DNA showed startling similarities with that of the Hanratty family members. It was then determined that to be absolutely certain of the identification Hanratty's body needed to be exhumed and DNA extracted from his teeth. Now, suddenly, the campaigners lost their enthusiasm for DNA analysis. The exhumation was opposed and denounced as disgusting, offensive and upsetting. The subsequent analysis indicated beyond all reasonable doubt that James Hanratty was indeed a murderer and a rapist.

The response from the campaigners was one of total denial. Bob Woffinden found the Court of Appeal's ruling "distressing and shattering". He insisted that "Hanratty's alibis cannot be dismissed in the way that they have been today. To me, the forensic evidence is incredible." He was echoed by Paul Foot, who breezily explained, "I'm a complete illiterate in relation to the science of DNA and physics and so on. I know nothing about it at all." But since he *knew* Hanratty was innocent, "There must be something wrong with the science."

Had they been Italian and around in the seventeenth century we can be certain that Woffinden and Foot would have rejected Copernican heliocentrism for its contradiction of the one true faith. Or to put it another way, although Paul Foot considered himelf to be a Marxist he romantically misperceived Hanratty as a working-class martyr, failing to recognise that he was in reality not a member of the proletariat (a revolutionary class) but rather of the lumpenproletariat, a "dangerous class" brusquely dismissed by Marx as "social scum".

The underlying theme of the slasher movie is now clear: it is women, the apparent victims, who are the true aggressors ... Men beware women: the frills and furbelows of feminity hide the knife.

Joan Smith, *Misogynies* (1989)

One recurring feature of the A6 saga is male writers confidently explaining matters involving women (and of course all the literature on this crime is written by male authors, including this one).

Nowadays it is impossible to overlook how gender may shape perception. The A6 murder and rape occurred at a time when sexism remained rife in British society, with stereotypical views of women, sexuality and rape common among large sections of the community, not least the male half. Detective Superintendent Acott made a notorious note that when Valerie Storie first described the events which followed the gunman's first appearance "it sounded so fantastic that from the start it was treated as highly suspect – like the majority of accounts by women who have made allegations of rape". Attitudes like that were institutionalised in the police service and commonplace in society at large.

Arthur Koestler, a famous writer, a friend of George Orwell, and an eloquent and effective campaigner against capital punishment, was, after his death, and to the shock of his admirers, exposed by his biographer David Cesarini as a sexual predator and rapist. Koestler at times exploded in rage and punched and hit women who were close to him. In 1952 Koestler raped Jill Craigie, who was Paul Foot's aunt. The politician Richard Crossman remarked that Koestler was "a hell of a raper". Behind the public persona of an engaged liberal intellectual and accomplished writer lay a much darker figure, whose true nature would only be revealed after his death. Of the rape of Jill Craigie, Cesarini comments: "Koestler had beaten and raped women before; over the next few years it would be almost a hallmark of his conduct."

To be fair to Detective Superintendent Acott, his initial scepticism about Valerie Storie's description of what had occurred evaporated when the forensic evidence confirmed her story. Acott's prejudiced views were to be expected of a serving male officer of his generation. But in the face of the evidence he set them aside and henceforth regarded Valerie as a very reliable witness.

What is plain is that prejudicial attitudes to women were not restricted to the police. One of the ironies of the campaign to clear Hanratty's name is that in defending a man who, all along, was indeed a murderer and a rapist, the campaigners pointed their accusing fingers at the two women at the centre of the case. It was, to the leading campaigners, substantially the fault of the victims. Valerie Storie was repeatedly told she was wrong about her identification of the man she said had shot her lover and then raped her. Janet Gregsten was regarded as a deranged, jealous wife who had hired a gunman to scare her husband and make him break off his affair.

Along the way other attitudes emerged. Louis Blom-Cooper used the A6 case as a peg on which to hang his ideas for improving the criminal justice system. Some were distinctly wacky. If an old woman alone in her bed at night was disturbed by a burglar, Blom-Cooper firmly advised her not to scream, as this might well provoke a fatal assault: "if old women in this predicament can learn that their lives may be saved by the exercise of considerable presence of mind in not shouting for help or screaming, then murders may be prevented".

Jean Justice had all the delicacy of a charging rhinoceros. *Murder vs. Murder* was deeply hostile to Valerie Storie, accusing her of letting her evidence be affected by "a slow and insidious process of police conditioning". *She* was to blame. Because of her a young man had "suffered martyrdom" on a "cold April morning". Jean Justice grieved for that "pathetic figure in the dock". He was haunted by the monstrous miscarriage of justice he had witnessed in that Bedford courtoom: "I could not cast from my mind the memory of the little man in the dock, vainly pleading his innocence".

To this lachrymose tribute to a psychopath he added a coarse challenge to a raped woman in a wheelchair:

> If Valerie will admit that I am right when I state that she and Gregsten were forced to have sexual intercourse together, then she will also realise that only one person could have given me the information.
> The murderer.

It evidently did not occur to him that he was almost certainly adding to her distress as a rape victim by including lurid anecdotes about sexual activity in which she was supposedly involved, which were based on nothing more than the erotic fantasies of the lonely, inadequate, attention-seeking Peter Alphon. Revealingly, even admirers of Jean Justice such as Paul Foot and Bob Woffinden chose not to recycle this unpleasant and entirely fictitious anecdote.

After Louis Blom-Cooper and Jean Justice came Lord Russell of Liverpool. He felt he understood James Hanratty, even though he had not attended the trial and knew little about him. There was no past evidence of Hanratty owning a gun and Lord Russell was convinced that "he was not the kind of young man who would ever want to do so".

Russell's interpretation of the events of the night of 22 August 1961 was opinionated and shallow. He coolly asserted that Gregsten and Storie were strong, calm individuals "not given to panicking and able to make sound and swift decisions". They must therefore, he blandly commented, not have been "unduly alarmed" at having a gun pointed at them. This was an easy thing for him to say. He had been a soldier during the First World War, winning the Military Cross. He was acquainted with weapons, danger, risk-taking and violent death. Valerie Storie and Michael Gregsten were leading quiet, lower-middle-class lives. They had no experience of criminality or firearms. In reality the couple were utterly terrified at the predicament they found themselves in. How could they be sure that the gunman wouldn't shoot? They couldn't. They knew nothing about him.

Lord Russell patronisingly suggested what Michael Gregsten should have done to liberate them from their predicament: "What could have been easier than to drive the car straight into one of the petrol pumps, which would quickly have brought someone on the scene and led to the gunman's capture?" This is a classic example of being wise after the event. Lord Russell was convinced that the gunman would not have opened fire. That was pure guesswork on his part. It is hardly surprising that Michael Gregsten chose not to risk it. Russell was also unaware that Valerie Storie had told police that Michael Gregsten had indicated to her that if he saw a policeman he intended to drive the car on to the pavement and stop by the officer.

Lord Russell was keen to offer pompous observations, while simultaneously displaying a basic ignorance of the geography of the crime scene. He stated that upon reaching the junction with the A4 Gregsten was "told to turn right in the direction of Maidenhead". Wrong: Maidenhead was to the left. To the right was Slough. Not that this mattered much. Lord Russell was in no doubt that Valerie Storie had made an incorrect identification of the killer. With a patronising sneer, he commented, "everyone knows the woman who is never more certain she is right than when she is wrong".

Next came Paul Foot. The 40-minute film about the A6 campaign, financed by John Lennon, features Foot with his Beatles haircut and his passionate certainties enlightening his audience about James Hanratty. "He never had any problems at all with his sex life," he assured his listeners. This raises the question of how Foot could possibly *know*. He had never met Hanratty. Besides, another person's sex life is always ultimately a mystery. When he made that remark Foot was recycling the complacent assumption that rapists are somehow abnormal individuals who are not involved in stable relationships. He was echoed by Bob Woffinden, who assured his readers that Hanratty was "Far from being sex-starved". But not only did he not know the truth about Hanratty's sexual history, he was evading the central point that rapists and murderers can both be sexually active individuals and "respectable" – husbands, fathers, professionals and pillars of the community.

Decades later Paul Foot admitted that at the time of writing *Who Killed Hanratty?* he was quite convinced that Janet Gregsten was a "jealous demon". To regard a woman as a *demon* is an interesting noun for a man of supposed progressive opinions to use. Foot died before the organisation to which he had dedicated his life imploded amid scandal and claims of a cover-up. In 2013 a leading member of the Socialist Workers Party, one of Foot's close associates, was accused of rape. The SWP leadership was widely perceived at the time as closing ranks over the matter and being more interested in protecting the alleged rapist and maintaining party discipline than in addressing the accusation. The scandal tore the party apart and resulted in an exodus of members and leading figures. Had he lived, Foot would have been forced to take a position on a matter which involved a close friend, who was, ironically, also involved in organising the celebration of his life and work held at the Hackney Empire on 10 October 2004.

After Foot came Bob Woffinden. Janet Gregsten met him and found him hostile. She rightly regarded his subsequent television documentary as a travesty. Woffinden also sought to meet Valerie Storie but she declined. She felt that she had been ambushed by the BBC when she agreed to be interviewed for

Panorama in 1966. She had no idea back then that the programme would question whether Hanratty was really guilty. Thereafter she distrusted television journalists.

Woffinden communicated with Valerie and told her that the wrong man had been convicted. This plainly insinuated that she bore some guilt in the matter for having erroneously identified Hanratty as her attacker. In the words of her biographer, "Valerie ignored him, and in time, would come to greatly dislike the man."

Woffinden wrote two more books arguing against historic convictions. In the year that *Hanratty: The Final Verdict* was first published another brutal crime gripped the nation. On Saturday 15 February 1997 a thirteen-year-old girl, Billie-Jo Jenkins, was found dead on the patio of her home in Hastings. She had suffered a brief, frenzied attack from someone who had beaten her over the head at least five times with a large, heavy iron metal tent peg, some eighteen inches long. The assault was so vicious it smashed in her skull. After two early suspects had been eliminated, attention turned to the dead girl's foster father, Siôn Jenkins.

The case against Jenkins was that his behaviour after the murder was highly suspicious in a variety of ways. The police believed that he had made a pointless twenty-minute car drive after the killing in order to create a hypothetical window of opportunity for someone else to have committed the crime. They discovered that he was dishonest, having invented qualifications which he lacked in order to obtain his current position of Deputy Headmaster. Most damning of all, forensic experts testified that the discovery of 158 microscopic particles of Billie-Jo's blood on a fleece jacket he was wearing on the day of her murder was "impact splatter" resulting from his savage attack on the child. On 2 July 1998 a jury unanimously found him guilty of murder. He was sentenced to life imprisonment.

Within days of the conviction Bob Woffinden rushed to Jenkins' defence, publishing two articles which proclaimed his innocence, one in *The New Statesman*, the other in the *Daily Mail*. Woffinden was "absolutely convinced" that Jenkins could not have killed Billie-Jo. He believed Jenkins had no motive for committing the crime and no opportunity. Had Jenkins carried out the crime, Woffinden believed, he would have been covered in blood. He could not have lost his temper "to a degree that none of us would find comprehensible", committed the murder, and then immediately returned to his normal behaviour.

This was classic Woffinden. He dealt in absolutes. He was not a forensic expert but he had a fixed opinion about blood splatter in a murder case where no one knew the relative positions of the attacker or the victim. He was not a psychologist yet he believed he understood human behaviour. He knew nothing about Siôn Jenkins but he felt he understood his character and his mind. Although Woffinden asserted that Jenkins had no motive for committing the crime and no opportunity, it was the prosecution case that he was a man who sometimes lost his temper, that he was an obsessive perfectionist, who might well have become furious when he saw the mess Billie-Jo had made of her painting task, and whose anger with the child might well have provoked an impudent and insulting response that detonated an explosion of rage. The claim that Jenkins had no opportunity to carry out the crime was denied by the prosecution. There was a window of opportunity when Jenkins was alone on the patio with Billie-Jo for a period of several minutes. Jenkins, according to his wife, had a history of violence. A family friend said that he had witnessed Jenkins physically attacking Billie-Jo on holiday. School friends remembered Billie-Jo coming to school with scratches and bruises, which the girl blamed on her foster father. But none of this influenced Woffinden. He was totally convinced that Siôn Jenkins was an innocent man, disgracefully traduced by the police.

Woffinden became part of a successful defence campaign. Forensic experts were found who argued that the blood on Jenkins' jacket might be "expiration splatter" which resulted from the dying girl releasing a spray of droplets. After six years in prison Siôn Jenkins was released. He faced two further trials. In each case the jury was divided and unable to agree a majority verdict. Jenkins was formally acquitted and applied for £500,000 compensation for loss of earnings and wrongful dismissal. This was rejected on the grounds that he had never been found innocent.

In the absence of a conviction the case remains officially unsolved. Aspects of the crime remain hotly contested, especially the timings and location of Jenkins' movements at the time of the murder, and the evidence of his two daughters. The major conflict is between the two interpretations of the significance of the blood on the jacket. The science is highly specialised and, as the judge at the first trial commented, it was impossible to reproduce the exact circumstances of the murder. Scientific experiments which attempted to do so were subject to many variables.

In 2008 the only book on this crime was published. Co-authored, *The Murder of Billie-Jo* was an account by Siôn Jenkins of the background to the case, his arrest, conviction, imprisonment and subsequent release, interspersed with chapters by Bob Woffinden providing further context to the crime and its aftermath.

The chapters by Woffinden are especially revealing. When the police interviewed Jenkins' wife Lois it was reported, "She said he has hit her throughout their marriage and that she has come to accept this as the norm, believing this is usual in a relationship." Woffinden found it "completely bewildering" that a woman like Lois could really have suffered in this way and told no one. He asserted: "Siôn is not a violent man and certainly not prone to domestic violence." To which one can only reply: how on earth did he know? The only two people who really know the truth are Siôn and Lois. In any case, Woffinden displays a stunning and crass ignorance of the subject of domestic violence. Even highly educated professional women can become trapped in coercive relationships and suffer abuse which they conceal from others. In *The Murder of Billie-Jo* Woffinden repeatedly exposes himself as a man who believes that domestic violence must be very visible to friends and neighbours. As far as he is concerned, if outsiders have not witnessed it, then it never occurred.

Feminists have a word for men who dismiss or underplay the experience and views of women: "mansplaining". Woffinden certainly fitted the definition of this term – the type of man who is condescending, overconfident and (arguably) clueless. A school friend, Holly Prior, said that Billie-Jo had come to school wearing a scarf, and had shown her scratches on her neck and a bruise. "She said Siôn was smacking Buster (her dog) and she told him to stop. He pinned her up against a door and told her it was up to him. He was really strict. She was really upset and crying. She told us not to tell anyone," she said. Holly Prior described the marks as "really red and sore, as if she had been bleeding". Woffinden explains this by seizing on the testimony of another witness, saying Billie-Jo had been in a fight and didn't want anyone to know.

Another school friend, Laura-Jane Conway, described how Billie-Jo had arrived at school with scratches on her neck and blood on her face. "She said she got punched in her nose by her dad. There was blood on her shirt and blood around her mouth." She also told the court that on another occasion, about a month before she died, Billie-Jo had gone to school with her mouth bleeding because of a cut. She also had bruises on her arms and legs, and said: "I had an argument with my dad again. You can guess what happened." Billie-Jo had also written "Hate" on her knuckles and "I hate my Dad" with "Siôn" in brackets, Laura-Jane Conway said. Woffinden briskly dismisses this evidence as "fantasies".

Of course the person who knew Jenkins best after fifteen years of marriage was Lois. She said she had witnessed his "vein-popping" anger when he lost his temper with Billie-Jo. She said he would sometimes flip and lose control, becoming "red in the face".

Denise Lancaster said she was with Lois Jenkins when

police told her blood spattering had been found on Jenkins's clothes which implicated him. "She said to me 'why did Siôn kill Billie? If ever he was going to kill anyone, I am sure he would kill me'."

Family friend Peter Gaimster said he had seen Siôn Jenkins kick Billie-Jo while they were on holiday in France in August 1996. He said Jenkins kicked his foster daughter as she lay on a bed settee after she twisted her ankle while playing nearby. Gaimster said: "There is no such thing as a playful kick. It was a proper, aggressive kick. He was furious, he was angry." Gaimster said Jenkins then turned round to see him standing in the doorway and afterwards "behaved very calmly". Woffinden regards Gaimster as another unreliable witness.

Woffinden was always adept at manipulating material to prove his case, while blanking out evidence that didn't fit his preconceived notions of what really happened. Thus in *The Murder of Billie-Jo* he evades the issue of the doctored CV, leaving the reader in ignorance as to precisely what lies Jenkins told on his application. Jenkins himself makes light of this stark evidence of his dishonesty, breezily explaining that he was only guilty of embellishment and exaggeration on his CV, like thousands of others.

Perhaps the most absurd part of Woffinden's contribution to *The Murder of Billie-Jo* is Chapter 17, entitled "Feed into Mum". This refers to an instruction given to the Jenkins family's two family liaison officers, Detective Constable Steve Hutt and Woman Detective Constable Julie Gregory. When it was discovered that there was blood on Siôn Jenkins's jacket, that it was Billie-Jo's blood, and according to the forensic expert who had analysed it, that the pattern indicated he was her attacker, the two officers were told to break this devastating news gently to his wife, Lois Jenkins – "feed into Mum". Woffinden is scandalised by this, which he regards as unfairly influencing the suspect's wife. Going into full outrage mode, Woffinden asserts:

"Feed into Mum" are the three most important words in the Billie-Jo murder case. The phrase is critical not just for the case itself but for the lives of all those who were unhappily caught up in it; its importance is such that it will become a key phrase in British criminal justice history.

This was preposterous hyperbole. The phrase was entirely innocent. It simply meant that the police were obliged to inform Lois Jenkins that her husband had come under suspicion. This information certainly had an impact. It was as if a dam had broken. Suddenly out poured the suspect's wife's revelations, including descriptions of his physical assaults on her, his violent temper, and his suspicious behaviour in not wanting to wear the fleece jacket after the murder, even though it was a cold night.

In February 2022 Channel 5 broadcast a documentary on the case involving four of the police officers (all now retired) who were centrally involved in the case. Detective Constable Steve Hutt rubbished the spin which Woffinden put on the phrase "feed into Mum". He also observed that in *The Murder of Billie-Jo*, Siôn Jenkins wrote, "I signed my forty-two page statement. I had not read what Hutt had written." Steve Hutt said that this simply wasn't true; Jenkins in fact had read the statement very carefully before he signed it.

Woffinden wrote one final book about supposed miscarriages of justice: *The Nicholas Cases*. The problem with it is that its treatment of the cases it covers, none of which has achieved any prominence, is very superficial. Woffinden might be right in his conclusions, or, infinitely gullible and naïve, he might equally be wrong about every single one of these cases. To form a conclusion would require further, extensive research. The A6 case revealed Woffinden to be good at discovering new material but bad at analysing it. As a guide to understanding he exposed himself as unreliable. He cherry-picked evidence when it suited him, he failed to grasp the significance of material which contradicted his belief in a convicted criminal's innocence, and when he was faced by tangible forensic evidence indicating guilt he simply went into denial. In short, he was not to be trusted.

Yet Bob Woffinden still has his admirers. Michael Rosen, for example, claimed in 2021 that "He made great TV programmes about miscarriages of justice." No, he did not – at least not where the A6 murder was concerned (and as far as I am aware Woffinden's other TV work did not involve any other criminal case). Meanwhile the journalist Richard Ingrams still clings doggedly to the notion that his old friend Paul Foot was right and Hanratty was innocent. As recently as 2018 he was still banging a very old drum, while managing to misspell Valerie Storie's surname, getting the year of the definitive DNA tests wrong and insisting that "two important experts who knew more about the case than anyone refused to accept the DNA evidence".

Needless to say the names of these two "important experts" do not require spelling out.

15   The Long Goodbye

> I didn't want it to end. I wouldn't let it end ... I could
> grow old in my search.
>
> James Ellroy, *My Dark Places* (1996)

The A6 Murder Committee fizzled out with the death of its
leading member, James Hanratty senior, who died in 1978. Ten
years later *Who Killed Hanratty?* was republished as a mass
market Penguin paperback. In a new Postscript (April 1988),
Paul Foot reluctantly acknowledged that "very little has come to
light in the last thirteen years to force the case once more into the
limelight". That remained so until Bob Woffinden became
involved. But by 2002 it was effectively all over for the long-
running campaign to prove that James Hanratty had suffered a
miscarriage of justice.

DNA analysis had established beyond all reasonable
doubt that it was Hanratty's semen on Valerie Storie's underwear
and Hanratty's mucus on the handkerchief used to wrap the
murder weapon. For aficionados of the crime my book *Shadows
of Deadman's Hill: A New Analysis of the A6 Murder* had shredded
the arguments of Justice, Foot and Woffinden, and asserted that
the conspiracy theories were nonsense and the crime had been a
random and arbitrary one. Everything about the gunman, I
argued, matched the personality and past of James Hanratty. On
top of all this the legal appeals came to an abrupt end with the
Court of Appeal's lengthy judgement upholding the original
conviction. Finally, Channel 4 and BBC TV both broadcast
documentaries asserting that James Hanratty was guilty of the A6
murder.

In 2004, some three years after *Shadows of Deadman's
Hill* was published, I received a long letter from the eminent New

York-based chess photographer Nigel Eddis. He said he was working on a book about British murder trials from the era before the final abolition of capital punishment, adding "of which I am a proponent!" The A6 murder would be one of the featured cases. Eddis, who was English-born, recalled that in 1973, visiting England, he had bought a copy of Foot's book on the case.

> When I opened it I found myself staring at an old friend of mine from my army days. This was Terry Evans – he and I were in the same troop in C squadron of the 15th/19th Hussars, in 1955.

> I thought it might interest you to know that despite his record, Terry was really at heart a very decent fellow. He was certainly capable of intense and even quixotic loyalty, though perhaps he was not the most astute judge of character. Obviously he was taken advantage of by Hanratty. But that he went out of his way to help the Hanratty family doesn't surprise me at all. As to honesty, well … You could leave your money lying around and Terry would never touch it. Of course I haven't seen him since 1956, so I have no idea of what he has been up to since, beyond what I read. But I hope Terry is well and prospering.

Hanratty's second bogus alibi hinged on the claim that he went to Rhyl to track down Evans and sell him a £350 diamond ring. It was an absurd claim since in the first place Hanratty knew professional fences in London, Bedford and, very probably, Liverpool. He did not need to go to a Welsh seaside resort and spend a day there wandering around in search of a man he barely knew. Secondly, Evans denied that he would have known how to dispose of such an expensive item. There was no reason to disbelieve him. Although he had a criminal record they were for motoring offences and petty theft. He was not a dealer in stolen property, nor was he a career criminal like Hanratty.

By now many of the leading figures involved in this long-running saga were dead. Jean Justice died in 1990; Janet Gregsten in 1995; Kenneth Oxford in 1998; Jeremy Fox and Mary Hanratty in 1999; Basil ("Bob") Acott in 2001. Two years after the Court of Appeal's judgement, Paul Foot died. It was perhaps unsurprising that *Socialist Worker* was in denial about the A6 case, listing among Foot's achievements his efforts in "exposing the faulty evidence that had led to the hanging of James Hanratty for murder in 1961". More surprising was that *The Guardian* newspaper adopted a similar ostrich-like attitude to the truth, with the paper's political editor Michael White and Sam Jones writing that among Foot's books were "exposés of miscarriages of justice, including … the execution for murder of James Hanratty".

Two decades have now elapsed since the A6 murder case came to its ultimate judicial conclusion.

In December 2010 it was reported that the Hanratty family's lawyers were preparing a case to go before the Criminal Cases Review Commission, urging a fresh review of the evidence on the basis that the material used in the DNA testing "could have been contaminated". However, if any such case was presented it was plainly rejected by the Commission as no fresh review of the evidence was ordered. Nothing seemed to follow this initiative in the years that followed. The misconceived, long-running campaign to clear Hanratty's name seems finally to have ended.

As it fizzled out, other central figures in the case dropped away forever. Peter Alphon outlived the two campaigners he had most influenced, dying in 2009. Michael Sherrard QC died in 2012; Valerie Storie in 2016; Bob Woffinden in 2018, and Michael Hanratty in 2020. The site of the crime is gone too, with the infamous lay-by at Deadman's Hill now absorbed into the northbound dual carriageway of the widened and improved A6 north of Clophill.

For a handful of people the case is still not closed. There are still some individuals living for whom the reverberations of Hanratty's savagery continue to this day. In 2007, some six years after publication of *Shadows of Deadman's Hill*, I was startled to receive a large envelope which had been sent to my publishers and forwarded. It was addressed to me and marked "PRIVATE AND CONFIDENTIAL". It had been posted from abroad and was from Michael Gregsten's youngest son, Anthony. He had exiled himself from his homeland, to create a new life in Scandinavia.

The contents included a short letter apprising me of the envelope's contents and thanking me for my book and its "penetrating insight". There was also a very long, deeply personal letter which left me in no doubt as to the catastrophic emotional impact which Michael Gregsten's murder had had on his widow and two sons. Other material included copies of correspondence about the case and the individuals who had become drawn into its orbit.

My feelings upon receiving this material were very mixed ones. I was fascinated by the revelations but also startled. Writing *Shadows of Deadman's Hill* had been a somewhat academic exercise. My primary intention was to deconstruct and demolish the case made by Hanratty's defenders, particularly Jean Justice, Paul Foot and Bob Woffinden. I cannot pretend that *Shadows of Deadman's Hill* is a particularly racy read. My emphasis was on the evidence put forward, not the characters or the human tragedies which lay behind the crime.

At the end of *Shadows of Deadman's Hill* I had quoted the American crime writer, James Ellroy, who wrote that where murder was concerned, closure "doesn't exist. It just goes on and on." Ellroy is himself the son of a murder victim and has written two eloquent memoirs of his damaged early years and the pain he had to struggle through to become what he is today. Anthony's bundle of material was a sudden, unexpected, shocking reminder of the raw suffering which endures long after a crime has been dealt with in the courts. James Hanratty wrecked many lives when he murdered Michael Gregsten and then raped and shot Valerie Storie. That pain was compounded by the long, wrong-headed campaign to clear him of the crime.

Pain was caused in other ways, too. When in 1978 the Home Office pathologist Professor Keith Simpson published his autobiography *Forty Years of Murder*, he included an account of his involvement in the A6 case. He also used (I would say mis-used) a police crime scene photograph, clinically and coldly captioned "Body of Gregsten lying in the lay-by on the A6, Bedfordshire". It is not an especially graphic photograph compared to some of the others in Simpson's book but in my view it should not have been reproduced while Michael Gregsten's widow and children were still alive. This very public exhibition of the crime victim's body, dumped on the ground like a heap of old rags, was like a second assault on Michael Gregsten. It was also ethically dubious to use, so close to the time of the crime, confidential material which was police property, for Simpson's own commercial gain.

"Do what you think best with this," Anthony wrote. At the time I had no intention of ever writing about the A6 case again. No publisher was interested in a paperback edition of *Shadows of Deadman's Hill*. Feeling somewhat discomfited by Anthony's revelations and by the raw suffering incarnated in some of the documents, I stuffed the material back into the envelope and filed it away with my modest collection of A6 press cuttings.

Only recently have I discovered that among Valerie Storie's possessions when she died was a copy of *Shadows of Deadman's Hill*. This, too, makes me feel both a little uncomfortable but at the same time relieved that I avoided discussion of intimate aspects of the crime which involved a victim who had survived and who had the opportunity of reading what strangers had to say about her experience. If she read the book I like to think she would not have dissented from its analysis and its conclusions.

Looking at the material sent to me by Anthony Gregsten again after the passage of some 15 years what I find of particular interest is what it reveals about Paul Foot. I had been startled to learn that Foot had had four long meetings with Janet Gregsten in 1995, in Soho, Penzance and Hampstead. He had quickly realised that his former suspicions of her were unfounded. His charm and genial demeanour worked their magic on her, with the consequence that now "She was strongly inclined to believe in Hanratty's innocence and agreed that his appearance in the Maidenhead field was, to put it mildly, unlikely."

Very soon after their final meeting Janet Gregsten died suddenly and unexpectedly of cardiac arrest. She was just 64 years old. The A6 murder had taken its toll from the day it happened and in 1980 she had suffered a stroke. Paul Foot, evidently remorseful for the way in which he had featured her in his telling of the A6 story, spoke at her funeral and "apologised both to her memory and to both her sons for ever having harboured any suspicions against Janet". This was a tribute to Foot's decency but did not, in my view, entirely absolve him.

Foot was a little ingenuous in his efforts to rewrite his own history. He argued, "I doubt very much whether anyone who reads the book [*Who Killed Hanratty?*] would conclude from it that Janet Gregsten had anything to do with the murder, and indeed my suspicions stopped well short of claiming any direct involvement by her." Yet the first sentence of the first chapter is simply: "The marriage between Michael and Janet Gregsten had been deteriorating for several months before the summer of 1961." The focus is on the private life of the murder victim. Before this first page has been turned the reader is coolly informed that "Janet Gregsten was irritated and depressed by her husband's affair with Miss Storie. She and her family did everything in their power to discourage the relationship." On the next page Foot informs his readers that "Other attempts at sabotaging the relationship had been made." He then cuts to a short account of the crime and how in the immediate aftermath the newspapers published an inaccurate story about the gunman having been a hitchhiker the couple had picked up. This false account of how the abduction began, Foot observed, ruled out the possibility that the couple were "the targets of a prearranged plot". It also deflected attention from the Gregstens' marriage and his affair with Valerie. Right from the start, Foot scented a conspiracy.

In reality the false hitch-hiker story probably originated with John Kerr, the teenager who had first spoken to Valerie as she lay wounded in the lay-by. In his distress he appears to have misunderstood some of the facts which Valerie was attempting to communicate. She was badly injured and he was understandably traumatised by the experience of stumbling upon a scene of horror. Later in the day, when he had recovered his composure, he told a television interviewer that the couple had picked up a hitchhiker at Slough. An innocent error later became part of the grist to Paul Foot's very active mill.

Foot's suspicions deepened. He firmly believed that Valerie Storie had told the police that the killer had "deep-set brown eyes". But this, too, was wrong. Valerie Storie had said no such thing. Another innocent error, this time within the police service and possibly derived from misread handwriting, became embedded in the narrative as another sinister component of a conspiracy. Foot connected this to the newspaper stories published shortly after Hanratty's conviction that Janet Gregsten had spotted Hanratty and his "blue staring eyes" at Swiss Cottage and the police had duly been informed that this man might be the A6 murderer. He insinuated that Janet Gregsten had helped to persuade Valerie that the killer's eyes were blue.

Alphon's fantasies supplied the framework which enabled Foot to tie all this together. Alphon said he had known a man named only as "X" for two years before the murder. "X" wanted to stop the affair between Michael Gregsten and Valerie Storie. "X" showed Alphon the cornfield where the couple used to go. Charles France knew both "X" and Alphon and supplied the gun. "X" arranged to pay Alphon £5,000 to frighten the couple and persuade Gregsten to end the affair. But when he held them up the couple laughed at him and told him to mind his own business.

Foot was careful not to name "X", who was in reality William Ewer. There were other grounds for suspicion, though they were not voiced. It is known that for some people the pain of bereavement can result in a heightening of sexual appetite. In the aftermath of her husband's murder Janet began an affair with her brother-in-law. This seems to have become known to journalists and helped feed the conspiracy theories that subsequently developed. For Foot, Ewer was the man who commissioned the crime for Janet's sake. For Woffinden, Ewer was the man who commissioned the crime to get rid of Michael Gregsten so that his widow would become available. Both plots were feverish fantasies but they supplied a satisfying explanation for those who found the crime inexplicable. Both versions, though articulated with carefully chosen words, insinuated that Janet was involved. Matters were complicated by the hidden involvement of others. Janet Gregsten was outraged when she discovered that an old acquaintance had contacted Ludovic Kennedy to inform him that she and Bill Ewer had been conducting an affair *before* Michael's murder. This information, which was malicious and untrue gossip, came from an individual with whom she and Michael had had no contact for several years. But it duly found its way to Paul Foot and surely helped to shape his perception that the crime was rooted in the murder victim's private life.

It remains a little ironic that, in a case which partly revolved around eye-witness testimony and the reliability of memory, Paul Foot's own account of his involvement displayed some blatant contradictions. One of his last articles about the A6 murder recalled how he first became involved. Four years after Hanratty's execution the reburial of the A6 killer was regarded as a newsworthy event. The news editor of *The Sunday Telegraph* sent along Paul Foot , then a 28-year-old journalist, to cover it.

"There may be trouble there," the news editor beamed. "This chap Alphon may cause a fuss." I had no idea who Alphon was, and after the burial in Wembley, I was none the wiser. There was nothing to report, so I gladly accepted the invitation of James and Mary Hanratty to join the wake for their son in their council house in Kingsbury ... Among the guests at the wake were Jean Justice, who told me he was a (rather elderly) law student, and his friend, a barrister called Jeremy Fox. I listened entranced to their assurances not only that Jimmy Hanratty had nothing to do with the A6 murder, but that they had been on intimate terms with the real killer: Peter Alphon. I was hooked on the case that gloomy February afternoon and, nearly 32 years later, I still am.

His memory was evidently failing him, because he had once written that he had first been told about Jean Justice in December 1965. He met him in person "about three weeks later" and heard all about Peter Alphon. Justice played Foot some of Alphon's secretly taped confessions, which Foot, initially sceptical, soon found "very convincing". All this preceded the reburial of Hanratty's remains. Foot, according to his earlier account, did not become "well and truly hooked on the A6 murder" until 25 August 1966, when he observed the trial of Peter Alphon for making threatening and abusive calls.

Human memory is fallible. But if the three eye-witnesses who identified Hanratty, and whose evidence was tested in court, were all wrong, why, logically, should the eye-witness testimony of residents of Rhyl be right? This last evidence was gathered in questionable, highly charged circumstances, never involved an identity parade, and lacked specificity when subjected to sceptical interrogation. The formidable intellect which Foot brought to other injustices deserted him when it came to James Hanratty. Hanratty's innocence became a matter of passionate faith, not reason.

Paul Foot was still in denial about Hanratty's guilt, which by 2002 had been comprehensively established. There was all the evidence set out at the original trial. A surprising number of alleged confessions by Hanratty had since come to light. There was no real mystery about Hanratty's presence in the cornfield. The crime had been a spur of the moment affair, which had evolved into murder and rape. It had not been pre-planned. There was no conspiracy. It had nothing whatever to do with the Gregsten marriage. Peter Alphon, an attention-seeking fantasist, was a red herring and an irrelevance. Finally, there was the DNA evidence, which was devastating confirmation of all the other aspects of the case which pointed time and time again to James Hanratty as the gunman.

But none of this mattered to Foot. "As far as I am concerned, the A6 murder is still unsolved," he wrote in 2002 – a position he stubbornly maintained until his own sudden, premature death just two years later. Ironically, at the end of his life, on the last page of his final book, which was published posthumously, Foot described how, when doubts crept in, he learned to squash them. By 1975 the social unrest of the previous decade seemed to be fading away: "I began privately to worry that the entire revolutionary project, and the ideas that gave rise to it, were misconceived." But a comrade told him not to lose hope: "there is nothing for us to do but what we are doing now". This may well be sound advice for a revolutionary but is less useful when campaigning to rehabilitate a supposedly innocent man who has been exposed by forensic science as a rapist and murderer.

Foot's books are now all out of print and were he still alive he would probably be dismayed by the disintegration and collapse of the Socialist Workers Party. But he would surely not have been surprised by the ongoing revelations of the so-called "Spy Cops" inquiry under Sir John Mitting, which has revealed that MI5 colluded with the police to spy on over one thousand entirely lawful left-wing and campaigning groups in the period

1968-2010. The Socialist Workers Party, which was hardly a secret or secretive organisation, was under near-constant surveillance from 1970 to 2007. An astonishing 139 undercover officers were deployed against a wide range of lawful campaigning groups, with at least twenty initiating sexual relationships with women who believed them to be fellow campaigners. This was both a scandalous waste of police time and a symptom of a deeply corrupt and highly politicised policing culture which even in its less political incarnations exposed itself as sexist, racist and casually violent. One of Foot's own comrades, Blair Peach, was coshed to death by a Met police officer, who was protected at the highest levels and who, like almost all the other killers who have passed through the ranks of the Metropolitan Police, was never punished for his crime. Conspiracies do exist – it's just that there wasn't one in the case of the A6 murder.

Likewise, spectacular miscarriages of justice have occurred, and continue to occur, as evidenced by the prosecution for fraud, theft and false accounting of 736 entirely innocent postmasters between 2000 and 2015. The financial discrepancies, it transpired, were not the result of dishonesty but caused by faulty software made by Fujitsu. The Post Office executives who oversaw the scandal have yet to be held to account and at the time of writing the Post Office is dragging its heels in compensating the victims.

None of this would have surprised Paul Foot and it would have reinforced his core beliefs. But he was wrong about Hanratty and did himself no favours by burying his head in the sand when the DNA analysis supplied a conclusion contrary to the one he was expecting. Detective Superintendent Acott was a senior officer in a police force with a dubious reputation but there was nothing shady, corrupt or scandalous about his investigation of Michael Gregsten's murder. Peter Alphon was an unfortunate distraction but an entirely understandable one. Once Alphon was out of the frame, the trail that led to James Hanratty was unambiguous.

In 2014 a book and a monograph were published, with some bearing on the A6 murder.

After *Shadows of Deadman's Hill* appeared I received a letter from Dick Taverne congratulating me on the book. Taverne had been on the receiving end of Paul Foot's sarcasm in the Postscript to the 1971 Panther paperback edition of *Who Killed Hanratty?* Taverne's offence had been to write a negative review in *The Sunday Times* of the original edition of Foot's book. Taverne, a QC, the Labour MP for Lincoln, and the Parliamentary Under-Secretary at the Home Office under Roy Jenkins, asserted that James Hanratty was guilty beyond all reasonable doubt and that a new inquiry into the conviction was quite unnecessary.

Taverne now published *Against the Tide: Politics and Beyond, A Memoir.* This book revealed aspects of the saga which Paul Foot either did not know or chose not to mention in his polemic. For example, Taverne was originally convinced of Hanratty's innocence. After learning of Peter Alphon's public confession to being the killer Taverne signed a Commons motion calling for a posthumous pardon for Hanratty. In short, Taverne was not a man with a closed mind but an open one. When new evidence presented itself he was prepared to change his mind – something which eluded Paul Foot, whose rigid belief in Hanratty's innocence was unshakeable. Foot took his delusion with him to the grave. Years later Taverne was remarkably generous in his assessment of Foot, describing him as "an investigative journalist of repute and a stalwart campaigner against injustice".

In 1966, by this time a junior Home Office minister, Taverne explained that in view of his interest in the case he had asked to see the bulky file of material on the A6 case. He hoped that establishing Hanratty's innocence would assist the campaign against the death penalty, which as a man of liberal persuasions he very much supported. To his dismay the material simply persuaded him that Hanratty was indeed guilty of the crime. When *Who Killed Hanratty?* was published the editor of *The Sunday Times*, Harold Evans, invited Taverne to review it. Evans promised him a full two pages – a truly handsome allocation in the golden age of broadsheets. Taverne duly read the book and also refreshed his understanding of the case by returning to the confidential file on the case held by the Home Office. He then furnished Evans with his review, which was entitled "Did Hanratty kill?" His answer was an unequivocal Yes. That was not the answer Evans wanted and at first he refused to print Taverne's review. Taverne spoke to his friend Roy Jenkins, who spoke to Evans. The review duly appeared but in a truncated version. The two centre pages which he had been promised instead featured an article asserting Hanratty's innocence.

Interestingly, Taverne based his belief in Hanratty's guilt not on the identification evidence of Valerie Storie and the two eye-witnesses who said they had seen him driving the Morris Minor but on the other evidence against him. Years later while appearing on BBC Radio 4's "You The Jury" programme Dick Taverne encountered John McVicar, a former criminal with a rich repository of prison anecdotes. He asked him what he thought about Hanratty. "Guilty as hell," came the reply. According to McVicar, Hanratty used to boast to other prisoners how he had raped Valerie Storie and how thinking about it still gave him an erection.

In the same year *Hanratty: The Inconvenient Truth*, a monograph on the A6 case by Alan Razen appeared. Self-published using the Amazon "CreateSpace" publishing facility, this work consists of 109 pages in a large font. It displays the peculiarities of format and style one might expect in a text which has not been subjected to any editorial processes. The author explains he has only read two books on the case – Foot's and Woffinden's – and his mission statement is that "I believe it is time that the original 'A6 Murder' case was re-evaluated from the perspective that Hanratty was probably guilty". Razen is plainly unaware that *Shadows of Deadman's Hill: A New Analysis of the A6 Murder* did just that, rather more substantially and accurately, thirteen years earlier, in 2001.

Razen states that Storie, Gregsten and the gunman set off on their journey from the cornfield "occasionally stopping to get more petrol". They stopped only once for petrol. They stopped before that for cigarettes. "Buying cigarettes was particularly strange, as Hanratty wasn't known to smoke ... " But there was nothing strange about it: the cigarettes were for Gregsten, who requested the stop in the hope that it would give him the opportunity to raise the alarm. Razen says that "the gun was found on the 36A bus the evening of the day of the murder". Not true – it was discovered the next day, Thursday 24 August. Razen asserts that Peter Alphon "was known to have frequented the pub that Gregsten/Storie used regularly and on the night of the murder". In fact there is not a scrap of persuasive evidence that Alphon had ever visited The Old Station Inn, Taplow, prior to 22 August 1961. Likewise the idea that Peter Alphon and Charles France "were acquainted" can also be safely dismissed as fiction not fact. Similarly, the notion that Louise Anderson "was associated with William Ewer" is equally devoid of substance.

Razen ends his monograph by calling for "the reintroduction of the death penalty for certain extreme crimes, provided that proper safeguards are incorporated and, only when the evidence is considered to have attained a particularly high level of probability". Leaving aside the standard ethical and practical objections to the reintroduction of capital punishment, I find it impossible to share Razen's rosy view of British justice. The fact that campaigners were spectacularly wrong about James Hanratty should not detract from the reality that miscarriages of justice do occur, police officers can sometimes be incompetent, prejudiced or dishonest, and Guilty verdicts are not always justified.

The next publication to appear on the subject of the A6 murder was altogether more impressive. Paul Stickler's *The Long*

Silence: The True Story of James Hanratty and the A6 Murder by Valerie Storie, the Woman who Lived to Tell the Tale (2021) is a handsomely produced, fluently written re-telling of the A6 saga by a retired police officer with considerable professional experience of murder investigations. It's an authoritative narrative which supplies a chronological account of the crime and the events leading up to the Guilty verdict and Hanratty's execution. Stickler is in no doubt as to Hanratty's guilt. He also sets out to retrieve the reputation of Detective Superintendent Acott and other officers involved in the investigation. It is difficult to disagree with his conclusion: "Acott was not corrupt. He was a police officer doing his best – occasionally he could have done better."

The last part of *The Long Silence* is devoted to the story of Valerie Storie's long years as a survivor, made worse for her by the campaigners, who repeatedly insisted she was wrong about her identification of Hanratty, and by recurring insensitive press intrusion. Stickler's subtitle is a little misleading, since few of the words in this book are by her, but he had access to her papers and her notes for a book she once planned. As an homage to Valerie Storie the book is a triumph. She emerges as a woman with an astonishingly strong and resilient personality, who coped as few would have done with a life sentence of fifty-five years of paralysis. *The Long Silence* supplies another reminder of the impact on the victim of a violent assault. There was the appalling physical disability, which robbed her of the life she might otherwise have expected. There were also the deaths of her father at 59 and her mother at 68 – premature deaths almost certainly connected to the shocking fate experienced by their daughter. But there were also the emotional and psychological scars for Valerie. For most of her life after 1961 she would wake up in the early hours of 22 August each year, reliving the moment her lover was shot in the head. She could no longer go into butcher's shops because the smell of blood triggered associations with the aftermath of the murder. She hated it if anyone came to her house and tapped on the window. A woman of conservative views, she remained a firm believer in capital punishment. Hanratty's execution had exorcised his ghost: "If he hadn't been hanged, with life sentences meted out today, he would be long out of prison. I would be terrified of every unusual sound or knock at the door. I could not ever relax."

Apart from having access to Valerie Storie's private papers, Paul Stickler was also able to access the case papers in the possession of Bedfordshire Police. This new information sheds light on hitherto unknown aspects of the investigation. For the first time the criminal records of several of the figures involved in the case are revealed, including those of Charles France, Florence Snell and William Nudds. There is also new information about the prison years of James Hanratty. Although portrayed by Foot and Woffinden as a rather timid, gentle, essentially harmless scallywag his numerous disciplinary offences included "damage to bedding, insolence, using obscene language" and, during his last period of imprisonment, nineteen cases of misconduct.

In retelling the A6 saga, Stickler brings a number of issues into critical focus. Much was made by the defence and the campaigners of Valerie Storie's mistaken identification at the first identity parade, involving Alphon. But, Stickler points out, Acott saw that Valerie was upset before the parade and contemplated postponing it. He was under pressure and so was she. Afterwards he regretted not delaying it. Others also made selections which cast doubt on their reliability: Edward Blackhall, William Nudds, Florence Snell and Harry Hirons. Stickler comments, "It would have been better if they had been told that the man they were looking for may not be there at all, as is now the practice."

The revelation of Hanratty's behaviour during his long first interview with Acott and Oxford supplies further indications of his guilt. The jacket was missing which Hanratty was almost certainly wearing when he shot Michael Gregsten at close range (which, whether the droplets were visible to the naked eye or not, must inevitably have been spattered with the victim's blood).

Hanratty admitted he had destroyed it but refused to say when and how: "I can't tell you that. You won't find out." That last observation turned out to be true: Hanratty had managed to dispose of it far more efficiently than the handgun and the ammunition. The jacket was never found and could therefore not be subjected to forensic analysis, which would surely have established the kind of tangible evidence connecting him to the crime which would not emerge until decades later with the DNA tests.

Whereas Alphon had responded to questioning in a fluent, casual, chatty manner, Hanratty's reaction was altogether different. There were long periods of silence as he thought about his answers. His response to questioning was at times unusual, with "great flushing up the face and the back of the neck ... the mouth twisted in an attempt to control it". Hanratty was a man under stress, and the detectives were struck by how at times his eyes bulged out and looked an almost transparent blue. None of this was admissible evidence for presentation in a courtroom but it underlined the similarities between the suspect and the killer.

Several of the myths and ambiguities of the case are ironed out by Stickler. It did not take twenty minutes for Valerie Storie to identify Hanratty on the ID parade. The contradictions surrounding John Kerr's account of events in the immediate aftermath of the discovery of Valerie Storie and the arrival of police at the scene can plausibly be explained as originating in the teenager's acute distress rather than an attempt by police to doctor the evidence.

Perhaps the most astonishing revelation in *The Long Silence* concerns attempts by a Hanratty family member to interfere with witnesses and evidence-gathering once Jimmy had been charged. The culprit was none other than James Hanratty senior (represented by Foot and Woffinden as something of a saintly figure). He had gone into Louise Anderson's shop in Soho and told her that if the missing jacket turned out to be in her possession she should give it to him, not the police. He had earlier telephoned Gladys Deacon and told her she was a liar regarding what she had said about her conversation with his son on the day he was arrested. That kind of behaviour would nowadays risk a charge of conspiracy to pervert the course of justice – an offence which, upon conviction, usually attracts a punitive sentence.

The Long Silence shows that there is still new material to come out about the A6 murder. However, the basic shape of the narrative is now unlikely to change, and Stickler's analysis of what happened between the hold-up in the cornfield and the shootings and rape at Deadman's Hill replicates the conclusions I reached twenty years earlier in Chapter 6 of Shadows of Deadman's Hill. The crime was not pre-planned. Valerie Storie and Michael Gregsten had the misfortune to be in the wrong place at the wrong time. James Hanratty stumbled upon the couple by chance. His new ownership of a gun made him light-headed and impulsive. Everything that happened sprang from his damaged, criminal personality. He was not very bright. Nothing was thought out. Hanratty took them on a ride through a part of west London he was very familiar with and on up the A6 towards a town he knew well. At some point that night the thought of raping Valerie had formed in his mind but it was only after shooting Michael Gregsten – another impulsive, unpremeditated action – that opportunity presented itself.

It was precisely the strangely meandering, elongated nature of the crime, heavy with conversation between the gunman and his victims, which made it seem so mysterious and compelling. The prosecution argued that Hanratty was motivated from the very beginning by lust but that never seemed satisfactory as an explanation. He could have coshed Gregsten with the gun and raped Valerie in the cornfield if this had really been his motive. That the long journey and its violent climax were explained by Hanratty's own indecisive, impulsive, sociopathic personality was, though accurate, a much tougher account to set before a jury.

For those troubled by the mysterious nature of the crime

there was a simpler explanation. Its origins lay in the fact that the murder victim was a married man and the woman in the car was his much younger mistress. They went regularly to the cornfield for their romantic assignations, sometimes having sex there. There were those who wanted this affair to end and for Michael to return to his wife. The killer had surely gone to their known rendezvous point to discourage the relationship, at gunpoint. Then matters had spiralled out of control. That this was what happened was later confirmed by Peter Alphon, the man first arrested on suspicion of being the A6 murderer. To Paul Foot and, later, Bob Woffinden, it all made perfect sense. Their belief that all was not what it seemed was nourished by the extraordinary coincidence of Alphon and Hanratty both having stayed at the hotel where cartridges from the murder weapon were later found, and by Janet Gregsten's supposed sighting of Hanratty in Swiss Cottage, long before he became a suspect. To this rich stew could be added Valerie Storie's apparent initial description of the killer having brown eyes. A supporting cast of shadowy figures from the underworld added extra colour to this lurid canvas.

It was an enticing conspiracy theory which gelled perfectly with a great deal of popular culture. In crime fiction and crime drama things are rarely what they seem. Almost always, the obvious suspect turns out to be innocent and only a quick-witted investigator manages to uncover the subterranean aspects of the crime and unmask the actual murderer. Alfred Hitchcock was a master of the genre. In *Young and Innocent* (1937) there is a mass of circumstantial evidence against the suspected murderer. He is seen apparently fleeing the scene. His raincoat belt was used to strangle the victim. In her will the victim left him a substantial sum of money, reinforcing the suspicion that they were lovers. But we, the viewers, know he is innocent because we see matters from his perspective and experiences. The real killer is the woman's jealous husband. The only person whose testimony supports that of the wrongly accused man is a tramp. This formula was repeated throughout Hitchcock's directing career. *The Wrong Man* (1956), based on a true story, is about sincere but inaccurate eye-witness testimony convicting an innocent man. Hitchcock's use of this theme climaxed with *Frenzy* (1972). Once again we, the viewers, know that the man convicted of murder is wholly innocent, yet the circumstantial evidence against him seems overwhelming.

True life crime is rarely as complicated or as compelling as the fictional variety. George Orwell asserted that middle-class murder was more interesting, because professionals planned their murders in advance, whereas working class transgressors killed on the spur of the moment. He was exaggerating, but he had a point. Diana Souhami's *Murder at Wrotham Hill* supplies an in-depth account of lorry driver Harold Hagger's savage murder of Dagmar Petrzywalski in 1946. She was a hitchhiker to whom Hagger gave a ride, then promptly sought sex from. When she resisted, he strangled her. The crime was sordid, brutal and opportunistic. Hagger was swiftly identified as the killer, tried, convicted, and hanged.

The case was a banal one. The victim was a rather sad, impoverished spinster. The murderer was a sly, devious individual with a long criminal history. Oddly, although there are obvious differences, there are striking parallels between Harold Hagger and James Hanratty. Hagger was a dustman's son, identified early on as having learning difficulties and being of low intelligence. His lengthy criminal career began in adolescence. He used aliases and was a compulsive liar. The image he projected to the world was that of a man who wore tailored jackets, clean shirts, polished shoes and, sometimes, a bowler hat. But the smart middle-class image clashed with his cockney accent; he had "the vocabulary and speech cadences of a dustman's son".

Another random, unplanned crime which sprang from a combination of panic and the ownership of illicit handguns occurred in London on an August day five years after the A6 murder. The Shepherd's Bush killings were every bit as sensational. Three plain-clothes police officers stopped a car to question the occupants. The three men inside were "criminal nonentities whose crimes up to that point had amounted to nothing more than acts of petty larceny for which they'd got nothing to show".

Harry Roberts, unnerved by the thought of going back to prison, responded to questioning by shooting Detective Constable David Wombwell in the face at point blank range, killing him instantly. Roberts then jumped from the car and fired his gun at Detective Sergeant Chris Head, hitting him once in the middle of his back. Robert's companion John Duddy shot the police car driver Constable Geoff Fox in the head, killing him. The car lurched forward, running over DS Head and leaving him wedged beneath. He, too, died at the scene. The murderers were quickly identified; Harry Roberts went on the run and eluded capture until November. It was a crime without mysteries or ambiguities, unique only because the brutal, casual gunning down of three unarmed police officers was unprecedented.

At the opposite extreme, lending further support to Orwell's argument, is the case of Jeremy Bamber. Here was a privileged, well-off young man living a very agreeable life. He was charming and very successful with women. At the age of 24 he lacked for nothing. But none of this satisfied him. The affluence he enjoyed wasn't enough. He was greedy for spectacular wealth and in order to obtain it immediately he massacred his adoptive parents, his sister and her two small children. It was an astonishingly cold-blooded, pre-planned mass murder which Bamber had been contemplating for some time. He was foolish enough to confide his plan to his girlfriend, whom he later dumped. Bamber executed the crime in such a way as to implicate his sister as the killer. Astonishingly inept and prejudiced policing resulted in him almost getting away with it. The full story is set out in an authoritative and persuasive manner by Carol Ann Lee in *The Murders at White House Farm*. Perhaps unsurprisingly, Bob Woffinden associated himself with the campaign to establish

Bamber's innocence but he later changed his mind and accepted that he was guilty of the crime. This is the only case that I'm aware of in which Woffinden showed any flexibility.

What is probably the finest crime non-fiction book ever written, Truman Capote's *In Cold Blood*, owes its power both to the author's eloquent literary style and to the depth of its characterisation. It is massively researched, with the author able to speak to the killers, the police, people who knew the victims, and many others. That kind of depth and comprehensive scope will always elude the telling of the A6 murder. Too many of the central figures remain enigmas and now almost everyone involved in the saga has died.

There are also still some unresolved matters about the basic narrative. For example, how did the police first come to discover that "J. Ryan" was James Hanratty? Paul Stickler says that Irish police were contacted on 19 September about the "J. Ryan" car hire correspondence: "A full description of Ryan was given together with the fact that he appeared to have hired a car in Dublin that had been found abandoned with some accident damage at the airport". It is very difficult to make sense of the chronology on offer here, because the first that Acott and Oxford learned about Hanratty's car hire in Dublin was when they belatedly visited the address which "J. Ryan" had registered at the Hotel Vienna on Monday 21 August 1961. The cartridges from the murder weapon were not discovered at the hotel until 11 September and Acott and his partner did not bother to visit the address (72 Wood Lane, Kingsbury) until the morning of 26 September. The householder, George Pratt, knew nothing about "J. Ryan" but was in possession of a letter sent to his address addressed to this elusive figure. When Acott opened the envelope he discovered material relating to the car hired by Hanratty using the name Ryan. Whether or not this material made reference to the car having been left damaged at Dublin Airport is an open question. If it did then it might well have been interpreted as meaning that Ryan had flown out of the country, which in turn would raise the question as to why Acott travelled to Ireland on 29 September in search of Hanratty.

It was at this point that an approach to the Irish police might well have been expected. But Acott was not really in a position to supply "a full description" of Ryan, if he was basing it on the hazy memories of the hotel staff who had dealt with him. Ryan was just another customer and there was no particular reason for him to have been remembered in any detail after the passage of some five weeks. But after visiting Pratt, Acott and Oxford went on that day to visit Hanratty's parents at their home nearby. It was obvious that they now knew that "J. Ryan" was James Hanratty. Acott cannot possibly have learned that in just a couple of hours from the Irish police. Although the Gardai were diligent in discovering Hanratty's visit to the Motor Registration Office in Dublin, his visit to Limerick, and his stay at O'Flynn's hotel in Cork, all this must have taken time. The Irish police also succeeded in tracking down Gerrard Leonard, who had shared a room with Hanratty at O'Flynn's. He remembered that Ryan had asked him to write some postcards for him to three addresses in London. One was to a Mrs Hanratty and began "Dear Mum". It seemed obvious that Ryan, who signed off "Your loving son, Jim", was not really called Ryan.

The conventional explanation that it was Gerrard Leonard who first put the police on to Hanratty is not remotely convincing. Paul Foot was justifiably sceptical about this. He also pointed out that the solution to this conundrum was given in an article in *The Sunday Times* magazine (18 December 1966). Charles "Dixie" France went to the police with a postcard which Hanratty had sent him from Ireland. France's widow Charlotte, interviewed some five years later, believed that this occurred on the 25 September. This was a significant date because it was just one day earlier that the case against Peter Alphon collapsed when Valerie Storie failed to identify him as her attacker. Plainly this revelation had a galvanizing effect on France. Paul Foot's speculation that he might have had "some motive for making the connection" was surely spot on. Two obvious ones spring to mind. Firstly, the discovery of the murder weapon in precisely the place that Hanratty had boasted to his friend was the perfect place to dump unwanted stolen goods must have aroused immediate suspicions on France's part. Secondly, France's wife thought that one of the photofits resembled Hanratty. Added to that was Hanratty's absence on the day of the abduction and the next day when the Morris was dumped. There may have been other grounds for suspicion. Hanratty had taken a suit to their local dry cleaners to have what he believed to be blood removed. Having collected the suit he went to London Airport to catch a flight to Dublin. He telephoned Charlotte France from the airport to say that he thought a man was watching him. Hanratty's paranoia may have heightened their growing suspicions.

Stickler says that France only knew Hanratty as "Jimmy Ryan". But France surely knew that Ryan was really Hanratty. When he delivered his postcard to Scotland Yard it would not have revealed anything of significance other than that the sender had been in Ireland. The handwriting would not have matched that in the register at the Hotel Vienna, since the card had been written on Hanratty's behalf by Gerrard Leonard. Whatever France told Acott (or someone else) it meant very little until the Detective Superintendent went to visit George Pratt the next day. That there was an envelope at Pratt's house addressed to "J. Ryan" about the hiring of a car in Limerick provided startling confirmation of France's suspicions, because now there was a direct connection between the false name and address in the hotel register, Ireland, and "Jim". Acott, of course, knew that when Valerie asked the gunman what his name was he had blurted out "Jim". It was surely only now that Acott contacted the Irish police, supplying them with the car hire details, the name Jim Ryan, and Charles France's description of Hanratty. When in due course they reported back that Gerrard Leonard remembered writing a card for Jim Ryan addressed to his mother, a Mrs Hanratty, it provided confirmation of the identity of their suspect.

Charles France knew that Jim Ryan was Hanratty and he plainly grassed on his friend. This explains why when Michael Hanratty went in search of his fugitive brother at The Rehearsal Club and attempted to speak to France he first of all tried to flee, then, trapped into a conversation, "turned white" and "couldn't get away fast enough".

All this is far more likely than the account given in *The Long Silence*, which attempts to downplay Acott's ineptitude regarding the room where the cartridge cases were found and argues, very unconvincingly, that "Alphon was never, as so many thought, 'the first suspect'." On the contrary, on 23 September, *The London Evening News* reported that Alphon was "expected to travel to Ampthill". The police had plainly tipped off the crime reporters and, as Woffinden correctly noted, this was the media's "carefully coded way of saying that he was expected to be charged with the A6 murder".

More information about Hanratty or others involved in this case may conceivably emerge in future years but two things seem clear. The first is that the definitive account of the A6 murder will never be written, because there are gaps in the story which seem unlikely ever to be filled. Who supplied Hanratty with the Royal Enfield .38 hand gun remains a mystery, as do Hanratty's activities on Tuesday 21 August prior to his encounter with the Morris Minor in the cornfield and where he went after he dumped the car on Avondale Crescent. The second is that any new information which may emerge in future years is unlikely to alter the basic configurations of the narrative of the A6 case. Every aspect of this convoluted tale points to Hanratty's guilt.

Notes

Abbreviations

The following abbreviations are used in the notes for frequently quoted sources, while surnames of authors are used for more occasionally cited sources. Where no page number is given the source is either a one-page article or an unpaginated online version. Fuller publication details for all sources can be found in the Bibliography.

BW   Bob Woffinden, *Hanratty: The Final Verdict* (Macmillan, 1997).

BW2   Bob Woffinden, *Hanratty: The Final Verdict* (Pan, 1999).

BW3   Bob Woffinden, *Miscarriages of Justice* (Coronet Books, 1989).

JJ   Jean Justice, *Murder vs. Murder* (Olympia Press, 1964).

JJ2   Jean Justice, *Le Crime de la Route A6* (Laffont, 1968).

LBC   Louis Blom-Cooper, *The A6 Murder* (Penguin, 1963).

LRL   Lord Russell of Liverpool, *Deadman's Hill* (Tallis Press, 1966).

PF   Paul Foot, *Who Killed Hanratty?* (Cape, London, 1971).

PF2   Paul Foot, *Who Killed Hanratty?* (Panther, 1973).

PF3   Paul Foot, *Who Killed Hanratty?* (Penguin, 1988).

PF4   Paul Foot, "Awaiting the Truth about Hanratty", *London Review of Books* (11 December 1997).

Introduction

"In the words of crime reporter Duncan Campbell": Campbell, p. 43.

"The case 'raised little public feeling'": LBC, p. 132.

"Because truth was suppressed ... the cases of the Guildford Four, the Maguire Seven and the Birmingham Six": Kennedy, pp. x and 309.

"Ronan McGreevy's recent well-received book ... mentions Hanratty as 'dubiously executed for murder'": McGreevy, p. 354.

1 Complicity

"you never seem to get a good murder nowadays": Orwell, *Decline of the*

English Murder, p. 10.

"some tiny unforeseeable detail": *Ibid.*, p. 11.

"he wrote on another occasion ... 'was uninteresting'": Orwell, *I Belong to the Left*, p. 347.

"As Jeremy Lybarger put it": https://www.theguardian.com/books/ 2018/mar/21/ill-be-gone-dark-michelle-mcnamara-golden-state-killer-quest.

"in his book on the campaigner Ludovic Kennedy": Ingrams, p. 11.

"Alphon was the son of a highly ranking Scotland Yard detective": https:// gcalers.wordpress.com/2019/03/26/james-hanratty-or-peter-louis-alphon-who-was-the-a6-murderer/.

"a short, error-riddled section on the A6 murder": Lane, pp. 311-13.

2 The Trial and Execution of James Hanratty

"Louis Blom-Cooper believed that Langdale was probably a police informer": LBC, p. 113.

"The confession made by Hanratty to Langdale was ... almost certainly true": *Ibid.*

"Justice excused Hanratty's conversation": JJ, p. 21.

"Superintendent Acott's satisfied grin": *Ibid.*, p 109.

"It is difficult to escape the conclusion that had the murder of Gregsten been committed a few hundred miles further north": LRL, p. 167.

"It is curious, but till that moment I had never realized what it means to destroy a healthy, conscious man": Orwell, *Decline of the English Murder*, p. 16.

3 The Campaign 1962-2000

"Most lawyers were of the opinion ... Hanratty should not have been convicted": LBC, p. 112.

"palpably false": *Ibid.*, p.20.

"the gap in the Crown's case might have been filled": *Ibid.*, p. 113.

"it is doubtful whether he should have been convicted": *Ibid.*

"one almost suspects that he disagreed with the verdict": *Ibid.*, p. 27.

"come to be wandering pointlessly in Buckinghamshire": *Ibid.*, p. 25.

"perverted design": *Ibid.*

"should we not explore it?": *Ibid.*, p. 41.

"to be hired to go out and scare the couple in the cornfield": *Ibid.*, p. 134.

"wildly fantastic": *Ibid.*, p. 134.

"he may nevertheless have told Hanratty where he could get hold of one": *Ibid.*, p. 131.

"distinct aura of guilt": *Ibid.*, p. 17.

"inexplicable": *Ibid.*, p. 124.

"the real story": *Ibid.*, p. 131.

"thought him not all a savoury character": BW2, p. 221.

"an extraordinary surrealist affair of criss-crossing horizontal and vertical lines": JJ , pp. 99-100.

"overwhelming": *Ibid.*, p. 79.

"a slow and insidious process of police conditioning": *Ibid.*, p. 70

"wildly fantastic": LBC, p. 134.

"a reliable witness": JJ, p. 39.

"told by superior authorities that Alphon was not to be touched": *Ibid.*, p. 82.

"Whitehall": *Ibid.*, p. 126.

"pornographic trash": Boyd, p. 266.

"a change in social attitudes toward the kind of love described in *Lolita*": *Ibid.*, pp. 266-7.

"What happened during that period was so nauseating": JJ, p. 45.

"a case which bristled with red herrings": LRL, p. 130.

"There is no class of evidence more liable to fall victim to the frailties of human judgement": *Ibid.*, p. 144.

"that only James Hanratty could have been responsible": *Ibid.*, p. 169.

"he was not the kind of young man who would ever want to do so:" *Ibid.*, p. 171.

"The following month Paul Foot reported": *Private Eye*, No. 135 (17 February 1967), p. 16.

"no further evidence which, if put before the jury, might have influenced the verdict": BW, p. 360.

"Hanratty reported the matter to the police": *Private Eye*, No. 140 (28 April 1967), p. 14.

"*Au cours d'une conference de presse donnée à Paris*": JJ2, p. 235.

"the latest book on the A6 murder": Paul Stickler, *The Long Silence* (2021).

"again by Girodias": BW, p. 373.

"A6 Murder: Breaking the Commons Law": *Private Eye*, No. 200 (15 August 1969), p. 18.

"histrionic performance in the witness-box": JJ, pp. 82-3.

"the victim of a nervous breakdown": *Ibid.*, p. 131.

"Alphon confessed to the murder and named the man": Paul Foot, "Further Confessor", *Private Eye*, No. 202 (12 September 1969), pp. 17-18.

"a rasping duel between the brains of Mr Swanwick": PF, p. 284.

"excruciatingly cocky": LBC, p. 70.

"Hanratty's insolence": *Ibid.*, p. 69.

"warm, gentle, determined people": PF4.

"living on her own in the most appalling conditions": PF, p. 170.

"jealous demon": PF4.

"as sure as it is possible to be that James Hanratty did not commit the A6 murder": PF, p. 404.

"Most people working in publishing would concede": Maschler, p. 64.

"Louis Blom-Cooper ate humble pie": *The Observer*, 9 May 1971.

"There were other sceptics": review quotations from *Private Eye*, No. 245 (21 May 1971), p. 24.

"The film was too amateurish in format ever to be shown on television": At the time of writing the following extracts are available on YouTube:

> https://www.youtube.com/watch?v=UCIP_r5Irc4
> https://www.youtube.com/watch?v=HGl9tzMNtpE
> https://www.youtube.com/watch?v=KWlnmeOYK4Y

"to shelter his family from an association with the crime": PF2, p. 437.

"Shirley Williams, supported a public inquiry": *Ibid.*, p. 449.

"Hawser concluded that the case against Hanratty": PF3, p. 426.

"Woffinden prefaced his account of the case": BW3, p. 89.

"The vision of a pack of pseudo-A6 killers": *Ibid.*, p. 135.

"bit by bit, he teased out the inconsistencies": *Ibid.*, 3, p. 41.

"he seemed temporarily bereft of his outstanding forensic abilities": *Ibid.*, p. 133.

"part of a madcap scheme to frighten the lovers apart": PF3, p. 425.

"initial work failed to produce a clear DNA profile": BW, p. 449.

"discrepancies, fabricated evidence and suppressed facts": *Ibid.*, p. 449.

"fatally failed to understand Alphon's psychopathic personality": *Ibid.*, p. 437.

"the intransigence of the Home Secretary himself": *Ibid.*, p. 451.

"every fragment of information to come to light": *Ibid.*, p. 443.

"a definitive result could be obtained": *Ibid.*, p. 449.

"tempting, but far from conclusive": PF4.

"By June 1999 further DNA testing": BW2, p. 445.

"his obituary of Fox": https://www.theguardian.com/news/1999/may/31/guardianobituaries4.

4 The Curious Case of Peter Alphon

"The police may have received casual information on the underworld network": PF, p. 70.

"The alibi ... was smashed": *Ibid.*, p. 71.

"Alphon shrewdly maximized his own advantages in his confrontation": BW, p. 423.

"A long extract from this interview is printed in Bob Woffinden's book": *Ibid.*, pp. 416-423.

"He bought an *Evening News* and started reading": BW, p. 269.

"he descended with his staff on the Hotel Vienna":PF, p. 56.

"Anyone who saw Superintendent Acott making his appeal on the television screen": JJ, p. 82.

"The first man the police pulled in for questioning": *Ibid.*, p. 81.

"shut himself in his room for five days": *Ibid.*, p. 23.

"He was so different from what I had expected": *Ibid.*, p. 92.

"little girl": *Ibid.*, p. 98.

"Alphon's aim was to maintain my interest": PF, p. 390.

"We will get Acott together": JJ, p. 112.

"One man in London has been confessing to every high profile murder for the past 20 years": Jane Clinton, "Confessions of a fake murderer", *The Daily Express*, 22 May 2001.

"Russell Keys confessed to murdering five women": *The Times*, 30 September 1999.

"It occurred to me, watching him carefully, that he didn't really know": PF4.

"The first consideration of the police": Hain, p. 104.

"officers are quickly implicated into marginal or off the books": Morton, p. 287.

"lies, brutality, planting, and the fabrication and suppression of evidence": *Ibid.*, p. 108.

"Peter spoke beautifully": *The Daily Mail*, 23 September 1961.

"The same recordings also demonstrate": JJ, p. 85.

"Alphon happens to be an excellent mimic": *Ibid.*

"a weak, insignificant man ... looking very small": BW, p. 433.

5 Hanratty's Alibi

"'a mountain of evidence' to support Hanratty's alibi": *The Guardian*, 25 July 2000.

"It is hard to see how, on his own timings, he could have missed the 10.20 and the 10.35": PF, p. 194.

"six sets of gold cuff-links with the initial 'E' on them": BW, p. 97.

"apprehensive about the prospect of photographs of himself appearing": *Ibid.*, p. 119.

"a few stops from the Scotland Road": PF, p. 190 on p. 341.

"the suspect was examined by a leading expert on speech and phonetics": LRL, p. 162.

"a normal and average young Londoner's voice": *Ibid.*, p. 161.

"Hanratty, of course, would have considered nothing less": BW, p. 100.

"so he could hardly have admitted on his return": *Ibid.*, p. 199.

"felt awkward": *Ibid.*

"The opening days of the trial must have been a shattering experience": *Ibid.*, p. 198.

"During the three days I was in Liverpool I stayed with McNally": PF, p. 216.

"rather small. No more than 5' 2"": *Ibid.*, p. 224.

"He knew as well as anyone that lies are often more convincing": Russell-Pavier, p. 122.

"He loved gambling": BW, p. 86.

"Hanratty's detailed description of the boarding house: *The Guardian*, 25 July 2000.

"most anxious to avoid publicity": PF, p. 264.

"had very clearly identified Evans, Evans's features, Evans's house": *Ibid.*, pp. 437-8.

"Richard most closely resembled James": PF2, p. 438.

"The behaviour which Mrs Hughes described to us": *Ibid.*, p. 438.

"Mr Gerald Murray, who said he may have been the barber": *Ibid.*, p. 438.

6 Conspiracy?

"an apparently motiveless crime": LBC, p. 41.

"the motive for the crime was not robbery but sex": JJ, p. 52.

"he pulled the trigger to prove his superiority": *Ibid.*, p. 158.

"*a reliable witness … once saw them together*": *Ibid.*, p. 39.

"*could have learned a great deal about Hanratty's movements*": *Ibid.*, p. 40.

"*Past attempt at cornfield*": Ibid., p. 118.

"*Couple in car fitted my mood and my main plan*": Ibid., p. 116.

"spectacular wins at the races": PF, p. 392.

"The articles presented a series of coincidences": Ibid., p. 51.

"irritated and depressed by her husband's affair": Ibid., p. 25.

"To us it always seemed a simple gas-meter case": BW, p. 380.

"*circle of friends*": JJ, p. 40.

a warning against jumping to hasty conclusions": PF4.

"someone who'd known Nudds in prison": BW2, p. 444.

"In no newspaper, radio broadcast or television bulletin": PF, p. 52.

"hastily scribbled and probably confusing [police] notes": BW, p. 50.

"*The Sunday Times* also settled out of court": Ibid., p. 384.

"a farrago of nonsense": PF2, p. 449.

"a man who I now know to be Peter Louis Alphon": Ibid., p. 441.

"a blonde woman who was, I would say, in her early thirties": Ibid.

"Through Justice, Lanz was drawn into the saga": JJ, p. 102 and JJ2, p. 250.

"Bob Woffinden worked himself up into a frenzy over this revelation": BW, p. 383.

"as though I was an associate of this filthy act": PF2, pp. 436-7.

"to shelter his family from an association with the crime": Ibid., p. 437.

"People in the grip of theories find it difficult to change": Ramsay, p. 55.

"in his own macabre way, helped to keep the case alive": PF4.

"All the bits and pieces of a confession at last became forged": PF, p. 364.

"Woffinden, bending the evidence yet again": BW, p. 432.

"a malicious jape that went disastrously wrong": Ibid., p. 437.

7 Hanratty Goes to Paddington

"The cornfield, although remote, lay between a small village": LRL, p. 170.

"I always work on my own ... I usually do night jobs": BW, p. 89.

"He was, he claimed, a regular client of a Soho prostitute": Ibid., p. 100.

"That he did say this ... one of the many pointers to Hanratty's innocence": LRL, p. 30.

"went to Ealing to sell a diamond ring ... He visited Donald Fisher": PF, p. 94.

"Paul Foot was very sarcastic ... dropped on to the chair": Ibid., p. 182.

"His attention span was short and he was careless by nature": I owe these points to Nigel Eddis (private communication, 4 March 2004).

"was the heyday of the armed robber": Campbell, p. 42.

"if the police heard of any burglary being committed by a light-haired man, they'd automatically associate it with him": BW, p. 92.

8 The Abduction

"Maybe Hanratty, in his frustration at finding too many people at home, even in the holiday season, thought he would try his luck in the next village, i.e. Dorney Reach": Robert Theil (personal communication, 10 December 2003).

"He said that Hanratty told him he was walking across a field": Stickler, p. 264.

"He was, as ever, thinking very short term": BW, p. 138.

"an Enfield .38 is a rather bulky weapon and awkward to conceal": Nigel Eddis (private communication, 4 March 2004).

"The whole thing seems without rhyme or reason": *The Daily Express*, 22 September 1961.

"His parents refused to accept this advice": LBC, pp. 64-65.

9 Night Ride

"told to turn right in the direction of Maidenhead": LRL, p. 5.

"Near London airport, the car turned into a Regent garage": PF, p. 29.

"an area he knew reasonably well": BW, p. 135.

"persuaded his parents to let him stay with his aunt": LBC, p. 65.

"frightened of his mother and had no filial feelings towards his father": *Ibid.*, p. 64.

10 Deadman's Hill

"borne out completely by the medical evidence": Simpson, p. 134.

"says that Acott could not find a single episode of violence in his past": PF, p. 280.

"it was all over for the gentle fugitive": BW, p. 113.

"Many were struck by his deference, his general mildness of manner": *Ibid.*, p. 222.

"He punched the one who'd spoken to him": *Ibid.*, p. 95.

"his large blue eyes did seem to be almost protruding from his head": *Ibid.*, p. 222.

"very large, pale blue, staring eyes and brown hair combed back": LRL, p. 13.

"fair auburn hair": BW, p. 90.

"one of the original identikit pictures had vaguely resembled Hanratty": BW2, p. 445.

"a form of spiritual stroke resulting in an emotional blackout": Cox.

"underlined Hanratty's social isolation from the prisoner group": LBC, p. 68.

"gross social and emotional immaturity": *Ibid.*, p. 68.

"He seemed sort of anxious to get it over with": Stickler, p. 44.

"the girl had not been raped in the classical sense of the word": JJ, p. 74.

"a difficult task just about possible even under the cramped conditions": *Ibid.*, p. 75.

"offered a few scraps of information about himself": BW3, pp. 89-90.

11 Hanratty on the Run

"did go very red": BW, p. 115.

"having found it, apparently abandoned, somewhere else": LRL, p. 144.

"This was plainly the murder car, and the man driving the car was plainly the murderer": PF, p. 40.

"I remembered this so well because I have always regarded 8 as my lucky number": BW2, p. 444.

"A couple reported an early morning encounter on the A6 at Deadman's Hill with a man and a stationary Morris Minor": *The Guardian*, 30 March 1999.

"the rather shocking fact that the murder car was nowhere near London at the time": *The Guardian*, 4 April 2001.

"This occasioned some raucous laughter, since he had earlier admitted that he could not drive": LBC, p. 70.

"drove zig-zagging, he was driving from side to side up the road": BW, p. 191.

"Hanratty had overlooked some glaring mechanical defects": *Ibid.*, pp. 133-34.

"Twenty cartridges to a box is standard. But there are smaller packages": Nigel Eddis (private communication, 4 March 2004).

"Paul Foot quoted from Hanratty's account of what happened": PF, p. 145.

"In other parts of his statement, Hanratty embellished his story": *Ibid.*

"Woffinden believed that a sexual encounter did take place": BW, p. 294.

"in this brief period he was at his happiest and most confident": *Ibid.*, p. 134.

"She was listening for a cockney accent": *Ibid.*, p. 116.

"He took Gladys for a drive. They headed north to Bedford": *Ibid.*, p. 135.

"according to the speech and phonetics expert who examined Hanratty": LRL, p. 162.

"There was not a trace of a confession to anyone": PF, p. 149.

"Peter Dunn, who had reported on the Bedford trial for *The Observer*": see *The Independent*, 20 August 1992, and *The Guardian*, 5 April 2001.

"she was in no doubt that he meant Michael Gregsten": *News of the World*, 27 November 1966.

"Now I've done something that scares. Something I've never done before": *Sunday Pictorial*, 18 March 1962.

"a very sombre thing, not a throwaway comment or anything like that": Cassandra.

"Jean Justice … remembered it rather differently": JJ, p. 110.

"the most insignificant and obvious errors in speaking … a thought-content which is at pains to remain concealed but which cannot nevertheless avoid unintentionally betraying its existence": Freud, pp. 146 and 123-4.

"Bush inadvertently acknowledged his own criminality": https://www.dailymail.co.uk/news/article-10831671/George-W-Bush-accidentally-calls-Iraq-invasion-unjustified-brutal.html.

"That's just it, I haven't a clue. I don't understand any of it": Carrère, p. 53.

"interested onlooker": BW, p. 269.

"I've sat here day after day, week after week": JJ, p. 109.

"empty boast": *Ibid.*

"discussed his inevitable release": PF, p. 280.

12 Tunnel Vision

"he was, without a doubt, a deeply stupid man": Ambler, p. 506.

"A man of Hanratty's mentality would be quite …": *Ibid.*, p. 508.

"There was, and is, no reasonable doubt that he was guilty": *Ibid.*

"The question of Alphon's guilt is debatable; the question of Hanratty's innocence is not": BW3, p. 137.

"if the DNA suggests otherwise there must be something wrong with the DNA": *The Guardian*, 13 May 2002.

"one of the most preposterous [theories] advanced in modern criminal history": Bob Woffinden, "McVicar's crime against Jill Dando" (review of *Dead on Time*), *The Observer Review* (14 April 2002), p. 15.

"by no means slim": JJ, p. 40.

"the case against Causley at trial was essentially non-existent": https://www.thejusticegap.com/two-trials-three-jailhouse-snitches-four-part-documentary-no-evidence/.

"it was riddled with quite basic errors of fact": Miller, *Shadows of Deadman's Hill*, p. 147.

"a series of clear miscarriages of justice ... James Hanratty": Morton, p. 320.

"withstood the closest examination": BW2, p. 445.

"numerous examples of serious misconduct by senior police officers": *Ibid.*

"nothing less than a 'martyrdom'": JJ, p. 158.

"powerfully attracted to me": *Ibid.*, p. 97.

"I needed Peter": *Ibid.*, p. 121.

"You – sick": JJ, p. 125.

"The police conform to the violence and bigotry of the rotten system ... campaigning can force concessions": Farrell, pp. 165-6.

"Stale evidence is often bad evidence": cited in Yallop, p. 379.

13 The Final Verdict

"The DNA findings conflicted grotesquely with the alibis": *The Guardian*, 13 May 2002.

"When I publicly challenged him in *The Guardian* newspaper": see Leonard Miller, "The case against Hanratty", *The Guardian* (14 May 2002), p. 17.

"an admiring piece by Julie Bundy": "Injustice", in *Paul Foot 1937-2004: A Tribute*, ed. Peter Morgan (London: Socialist Review, 2004).

"a sympathetic obituarist in the *Guardian*": https://www.theguardian.com/law/2018/may/11/bob-woffinden-obituary.

"The wrong man was not hanged": https://web.archive.org/web/20050212101709/http://www.clsg.org.uk/hanratty.htm.

"The Court of Appeal's 2002 judgement": https://www.bailii.org/ew/

cases/EWCA/Crim/2002/1141.html.

"Maxwell Confait is one of the rare instances": Morton, p. 320.

"We had hoped that state-of-the-art forensic analysis might be able to provide a DNA profile of the gunman": BW2, p. 445.

"To me, the forensic evidence is incredible": *The Guardian* (11 May 2002).

"dismissed by Marx": *The Communist Manifesto* (1848).

14 Men / Women

"Koestler had beaten and raped women before": Cesarini, p. 401.

"if old women in this predicament can learn that their lives may be saved": LBC, p. 40.

"suffered martyrdom" on a "cold April morning": JJ, p. 158.

"pathetic figure in the dock": *Ibid.*, p. 109.

"the little man in the dock, vainly pleading his innocence": *Ibid.*

"If Valerie will admit that I am right": *Ibid.*, p. 45.

"he was not the kind of young man who would ever want to do so": LRL, p. 171.

"What could have been easier than to drive the car straight into one of the petrol pumps": *Ibid.*, p. 6.

"told to turn right in the direction of Maidenhead": *Ibid.*, p. 5.

"everyone knows the woman who is never more certain she is right than when she is wrong": *Ibid.*, p. 146.

"Far from being sex-starved": BW3, p. 110.

"The scandal tore the party apart and resulted in an exodus of members and leading figures": see Platt.

"Valerie ignored him, and in time, would come to greatly dislike the man": Stickler, p. 229.

"Siôn is not a violent man and certainly not prone to domestic violence": Jenkins, p. 112.

"Woffinden briskly dismisses this evidence as 'fantasies'": *Ibid.*, p. 410.

"its importance is such that it will become a key phrase in British criminal justice history": *Ibid.*, p.106.

"I had not read what Hutt had written": *Ibid.*, p. 93.

"He made great TV programmes about miscarriages of justice": https://twitter.com/MichaelRosenYes/status/1474376105478045698 (24 December 2021).

"two important experts who knew more about the case than anyone":

https://catholicherald.co.uk/a-reasonable-doubt/.

"In short, he was not to be trusted": Perhaps Bob Woffinden's judgement was always a little faulty. I first came across his name in my younger days when I bought his book *The Illustrated Encyclopedia of Rock* (1976), co-authored with Nick Logan. This is a work which reverentially treats Frank Zappa as equal in achievement to The Beatles, The Rolling Stones and Bob Dylan. The encyclopedia's critical assessments have not always worn well. The reader is authoritatively informed that Leonard Cohen "is too self-consciously a poet ever to develop into a first-rate song-writer".

15 The Long Goodbye

"very little has come to light in the last thirteen years to force the case once more into the limelight": PF3, p. 433.

"a long letter from the eminent New York-based chess photographer Nigel Eddis": dated 4 March 2004.

"a book about British murder trials from the era before the final abolition of capital punishment": This work, if completed, does not appear to have been published.

"exposing the faulty evidence that had led to the hanging of James Hanratty": Chris Harman, "Paul Foot 1937-2004", *Socialist Worker* (24 July 2004).

"exposés of miscarriages of justice, including ... James Hanratty": Michael White and Sam Jones, "Paul Foot, radical columnist and campaigner, dies at 66", *The Guardian* (19 July 2004).

"reported that the Hanratty family's lawyers were preparing a case to go before the Criminal Cases Review Commission": *The Guardian*, 30 Dec 2010.

"She was strongly inclined to believe in Hanratty's innocence": Paul Foot, letter to Dr Rudi Vis MP, 17 July 2002.

"apologised both to her memory and to both her sons": *Ibid*.

"my suspicions stopped well short of claiming any direct involvement by her": *Ibid*.

"Janet began an affair with her brother-in-law": BW, p. 446.

"One of his last articles about the A6 murder recalled how he first became involved": PF4.

"very convincing": PF, p. 353.

"when he observed the trial of Peter Alphon for making threatening and abusive calls": *Ibid.*

"Foot described how when doubts crept in, he learned to squash them": Foot, *The Vote*, p. 451.

"Spy Cops": see https://www.theguardian.com/uk-news/2022/may/20/spy-cops-inquiry-delays-beyond-belief-say-women-deceived-by-officers and https://www.theguardian.com/commentisfree/2022/may/22/the-guardian-view-on-the-spy-cops-inquiry-not-enough-answers.

"coshed to death by a Met police officer": see https://www.theguardian.com/commentisfree/2010/apr/28/death-of-blair-peach-editorial and https://www.theguardian.com/uk-news/2021/may/06/met-spied-on-blair-peach-partner-for-more-than-two-decades-inquiry-hears.

"736 entirely innocent postmasters": Mario Ledwith, "Most Post Office victims have yet to receive a penny", *The Times* (19 February 2022), p. 16.

"re-evaluated from the perspective that Hanratty was probably guilty": Razen, p. 10.

"occasionally stopping to get more petrol": *Ibid.*, p. 41.

"the gun was found on the 36A bus the evening of the day of the murder": *Ibid.*, p. 58.

"was known to have frequented the pub that Gregsten/Storie used": *Ibid.*, p. 76.

"were acquainted": *Ibid.*, p. 83.

"was associated with William Ewer": *Ibid.*, p. 91.

"the reintroduction of the death penalty for certain extreme crimes": *Ibid.*, p. 102.

"It's an authoritative narrative": Although a fluent and impressive book which is likely to become the enduring account of the A6 murder, *The Long Silence* has a sprinkling of minor errors. It is not true that when he returned to London from Liverpool on 24 August 1961, Hanratty "stayed on the Friday night in a hotel" (p. 271). He spent that night travelling on an overnight train, which arrived in London at dawn. The crime of course did not take place on 22nd/23rd October 1961 (p. 66) but two months earlier. Stickler consistently gets the title of my book wrong (pp. 248 and 249 and Bibliography). There is a slight misquotation from it (p. 249). But these are minor slips of the sort that any author might make; hardly any books achieve perfection.

"Acott was not corrupt. He was a police officer doing his best": Stickler,

p. 253.

"If he hadn't been hanged, with life sentences meted out today ...": *Ibid.*,
     p. 249.

"It would have been better if they had been told that the man they were
     looking for may not be there at all": *Ibid.*, p. 87.

"the vocabulary and speech cadences of a dustman's son": Souhami, p.
     231.

"criminal nonentities whose crimes up to that point had amounted to
     nothing more than acts of petty larceny": Russell-Pavier, p. 140.

"A full description of Ryan was given": Stickler, pp. 89-90.

"Paul Foot was justifiably sceptical about this": PF, p. 87.

"some motive for making the connection": *Ibid.*

"France only knew Hanratty as 'Jimmy Ryan'": Stickler, p. 93.

"couldn't get away fast enough": BW, pp. 105-6.

"Alphon was never, as so many thought, 'the first suspect'": Stickler, p.
     252.

"carefully coded way of saying that he was expected to be charged with
     the A6 murder": BW, p. 77.

Bibliography

Books About the A6 Murder

Blom-Cooper, Louis. *The A6 Murder: Regina v. James Hanratty, The Semblance of Truth* (Harmondsworth: Penguin Books, 1963).

Foot, Paul. *Who Killed Hanratty?* (London: Jonathan Cape, 1971; Frogmore: Panther Books, 1973; London: Penguin Books, 1988).

Hawser, C. L. *The Case of James Hanratty: Report of Mr. C. Lewis Hawser QC of His Assessment of the Representations Put Forward in the Case of James Hanratty and of Other Relevant Material: Presented to Parliament by the Secretary of State for the Home Department* (London: HMSO, 1975).

Justice, Jean. *Murder vs. Murder: The British Legal System and the A6 Murder Case* (Paris: Olympia Press, 1964).

Justice, Jean. *Le Crime de la Route A6* (Paris: Robert Laffont 1968).

Lord Russell of Liverpool, *Deadman's Hill: Was Hanratty Guilty?* (London: Secker and Warburg, 1965; London: Icon Books, 1966; Oxford: Tallis Press, 1966).

Miller, Leonard. *Shadows of Deadman's Hill: A New Analysis of the A6 Murder* (London: Zoilus Press, 2001).

Razen, Alan. *Hanratty: The Inconvenient Truth* (n.p.: CreateSpace, 2014).

Stickler, Paul. *The Long Silence: The True Story of James Hanratty and the A6 Murder by Valerie Storie, the Woman who Lived to Tell the Tale* (Cheltenham: The History Press, 2021).

Woffinden, Bob. *Hanratty: The Final Verdict* (Basingstoke: Macmillan, 1997; London: Pan Books, 1999).

Other Material

Adam, Craig. *Forensic Evidence in Court: Evaluation and Scientific Opinion* (Chichester: Wiley, 2016).

Ambler, Eric. "James Hanratty: The A6 Murder" in *The Ability to Kill* (London: Bodley Head, 1963), reprinted in *The Mammoth Book of Murder*, ed. Richard Glyn Jones (London: Robinson Publishing, 1989), pp. 498-508.

Barton, Fiona. "If I shut my eyes I'm just head and shoulders. I'm completely paralysed ... Hanratty did this to me" [interview with Valerie Storie, Part One], *The Mail on Sunday* (28 April 2002), pp. 46-48.

Barton, Fiona. "Hanratty killed my lover and left me paralysed for life ... but 40 years on, I still believe I'm lucky" [interview with Valerie Storie, Part Two], *The Mail on Sunday* (5 May 2002), pp. 56-57.

Blom-Cooper, Louis. *The Birmingham Six and Other Cases: Victims of Circumstance* (London: Duckworth, 1997).

Boyd, Brian. *Vladimir Nabokov: The American Years* (London: Chatto and Windus, 1992).

Campbell, Duncan. "The man in the mac", *The Guardian Weekend* (5 September 2009), pp. 40-43.

Capote, Truman. *In Cold Blood* (London: Penguin Books, 2000).

Carrère, Emmanuel. *The Adversary: A True Story of Murder and Deception*, trans. Linda Coverdale (London: Bloomsbury, 2000).

"Cassandra" [pseud.], "I would rather his family didn't read this ... but here is the awful truth about the awful James Hanratty", *The Daily Mirror* (25 May 2002), p. 17.

Cesarini, David. *Arthur Koestler: The Homeless Mind* (London: Heinemann, 1998).

Cox, Brian . "The face of evil", *Guardian*, 21 May 2001. https://www.theguardian.com/culture/2001/may/21/artsfeatures.

Ellroy, James. *My Dark Places: An L.A. Crime Memoir* (London: Arrow Books, 1997).

England and Wales Court of Appeal (Criminal Division) Decisions: Regina and James Hanratty deceased by his Brother Michael Hanratty (10 May 2002), https://www.bailii.org/ew/cases/EWCA/Crim/2002/1141.html.

Farrell, Audrey. *Crime, Class and Corruption: The Politics of the Police* (London: Bookmarks, 1992).

Foot, Paul. "Awaiting the Truth about Hanratty", *London Review of Books* 19 (24), https://www.lrb.co.uk/the-paper/v19/n24/paul-foot/diary.

Foot, Paul. "Hanratty's appeal is over, but justice is yet to be done", *The Guardian* (13 May 2002), p. 18.

Foot, Paul. *The Vote: How It was Won and How It was Undermined.* (London: Viking, 2005).

Fowles, John. *The Collector* (London: Jonathan Cape, 1963).

Fowles, John. *The Ebony Tower* (London: Jonathan Cape 1974)

Freud, Sigmund. *The Psychopathology of Everyday Life*, trans. Alan Tyson (Harmondsworth: Penguin Books, 1975).

Hain, Peter. *Mistaken Identity: The Wrong Face of the Law* (London: Quartet Books, 1976).

Ingrams, Richard. *Ludo and the Power of the Book: Ludovic Kennedy's Campaigns for Justice* (London: Constable, 2017).

Jarossi, Robin. *The Hunt for the 60's Ripper* (London: Mirror Books, 2017).

Jenkins, Siôn and Bob Woffinden. *The Murder of Billie-Jo* (London: John Blake, 2008).

Kennedy, Ludovic. *Truth to Tell: The Collected Writings of Ludovic Kennedy* (London: Bantam Press, 1991).

Lane, Brian. *The Encyclopedia of Forensic Science* (London: Magpie Books, 2004).

Lee, Carol Ann. *The Murders at White House Farm* (London: Pan Books, 2016).

Maschler, Tom. *Publisher* (London: Picador, 2005).

McGreevy, Ronan. *Great Hatred: The Assassination of Field Marshall Sir Henry Wilson MP* (London: Faber, 2022).

McNamara, Michelle. *I'll Be Gone in the Dark: One Woman's Obsessive Search for the Golden State Killer* (London: Faber, 2018).

Miller, Leonard. "The case against Hanratty", *The Guardian* (14 May 2002), p. 17.

Morton, James. *Bent Coppers: A Survey of Police Corruption* (London: Warner Books, 1994).

Orwell, George. *Decline of the English Murder and other essays* (Harmondsworth: Penguin Books, 1965).

Orwell, George. *I Belong to the Left: 1945*, ed. Peter Davison (London: Secker and Warburg, 2001).

Platt, Edward. "Comrades at war: the decline and fall of the Socialist Workers Party", *The New Statesman* (20 May 2014) https://www.newstatesman.com/uncategorized/2014/05/comrades-war-decline-and-fall-socialist-workers-party.

Ramsay, Robin. *Conspiracy Theories* (Harpenden: Pocket Essentials, 2000).

Russell-Pavier, Nick. *The Shepherd's Bush Murders* (London: Arrow

Books, 2016).

Seabrook, David. *Jack of Jumps* (London: Granta Books, 2006).

Simpson, Keith. *Forty Years of Murder: An Autobiography* (London: Harrap, 1978).

Smith, Joan. *Misogynies: Reflections on Myths and Malice* (New York: Fawcett Columbine, 1989).

Souhami, Diana. *Murder at Wrotham Hill* (London: Quercus 2012)

Taverne, Dick. *Against the Tide: Politics and Beyond, A Memoir* (London: Biteback Publishing, 2014).

Woffinden, Bob. *The Nicholas Cases: Casualties of Justice* (London: Bojangles Books, 2016).

Yallop, David. To *Encourage the Others* (London: Corgi, 1990).

Index

L

M

N

Y

Printed in Great Britain
by Amazon